Diary from the Edge
1940 –1944

A wartime adolescence

Diary from the Edge 1940–1944

A wartime adolescence

Anthony Ryle

The Hedge Press
London

Published by The Hedge Press
246 Alexandra Park Road
Wood Green
London N22 7BG

www.thehedgepress.co.uk

Printed and Production managed by Jellyfish Solutions, Swanmore

British Library Cataloguing-in-Publication Data
A catalogue record for this book is available from the British Library

ISBN 978-0-9571080-1-1

Contents

Illustrations

Cover: Sandbagging Newquay Hospital, 1939 [George Ellis, Cornish Studies Library]; Crashed fighter, Sussex, 1940 [Agency photograph, Imperial War Museum (HU88412)]; RAF Initial Training Wing inspection [as above]; Exhibition of toys made to support Russian refugees, St. Martin's School of Art, London, 1943 [Ministry of Information, Imperial War Museum (D9087)].

Drawings by the author from the original diary appear in the text of the diary entries.

Drawings by Ellen King

Maps

A note about this edition

The original diary was written as a direct record of thoughts as they occurred during the brief time each day devoted to writing it. During term-time at boarding-school, this was in the few minutes of quiet, late in the evening, intended officially for private prayers. When days were missed due to being away on expeditions or at conferences, the omissions were filled in later as the opportunity arose, but no day was left out completely. During the holidays the writing followed a fairly similar pattern.

Though conscious of a possible future reader (the diarist mentions himself), the diary was written without literary pretensions, or the ambition to present an autobiographical narrative. Writing essentially for himself, he had little need to explain who people were, or the background to contemporary events, so these details have been added where necessary. This edition consists of about half the available manuscript (the last, fifth, volume was lost). Omissions—indicated by ellipses—are often of repetitive remarks about routine events. Irregular punctuation and spelling have sometimes been corrected for clarity; double dashes and question marks are in the original text.

The names of most school pupils have been replaced by single initials (many share the same initial), but close friends and other important figures who appear regularly are named. Some friends are referred to in a variety of ways: Martin Wood = MFW, Roger Cruickshank = RJC, Cym Smith = Wallop = CMGS = Smith iii, Alan Watkinson = AWW.

Thanks are due to the following people for their generous help in preparing this book: Roger Browning, Richard Glassborow, John and Indijana Harper, Peter Holloway, Wendy Jotcham and Sophie Ryle; also the staff of the Cornish Studies Library, the East and West Sussex Record Offices, and the Imperial War museum, for help in choosing photographs connected with the diary story.

Introduction

The origins of the diary

I started keeping a diary when I was given an engagement book for 1940 with a separate page for each day. In subsequent years, I maintained the habit of almost daily entries, and have a series of volumes containing these, up until February 1944. I was nearly 13 when the diaries started, and nearly 17 at the time of the last entry—a further volume was lost. Reading the diaries 70 years later, I can identify the events, thoughts and feelings they record as mine, but I know that without this written record, the reconstructions and editings which are a part of memory would have generated a less reliable piece of personal and social history.

My growing up was shaped by historical and social circumstances, and many of the assumptions that I held then will be strange to the generation of my grandchildren and great-grandchildren. They will perhaps find in this book some sense of how life has changed.

The four years for which I have diaries were affected by the impact of war, and they also record my transition from childhood to near-adulthood. This period coincided with the national transition from the denials and disasters of the first years of the war to the first emergence of realistic hope. The diary reflects the general activities and interests of an adolescent in those days—many of which were surprisingly unaffected by the war—my evolving sense of self, and my developing social and political views. I have also included most of the war-related events that I witnessed, as well as many of the reports of the progress of the war that I gathered from newspapers and the wireless, especially those which, for a while, were of continuing concern. Meeting my adolescent self, I have sometimes been embarrassed by his combination of arrogance and naivety, but I have not edited out these passages.

I started this piece of writing when I had finally retired from my work and had time to fill. As the diary records, I decided to become a doctor at the age of 16, but after 1970 I was concerned primarily with the practice and teaching of psychotherapy, and with research into the model I had developed. This had involved me in writing a large number of papers and books, but now I felt I had said what I had to say, and was too distanced from clinical practice and teaching to develop new ideas. But I missed having a daily task to return to, and reading and commenting on the diaries filled the gap.

I had no audience in mind beyond a vague wish to tell the story to my grandchildren's generation, but as I followed my evolution as a diary-writing boy, my attitude to what I was writing also evolved and became increasingly reflective. I had always resisted suggestions that I should write some kind of autobiography recording the perspective and values I acquired from my family—a resistance owing something to the view expressed in the proverb (I believe a Spanish one) which states that keeping a diary is like blowing one's nose and then looking at the handkerchief. But of course the young diary writer and the old commentator are the same person, and as I wrote I became increasingly interested in how the two are related. I thought this might interest others too, so both voices will appear in the text—the retrospective comments being presented in square brackets within a diary entry, or between entries (together with explanatory comments). I have added a final chapter—*Retrospect*—summarising more general reflections.

As the title suggests, I did not experience the war as an active participant but rather as a witness from the edge of the action. I was myself on the edge of adulthood, and the world too was on the edge—first of catastrophe and then of victory and change. In the early diaries, I was particularly fascinated by events which I witnessed myself, by the relics I collected (shrapnel, bits of crashed planes and so on) and with the progress of the various military campaigns. As the war continued, I was increasingly concerned with recording and responding to the cumulative human cost, and expressing an idealistic determination that the world should be better.

Family background

This is the diary of a single individual, and my understanding of the world was clearly influenced by who and where I was. I must have been one of the most protected adolescents in Europe, for I did not experience invasion or occupation, I did not live in any of the heavily bombed towns, and within Britain I was among the more socially privileged. Living in a house with servants and being privately educated, my childhood was typical of the professional middle classes of the time, and different from that of the great majority of my contemporaries. But I like to believe that aspects of my family background protected me from complacency and from too narrow a perspective, and meant that I was an engaged and relatively informed witness. In particular, the effect of being privileged was to some extent countered by family traditions of dissent.

My mother's parents had been Irish immigrants to South Africa in the latter half of the 19th century. Her father, W.C. Scully, had left an impoverished Ireland and emigrated at the age of 14, bringing with him no great love of the English. Following the painful death of a friend, he had already abandoned Catholicism. His experiences included pioneering expeditions to land not yet colonised, and working in the Kimberley diamond mines, where he sold his claim (and probably saved his soul) just before diamonds were discovered. For a time he worked for Cecil Rhodes (mining entrepreneur, imperialist and colonial politician), an experience which reinforced his opposition to British imperialism. My mother had clear memories of visits to her childhood home by Sir Roger Casement, a British consul who was then engaged in exposing the conditions of life in colonies around the world. His revelations contributed to his eventual rejection of British rule, and he later sought German support for rebellion in Ireland. He was executed in 1916 having been landed in Ireland from a German submarine. The revelation that he was homosexual played a part in determining his death sentence.

My grandfather had become a magistrate and was one of South Africa's first authors. During the Boer war, they had lived across the road from the world's first concentration camp, built by the British for Boer families removed from their farms. My mother used to tell how my grandmother visited sick families with fruit and vegetables and, when told by the guards that she must not enter, would say 'shoot me if you dare', and proceed.

My father's father was a doctor and a Darwinian humanist who was somewhat alienated from his father, J.C. Ryle, the Church of England Bishop of Liverpool. He believed that humanists needed to be more moral than Christians and transmitted to his children a strong sense of duty and of responsibility. This could be puritanical; for example, when, as a child, my father took a handful of hay from a passing wagon, he was told to put it back and apologise. My grandfather was a principled man, and as a General Practitioner in Brighton, he lost many patients through his opposition to the Boer War.

My father, J.A. Ryle, qualified in medicine in 1913. His pacifism forbade any participation in killing, but did not stand in the way of his joining up as a doctor, and he served in the RAMC (Royal Army Medical Corps) in France throughout the First World War. My parents married in 1914, shortly after the outbreak of the war. A sense of the times and of my father's family is conveyed by a letter to my father John and my mother Miriam from my father's sister Meg, written from Russia, where she had been a governess and was now working with the Red Cross:

Sanitatial train 182. November 18th [1914]

I have just been back to Moscow for a night and got your letters. Here's my blessing in return, and may these three days at the George Inn [their honeymoon] *come true many times when the war is over. I dare say by now John is in France (hearing the thump and thunder of artillery that one so soon gets used to) but nothing can make you really apart again. I'm happy and sad all at once when I think of you two—and that's very often. I'm scribbling this, to the jogging refrain of my caravan, on a page of my war diary, with a pencil stump I found in the trenches after the battle of*

Augustova. P'raps the last thing it wrote was a dispatch praying for reinforcements—or perhaps a picture postcard to liebe Minna and the kinderlein. I found letters there from German wives that have washed my heart clean of any hatred against Germans. Also I've been nursing young Austrians—dear honest peasant boys with shy smiles when you say 'AuchWeidenschen, bruder', and a few broken words when you've bandaged them up. You can't feel enemies; certainly my Russian soldiers don't.

We're off on our fourth journey now, to which frontier is uncertain. Our train alone has now fetched over a thousand wounded, and we are one of hundreds, and this is only Russia. Where is the end of it to be?—and still trainloads [of recruits] *go pouring westward every day, from the far depths of Siberia, and the Ural Mountains and the Caucasus, beautiful giant peasants staring at all this new world and singing as they go. We shall live through very strange times before we meet again. Perhaps your love will help you to puzzle some meaning out of even the darkest days. God bless you both.*

Your loving sister Meg.

Meg died in Serbia, where a number of intrepid war-time women volunteers were working, probably from typhus.

Glatting by E.T. Holding

My childhood

As a result of these influences, I grew up in a home that was sceptical about patriotism, had no connection with organised religion, was opposed to militarism and put a positive value on non-conformity. But the life we led was in most respects conventional.

I was born in 1927, less than ten years after the end of the First World War, the youngest of five children. The eldest, John, was twelve years older than me, followed by Martin, Nora and Margaret. By that time my father was a consultant physician on the staff of Guy's Hospital, London. Consultants were unpaid, but being on a London teaching hospital's staff attracted private patients. This also more or less determined where you lived, as a result of which I was born in Wimpole Street, in a house once occupied by Nelson's Lady Hamilton. These handsome houses were built when ground rents were high, but labour was cheap, so servants slept in the attic and the kitchen was five or six floors below in the basement. As I recall, we employed a cook, at least three maids, my Irish nurse Hannah, a secretary and, as my father never learned to drive, a chauffeur. My lifelong discomfort at the idea of servants dates back to memories of that house.

In 1928 my parents found an empty farmhouse called Glatting (near Sutton, in West Sussex) and rented it for £25 a year. Part of it was built of vast oak beams, probably in the 10th or 11th century, and it is recorded in the Domesday Book. It was without electricity, and water came from a spring in the nearby woods and had to be pumped to an upstairs cistern by hand. It provided weekend and holiday respite for my father, who never learned not to overwork, and land on which my mother planted an orchard and made a garden yielding flowers, honey, eggs and vegetables, with the help of the family and an unemployed villager called Francis who was soon taken on as the gardener (one more servant). My idyllic memories of childhood are mostly located at Glatting.

My father was on the staff of Guy's Hospital until moving to Cambridge as the Regius Professor of Physic (medicine) in 1935. He returned to Guy's during the blitz, as my diary records, and then became the first Professor of Social Medicine at Oxford. This new role reflected his belief that the social conditions associated with illness—the ultimate causes—deserved as much attention as the intimate causes, such as bacteria and cancer, which dominated medical thinking and teaching.

In Cambridge we lived at 5 Herschel Road. The number of servants was reduced to one or two, except for a brief period when, under a scheme meant to ease the situation of the long term unemployed, three Durham miners were employed as domestic servants. They enjoyed playing cricket with me in the garden, but soon left for less humiliating work. The house was a short walk from King's College Choir School where I went as a (non-singing) dayboy, until a friend referred in my mother's presence to the fact that I had blubbed when I had been beaten. I had kept this beating (for something I had not done) a secret, knowing that my parents had told the school that I was not to be beaten—that I would do nothing to justify it, and they would remove me from the school if this was not understood. They were as good as their word, and I was taken from the school. Just after the outbreak of war I went as a boarder to Gresham's School, where there was no corporal punishment and where, as an added advantage, the curriculum included much more science than was usual in British public schools.

Political influences

I recall our London house as being a centre for anti-war activity, notably for people involved in organizing the Peace Ballot of 1934–35—for which over 10 million signatures were collected—calling for the active implementation of the League of Nations' principles of multilateral disarmament, and the use of international sanctions or armed force to curb aggressors.

After Franco's insurrection in 1936 and the subsequent German and Italian military intervention in the civil war, Spain became the chief topic in the conversation of the Cambridge students who came to my parents' open evenings—and to whom, with wide open ears, I used to distribute sandwiches and cider cup. My basic political orientation was formed at this time. My mother was active in supporting a hostel for Basque children at Pampisford, near Cambridge—one of many set up by volunteers around Britain to care for the large numbers of child refugees who had been sent to England to escape the bombing in Spain. Seeing her weep when she returned from the hostel on the day that Bilbao had fallen to the Fascists was one of the moments which made me realise that the safety of childhood was illusory.

The Munich crisis in 1938 brought this realisation closer, with the issue of gas masks and the digging of zig-zag trenches in the school playing fields. The Munich agreement was the final act of a shoddy decade of British appeasement which made war inevitable. Meanwhile the trenches in the school playing fields were filled in, and the hole dug in our garden for an air raid shelter quickly filled up with water, and was converted to a lily pond.

At this point, in order to describe the wider context for this personal account of the pre-war years, I offer a brief historical survey.

The world in the 1930s

In many ways, the Second World War was a continuation of the first. The Versailles treaty imposed reparation payments on Germany at a level many regard as having been economically unsustainable, and also determined that she lost her colonial possessions in Africa. When Hitler came to power in 1933, Germany proceeded to break the terms of the Versailles Treaty, embarking on a rearmament programme and later uniting with Austria. Plans for German expansion were clear for all to see. The regime was marked at home by increasingly violent anti-Semitism, and the suppression of all trade unions and left-wing organisations.

Franco's rebellion against the elected Spanish Government was supported by Germany and Italy. The official policy in Britain and France of non-intervention starved the Spanish government of supplies, but did nothing to stem the supply of German and Italian weapons and troops to the rebels. Popular support for the Spanish government in this first resistance to Fascism was widespread, and over 30,000 volunteers from all over the world joined the International Brigade. But in the end the Spanish government was defeated. In 1938 the Munich agreement transferred the Czechoslovakian Sudetenland to Germany, and a few months later Germany occupied the rest of the country, provoking only mild international protests.

During this period Litvinov, the Soviet foreign minister, had proposed an alliance with France and Britain, but no agreement had been achieved. He was replaced by Molotov who in August 1939—as German troops assembled for the invasion of Poland—signed the Nazi-Soviet pact whereby Poland was partitioned between Germany and the USSR. It is common to see Molotov's signing of the Nazi-Soviet pact as cynical, and responsible for the outbreak of war, but a more realistic view in my opinion would be to regard it as a recognition by both countries that the utter passivity of the West left Germany free to turn East.

Over the same period Japan and Italy, both militarist regimes which lacked colonies as sources of raw materials and as markets, had used military force to acquire or extend their colonies. Japan was at war with a corrupt and disorganised China, and Italy had occupied Ethiopia. Neither had met with serious resistance from the rest of the world.

The world at the start of 1940

My diary begins three months after the German invasion of Poland had provoked the declaration of war by Britain and France. At this point, the present and future combatants of the Second World War were divided into four main groups. Of these, Germany, Italy and Japan were later to formally join together as the Axis powers. Three other contrasting groups were eventually to unite as the allies against this Axis.

One group, the victors of the First World War—centrally Britain and France—were old colonial powers, incompletely recovered from the major world economic crisis which had started in 1929. Their appeasement of Germany, and their feeble and late response to the threat of war, had been influenced by the fear of communism and the fresh memory of the carnage of the First World War. Britain had retained or extended colonial rule of India, Burma, Malaya and Hong Kong, and had taken over German colonies to extend its African possessions. It could count on the loyalty of at least the white populations of the Commonwealth and colonies. France retained substantial colonies in North Africa and, along with Holland, in the Far East. India's demand for independence from Britain remained unsatisfied, and throughout the Far East and Africa, resentment of the white colonial powers was widespread.

Loosely linked to this group was the USA, a late entrant in the First World War and now the world's dominant economic power. America guarded its spheres of influence in Latin America and the Far East, but it was otherwise isolationist; it had refused to support the League of Nations, and was reluctant to become involved in another European war.

The third group was the USSR. Russia had been deprived of a substantial proportion of its pre-war territory and population by the treaty of Brest-Litovsk, signed when Russia was undergoing revolution and civil war—at which time armies from Western Europe had supported the anti-Bolshevik 'Whites' against the ultimately victorious Reds. But the Soviet Union had survived. By 1940 it had accomplished a rapid and ruthless process of agrarian reform and industrial development.

For many on the left—disillusioned by the failure of the Second International (an international organisation of socialist and labour parties founded in 1889) to resist the nationalism and mutual murder of the First World War—Communism and the Soviet Union seemed to promise a new civilisation. But there was a huge gap between communist ideals and the reality of the paranoid authoritarian regime evolving under Stalin, which had caused mass starvation by imposing a brutal and too-rapid programme of agrarian reform, as well as carrying out the purges of the late 1930s, and the murder of Leon Trotsky.

France and Britain declared war on September 3rd, when Germany invaded Poland. The partition of Poland was swiftly accomplished, and the Soviet Union was soon engaged in a war with Finland aimed at reducing the vulnerability of Leningrad. There was little military activity in the West, where this period was referred to as the 'phoney war', but it was real enough in the East. In Poland, deportations and massacres occurred in both zones, with the Germans picking on Jews, communists and intellectuals, and the Russians on capitalists, landowners and army families. Older enmities were also active—particularly in the Russian-occupied areas—Polish-Ukrainian hatred led to mutually genocidal wars. Pre-existing anti-Semitism contributed to the millions of murders carried out by the Germans over the next few years.

The Allies who eventually defeated the Axis were united by the common threat which they faced, but there were immense differences between both countries and individuals in how the war was understood. In occupied Europe, an uneasy alliance developed between those motivated by the conscious anti-Fascism of the political left—which had developed especially as a result of the war in Spain—and nationalists of varying political attitudes.

It took time for Britain to recover from the years of appeasement. Despite memories of the appalling losses of the First World War, the dominant belief across the political spectrum was that the Second World War was a necessary war. Some on the right saw it as a defence of the (declining) empire, while most of those on the pacifist wing of the left understood that it was not just another round of imperialist rivalry. Fascism was a racist ideology which justified ruthless suppression at home and military conquest abroad, and which murdered millions—simply because of who they were. It had to be resisted.

Chapter 2: 1940

World events: 1940

In Europe, 1940 started with re-drawn boundaries. Czechoslovakia and Poland had disappeared. Finland was fighting Russia, which sought territory to extend the distance of Leningrad from her borders.

There was little military activity in Western Europe in the early months of the year, and this period was called, with typical British insularity, the 'phoney war'. All this changed in April, when Germany invaded Denmark and Norway, and Chamberlain's Conservative government—which had been responsible for years of appeasement—was replaced by a national government under Churchill. Naval battles involving British, French and Norwegian forces were partially successful, but on land, troops sent from Britain were soon withdrawn, and the Norwegian army was forced to surrender.

The Germans then invaded Holland and Belgium, and entered France through the Ardennes in a 'blitzkrieg' which gave them a rapid victory and control of the Channel Ports. A large proportion of the British Expeditionary Force in France, minus tanks and heavy arms, escaped from the beaches of Dunkirk. France surrendered, and was divided between a German occupied Northern part, and a regime under General Petain at Vichy. The Battle of Britain (July to September), fought over southern England, denied the Germans air control. Their plans to invade Britain were abandoned, but a sustained campaign of night bombing ensued.

Italy had entered the war when France collapsed, and attacked British Somaliland; it met strong resistance when invading Greece and Yugoslavia. Its bases in Libya and Ethiopia were attacked by the British, and North Africa became an important theatre of war in which a small British force achieved considerable early successes.

The Italian Navy lost half its major warships to a British attack on Taranto carried out by carrier-borne obsolete biplanes (Swordfish)—a victory which inspired the later Japanese attack on Pearl Harbour.

By the end of 1940 much of Europe was allied to, or occupied by, Germany. In the West, Switzerland, Spain, Portugal, Eire and Sweden remained neutral; of the rest, only Britain was free from occupation, defended by its depleted army, its undefeated air force, its navy, and the Channel. Food and other crucial supplies were dependent on the merchant navy, and by the end of the year the German U-boats, based now in France's Atlantic ports, were sinking a frightening number of ships. The war was generally presented as a national or patriotic struggle, but with none of the jingoism which had characterised the First World War.

Diary for 1940

When I began the diary I was shortly to start my second term at Gresham's School at Holt, which was a market town near the northern coast of Norfolk. Home was currently Cambridge, where my father was Professor of medicine, with parts of holidays spent at Glatting, the farmhouse in West Sussex tucked into a fold in the steep northern escarpment of the South Downs (see above pp. 6–7).

In the diary I used the family names for my parents—*Daddy* for my father and *Mommy* (rather than the middle class *Mummy* or more democratic *Mum*) for my mother. At that time, school friends and male working class men were usually addressed by their surnames only, single female servants were called by their first names, and those who were married were granted the title *Mrs.*

at Glatting

January

Monday 1st
Today is my last day at Glatting [before going to Cambridge]. … *As nearly all the snow has gone, I spent the day in my house. Mother came to lunch, we had hot sardines on toast and cocoa, and lots more toast and some Glatting nuts. After lunch I tidied the house up and then read Lorna Doone as there is a lovely fire there.*

After tea which I had indoors, I collected my belongings and pumped up the bicycle tires, as we are biking to the station tomorrow (Fittleworth). I had a farewell sit in my house, and then locked it up.

My 'house' was a small wooden hut with a stove which my mother and I had built the summer before in the orchard, some way from the house. It was a much-valued private space where I sometimes entertained and fed members of the family. I remember on one occasion my brother Martin asking if I had put an OXO cube in the stew, and when I nodded, he said "I thought so, I've just found it".

to Cambridge

Tuesday 2nd
We had breakfast horribly early, and started out with Tinker [my Airedale] *at about 9 o'cl. We bought some labels at Mrs. Harris', and corrected a hitch in the little racer which I was riding, and then we had to walk down Sutton Hill as that was the one place they hadn't sanded!*

We went on our way, getting very cold, and going slowly down all hills with our feet on the ground until we eventually reached Fittleworth. Here we found that Mother had bought us bike tickets which said we had to accompany the bikes—right across London and changing at E. Croydon. However, we lost them so it was all right. At East Croydon we saw the balloon barrage [tethered balloons to deter low-flying attacking aircraft], *which I had not done before.*

January 1940

Arrived back at 3.30 to find there is skating. I shall get my skates which were promised at Christmas tomorrow. WHOOPEE!

It was an exceptionally cold winter, and the flooded fens around Cambridge offered extensive areas for skating.

Wednesday 3rd
… We got my skates and had them fixed [to] *the boots. … We went to Grantchester meadows, which were rather rough, but all the same quite fun, and then we went out to lunch with the Bushells …*

José Cisneros came to supper; apparently he is working on a farm until he returns to Spain.

José was one of the Basque refugee children housed at the hostel my mother had helped set up at Pampisford, in an empty vicarage. The boys and girls who came to Cambridge were from an anarchist orphanage in Bilbao. My parents took particular responsibility for José.

After the fall of Bilbao in June 1937, when some children from other hostels began to return to Spain, the Cambridge group remained intact. They had to move out, however, because the vicarage and its garden, which had been refurbished by volunteers from Cambridge trades unions and students, were acquired by a new incumbent who gave them notice to quit by the next quarter day, which was December 25th. Before leaving, my mother planted the lawn with crocus bulbs in a pattern which read 'Mark 10-14' ('Suffer the little children to come unto me …') and let a goat loose in the vegetable garden.

Thursday 4th
Almost immediately after breakfast Margaret, Clara and I set out to walk to Lingey Fen [to skate]. … *To begin with, there were very few people there, but the number gradually increased. The ice was perfect compared to Grantchester meadows …*

Clara and her sister Lorna were evacuees from London who were staying with us, among the thousands of children sent out soon after the outbreak of war in the expectation of the bombing which, so far, had not happened. They were daughters of a First World War holder of the Victoria Cross who had been unemployed through much of the 1930s. She was a little older than I was, and was almost the first girl—and the first working class contemporary—I had had any chance to know. I thought she was wonderful.

Evacuees played an important part for many people in diminishing the incomprehension and prejudice derived from British class divisions, although the opposite was also sometimes the case. For all the liberal and left wing beliefs of my family, my mother and sister never questioned that their way of doing things was right. In retrospect, I think Clara dealt with this in a dignified way, even when having to submit to having her nits (head lice) treated by my sister, by having her hair washed with kerosene. Her younger sister Lorna, who was an unhappy child, earned a place in my heart by resisting my mother's attempts to make her eat parsnips with the heartfelt explanation: "they make me spew".

My diary records that over the next 2 weeks Clara, or Clara and Lorna, often accompanied me and my sisters skating or taking Tinker for walks. Soon after I went back to boarding school, they returned to London, as did most evacuees at that time.

The bikes have arrived at the station, so we will be able to ride to skating, if there is any (it was thawing a little last night and yesterday).

Friday 5th

... I played [ice] *hockey with Leake and an air raid warden friend of his. Returned just in time for tea.*

Washed up supper and listened to Lord Haw-Haw ...

Lord Haw-Haw was a name given to a number of broadcasters of German propaganda. The most infamous was William Joyce. The broadcasts had a considerable audience in Britain.

Saturday 6th

There was quite a hard frost last night, which seemed even colder as there was a mist which froze in the trees. ... I went to Lingey Fen by myself. As there was a mist I could not see far, so I spent some time patrolling about looking for Leake. After I had been there about half an hour, he arrived with two hockey sticks and a puck (all home made) so we played hockey. After that we skated about together for the rest of the morning ...

Margaret's instep has been hurting her since she started skating this year, which is rather bad luck as she does not enjoy herself much ...

I am reading a book called Larkrise, by Flora Thompson.

Sunday 7th

... I developed a film in the morning, and then played marbles with Lorna.

After lunch I went out to spend the afternoon with Charles Pickthorn [a close friend from Prep school who was son of the current Tory MP for Cambridge] *... we tried to cast a piece of lead in a mould of his but it did not work and he burnt his hand. After he had had some 'Tannofix'* [ointment] *put on it, he was sick (he had already been sick once before I arrived), so I took my leave, so he could be sick in peace ...*

Tinker has scratched a nasty hole in himself and he wouldn't touch his dinner, so I don't think he can be very well.

(Add. Tinker had the worst epileptic fit he has ever had, and was very excited when he came to, so we gave him some warm milk and Bromide).

Monday 8th

Last night Tinker had two more fits, and the vet came at 5 o'clock to see him.

… the Bushells came to lunch. Afterwards we played ping-pong and at 2.45 they left. For the rest of the afternoon I learnt to knit—I am making a blue scarf.

Mr. Runciman (the vet) said that Tinker might have worms, that he was only to eat meat and vegetables (not biscuits), that he must not sleep indoors, and that his ear should have drops put into it as it hurts. He said that having fits does not matter at all [they were probably the effect of the 'improver' added to flour—agene].

Tuesday 9th

Wonderful news this morning. The Finns have won an even greater victory [against the Russians, who were not then Britain's allies], *and Russians are digging themselves in for the winter …*

Tinker is much better, he had a pound of Horse or Worn-Out Cow Meat today and enjoyed it immensely.

The temperature is below freezing, and has been as low as 27 ℉ [-2°C].

Saturday 13th

… In Romania and central Europe several people are dying of the cold, while in S. America twelve have died of the heat.

We did the News Chronicle £100 crossword after tea. There are hundreds of alternatives, so it is very unlikely that we will win.

Monday 15th
… Martin has gone to 'somewhere in England' to see the naval authorities about his hush-hush job. I will not see him until next holidays …

José Cisneros goes off back to Spain tomorrow, he came to supper tonight—we will go to see him off at the station tomorrow morning.

Tuesday 16th
Immediately after breakfast we went in the car to see José off. He was rather worried about the journey and Marie-Thérèse (his sister) was very sad and frightened about the sea journey …

José re-appeared in my life after the war. Following his conscription to—and desertion from—Franco's army, he had spent a period in the Pyrenees in a Resistance group, carrying out sabotage. They hoped that Franco might fall when the war ended, but in the event they were interned in France. José contacted my parents, who managed to get him to England, where he soon became known as Joe. He settled in London, working as a refrigeration maintenance engineer. But for many years, until he married, he took some months off in the summer so he could visit old Basque friends in France and work on the grape harvest. He became a good friend and a wonderful honorary uncle to my older children.

Wednesday 17th
The snow was only about 2″ deep in the morning, but it has scarcely thawed at all, and in fact most of the taps are frozen, even the hot taps.

One day more of holidays!

On the 19th January, I went back to Holt for my second term at school. The main diary entries recorded during the first weeks of school concerned my frustration at not being able to toboggan (using a sledge I made myself in Manual Training classes) due to a persistent swelling of one knee. Although I was extremely homesick, I had got used to the dormitories, the tuck box of jams and other treats stored under the iron beds, and the unfamiliarity of collective living. Being one of the older boys in the junior school, I did not suffer from bullying.

to Holt

Friday 19th
... After an early lunch Mommy took me to the station. ... At Kings Lynn we had to wait two hours, during which we went into the cabs of the engines ... arrived at Holt an hour overtime ...

Wood, the new boy in the dorm, is in quarantine for German measles, and will not be coming for a fortnight ...

Saturday 20th
... I am slightly homesick, but I expect it will wear off after the first week. I had a hot bath in the evening, my [bath] *nights are Tuesday and Saturday this term.*

Sunday 21st
I was much warmer last night, as my travelling rug and dressing gown had been unpacked. Woke up to find that there was a 'blizzard' outside, which had added about 3″ of snow ...

There are hundreds of seagulls about here, escaping from the sea or looking for food, I expect.

The navy lost another destroyer flotilla leader today by mine or torpedo. This makes our losses so far 1 aircraft carrier, 3 submarines, 1 destroyer and 1 other ship. The Germans have lost the pocket battleship Deutschland, 1 cruiser and about 40 submarines.

Noting the casualties as reported in the press became a regular feature of my diaries.

Monday 22nd
... In the afternoon I had my first French lesson with Mr. Frietters (?) who is a new master—a refugee from Germany—in place of Mr. Stubbs. He gave us rather a lot of prep.

He was, I imagine, Jewish, but this was not mentioned. Anti-Semitism was widespread in Britain, and the racial policies of the Nazis were little emphasised at this time.

Wednesday 24th
… It seems I was wrong about our naval losses, another destroyer was lost by mine today, making 5 in all. All hands were lost, 175 of them.

Thursday 25th
It thawed a lot today—all the roads are getting slushy and it is all wet everywhere. … In the afternoon I tuned up my bicycle, while nearly everyone else snow fighted on the Beach …

I got a letter from Daddy in the morning, he told me all about the election, and said he did not expect to get in.

The election was for the University seat. At that time, anachronistically, Oxford and Cambridge graduates each elected one MP. My father was a candidate.

Saturday 27th
… We had a library period in English, I am reading 'Stalky & Co.' [by Kipling].

In the afternoon I helped Watkinson rearrange the library, and lost two games of chess to B. … And then to end up with there were school films, '100 men and a girl'. It was rather funny as it was a very old film and kept on breaking at critical moments.

Sunday 28th
I was bell fag today. I prefer Sundays for that job as there are fewer bells to ring. … Mr. Habershon [school chaplain] *preached about the war. Quite good.*

February

Thursday 1st
Mr. Spencer [in charge of the junior house, Kenwyn, therefore my Housemaster at the time, and a Cambridge graduate] *talked to me*

about the election at Cambridge, and said he was a Conservative, BUT he knew who he would vote for, and afterwards he emphasised the But.

I have kept my diary for one month now.

Friday 2nd

In the morning I had to take the absentees list down, as Sweet has a cold. There were two at home, 4 in the San and 13 at Kenwyn, of whom only about eight really had colds …

Sunday 4th

… An awful Russian person came and preached, and there was a collection for 'promoting good relations between Eastern and Western Christians' to which I gave 2d. After the service I went up into the organ loft and listened to Hubby [Mr. Hales, music teacher] *playing something. Lovely to look at the organ; all knobs and pedals and things …*

I had become accustomed to compulsory prayers and chapel services and had got over my initial embarrassment at my ignorance of the rules. In my first term I had noticed that boys were sometimes called away from prep for 'remedials', and I thought that they were attending some religious mystery, but I now know they were having treatment for conditions such as flat feet.

Monday 5th

… On the six o'clock news, they said the following: "Today the candidates for Cambridge have been announced; there will be a straight fight between Dr. Hill, Independent Conservative, and Prof. J.A. Ryle, Independent Progressive". A straight fight! Hooray! but I don't expect he'll get in because of the parsons.

Wednesday 7th

… we were called to Big School [the main assembly hall], *and the headmaster said that the police had told him that the enemy was dropping toy balloons filled with gas or explosive which burst when touched. Accordingly he asked us to give up touching stray toy balloons*

for Lent. It turned out, in the six o'clock news, that a man had found an escaped meteorological balloon and had dropped some cigarette ash on it. A very widespread and silly rumour.

Thursday 8th
... the head-master revised his statement of yesterday, saying that our Lent resolution must now be not to touch stray meteorological balloons with cigarettes in our mouths ...

Baines had a wizard model of a Supermarine Spitfire. It was a Frog Penguin. It cost 4/-, was quite easily put together, and looked much better than the Skybirds. I think I will get one if my bank-balance is favourable ...

Skybirds was a pioneering range of 1/72nd scale model aircraft construction kits, made of wood and metal, launched in the 1930s. The Frog Penguin brand introduced plastic models a little later.

Friday 9th
... In the evening Mr. Escott North came and gave a wizard lecture on 'The trail of the Cowboy'. There were some wizard [film] *reels showing broncos bucking, and at the end he roped someone up from a distance of 3 yards.*

Sunday 11th
... I wrote home and brought my diary up to date. ... I have now to do Watkinson's black-out, as he has got the disease and gone to the San.

Wartime regulations required that no lights should be visible from buildings after dark. This usually meant having very heavy curtains in windows, but windows could be painted over permanently instead. Coastal areas were especially sensitive on the matter.

Sunday 18th
... Mr. Bagnell-Oakley took E, S and B (the 3 favourites) to Blakeney [known for the wildlife of its surrounding marshes] *in the afternoon. They saw a cargo vessel which had been set on fire by enemy action a few days previously. They brought back a few trophies—E got half a*

chronometer [a very accurate naval clock] *and some gas mask ends. S some uniform buttons. Lucky devils!*

Tuesday 20th

… Mr. R. drove us [three boys] *and Mr. D'Aeth* [a very nice Biology master who had been in a car accident a few days previously] *to Cromer. … He* [Mr. D] *was going to the hospital to have his foot X-rayed as it was bruised. When we were there we saw the X-ray apparatus and the Iron Lung. This was very simple indeed, being just a 3-ply wooden box with an airtight joint at* [i.e. collar round] *the patient's neck and an electric pump working a pair of bellows. We talked a lot on the way to and fro; Mr. R. is nicer than I thought, and Mr. D'Aeth is just 'wizard' …*

Wednesday 21st

… I bought a rubber at the school shop, and when I got back I found studies 1 and 3 besieging our study. Of course the odious boy M was the chief offender. I managed to squeeze in, and we held out until tea with Wood, P, F and myself, plus B for a time until tea.

After tea we had S, but they had captured F and B and were bullying them in Study number 3. Frank [Spencer, housemaster] *came along just at the right moment and blew M up, though not quite as well as he deserved. Last night the Pink* [dormitory] *was attacked, they bagged F's slippers and a hairbrush and a clothes brush …*

Thursday 22nd

… After breakfast studies 2 and 3 united against study 1, which was much funnier from our point of view. While they were wedging the door shut with a sledge runner, S and I bent the end outside the door up, so they couldn't pull it back. Mr. Spencer arrived quite soon and we stopped.

In the evening I found their door handle loose and 'borrowed' it. I gave it back later, whereupon M made a loud remark for Mr. Spencer—who was along the passage—about taking other people's door handles, and looked injured innocence at him, the lying, double-crossing skunk that he is. More raids tonight? …

Friday 23rd
No; there were not any raids. It has now completely thawed, and we played beach hockey sometimes in breaks etc. …

Saturday 24th
… Con club this evening, Mr. D'Aeth was there and [we had a talk by] *an old boy, Christopher Swainson, just back from the Maginot line. He showed us a medal he got for being in the Maginot Line. He told us what little he could. He was very nice, short and stocky. I wonder if he will last out the war; he goes to France on Monday.*

The Maginot line was an extensive construction of 'impregnable' fortifications along the French frontier, connected by underground road and rail tunnels, stretching from Switzerland to Luxembourg and linked to Belgian defences. It was intended to prevent any repetition of the horrors of trench warfare. Like so many military developments, it was a solution more relevant to the past than the present. For me, what 'France' meant was derived from the First World War. My knowledge about that war owed little to my father, who, in common with so many participants, seldom discussed his experiences, but at some point I had discovered in the attic a bound edition of the *Illustrated London News* for the war years which provided an adequately documented and gruesome account. Maybe I was less reassured than was the French Army by the comforts and supposed impregnability of the Maginot Line.

Sunday 25th
… Summer time started today, so it gets dark at about 7 o'clock now.

Summer time started two months early this year and remained in force all through the winter of 1940–41. Another hour of (double) summer time was introduced from May to August in 1941.

Wednesday 28th
The latest craze is stilts, I expect I will make some …

In Louis Malle's great film *Au Revoir les Enfants,* my near-contemporaries in a French boarding school were depicted as sharing the same craze.

March

Saturday 2nd
My birthday! I woke up at about 4 o'clock and opened the parcel -- A watch! a beautiful Mappin and Webb watch with a second hand … and a lovely velvet case to keep it in. After breakfast Martin's present came, a wizard geometry set, all shiny …

I had to teach in Maths today—the headmaster said 'Professor Ryle junior is going to show the class how to do compound interest'. He played Boston's part of not attending and drawing pictures with heelball.

Boston, a fellow pupil, was an enthusiastic brass rubber, taking images of brass plaques in surrounding churches by rubbing overlaid paper with a black substance called heelball.

Sunday 3rd
I stilt-walked a little in the evening, but the craze is definitely wearing out. … J has gone to the San, and I've got the filthy job of looking after the Junior Dorm. F, S and B have all got German measles …

Monday 4th
… I made a shove-halfpenny board in MT [manual training]. *It works quite well.*

Thursday 7th
… I saw in the BOP [Boy's Own Paper] *an article by Patrick Halnan* [an ex-schoolmate]. *He was in a boat when it was torpedoed, and had seen a British plane shot down by the submarine.*

Sunday 10th
Junior dorm a little rowdy before the bell went so I gave three people lines. … Frank sat with us at lunch. We discussed the war.

… my last night in Junior Dorm for a week. A few people will have to report at 7.10; 7.15; 7.20 and 7.25, undressing and dressing again between each time.

I had been made a House prefect and this was one of several reports of my distressingly officious exercise of my powers. Hierarchy was a dominant theme in the social structure of the school.

Monday 11th
… Lovely—I spent my first night in the Pink dorm, and did not have to go to bed until after 8 o'clock.

Tuesday 12th
We had double biology. B and I made a slide of the mouth parts of a cockroach, it was very difficult dissecting them, but wizard fun …

Thursday 14th
… In Maths the headmaster could not do a rider and I showed him how and got 7d. I had a 'booze' at the school shop …

A rider, as I recall, is an extension of a mathematical proof. This was probably the high point of my mathematical ability and left no trace.

Saturday 16th
… I went out to Salthouse with Mr. Oakley, E and G. We saw on the Salt Marshes a redshank, mallard, thousands of coots and a flock of Brent geese, at which Mr. Oakley fired, but they were too high and the bullets bounced off. We saw an extraordinary pair of ducks—crosses between mallard and farm ducks. On the way back we saw a large brown barn-owl flying round a gravel pit. It flew across the road and E saw it pounce on something, and then it flew away.

Sunday 17th

Mr. A.C. Candler [physics master] *preached in chapel. He preached a jolly good sermon I think—how Democracy is based on Christ's teaching …*

A miserable day, pouring with rain, so study rags [fights] *started. We were besieged and had bad banana smeared on the windows. Mr. Spencer put all study members off bikes tomorrow, not as a punishment, but as a token of disapproval. He said that there were visitors coming round, and they might have found banana on the windows of the proud housemaster's studies …*

Forty German planes raided Scapa floe [a natural harbour in the Orkneys where the Royal Navy's Home Fleet was based], *damaged one warship slightly and killed a civilian who was watching the raid. 40 HE bombs dropped on mainland.*

Wednesday 20th

… Possibility of war being declared against Russia soon. I wonder? Since 8 o'clock last night the RAF has raided Sylt [a fortified island off the northern coast of Germany] *almost continuously, except for this morning. This is because a few German planes had raided Scapa Floe. … I saw three Wellingtons returning just after tea, I expect they'd been raiding Sylt.*

Thursday 21st

Last night when we were in the dormitory, and after lights out, I saw the port lights of two aeroplanes and later their rear lights. After watching them for about two minutes we saw them drop two extremely bright flares, so that they could be recognised I suppose …

Sunday 24th

… In the afternoon Wood and I went for a long walk in the school woods. We saw about 15 toads, about 6 in the school ponds and the rest on the paths. I saw a dead toad which was horribly bloated. We also got a jolly good view of a bird climbing on a tree near some woodpecker holes which we identified as a Nuthatch when we got back.

Tuesday 26th
… In prayers the headmaster announced that as a war measure, straw hats and stiff collars would be abolished. I think we should have a bonfire.

Public schools, in addition to daily uniforms of blazers and grey flannel trousers, marked Sundays by requiring boys to wear black suits and straw 'boaters'.

Saturday 30th
… Freiter's French period, and [we] *tried to sing the Marseillaise, everyone ragged about. I'm afraid I haven't been behaving very well this term with him—it's very difficult to, he's so hopeless. He is quite nice really, but just can't keep order …*

Sunday 31st
… After lunch B, B, H and I all went for a bike ride. We went eleven miles altogether. Jolly good fun. While we were having a rest, some yokels offered to take our bikes for a spin and then began throwing stones at us. H and B replied with fir cones, and somehow or other a man who looked like a retired colonel was hit. After a lively lecture, he went away with the words 'You damn scum of the earth'. I think and hope he was addressing the yokels …

to Cambridge

April

Tuesday 2nd
Got up at the horribly early time of 6 o'clock and after a cup of tea I bicycled to the station. Home by train for Easter holidays. Lovely to get home again. Everyone very well, but Martin working almost continuously …

Wednesday 3rd
… After tea I put a 60 bulb in the dark room and printed my three best pictures yet. I am very pleased.

Thursday 4th

… Boston rang up and asked me round. … He has a lovely Trix twin layout, and his mother had painted some very realistic scenery all round. He had lots of trucks etc. He also showed me his lovely gauge 3 steam engine, the 'County of Northumberland'. That was a marvellous model.

Then in the afternoon he came round. … We sent my Basset-Lowke Enterprise twice, she went beautifully—made a station and painted it and lay out the gauge 00 track. Martin says we could run that off the little car battery as it has got to be taken out.

The gauge 3 and Bassett-Lowke gauge 0 (such as the Enterprise) model locomotives were steam-powered.

Friday 5th

… After lunch Margaret and I went to the Bird Sanctuary (Dr. Hopkinson has obtained a key for us). It was very nice, we saw as we went along a robin close up and two or three chaffinches. Then Margaret saw something lying by the edge of the water, and when I saw it I thought it was a dead duck. Then it began to struggle, and we saw it was a rabbit. Thinking it was caught, I went down to see it, and it jumped into the water and breathed a little of it. I pulled it out and Margaret held it upside down, which made water pass out of its nose. As we thought we might make him better we took him home and put him in the hot-cupboard.

Saturday 6th

The rabbit was dead in the morning. After breakfast Margaret and I dissected it. Its chest was covered with bubbles, showing that he had been drowned, and there was a big clot of blood showing where he had ruptured his chest. Also at the top joint of his right hind leg there was a big clot. Very interesting dissecting him, he had about eleven feet of intestine …

Tuesday 9th
I rang up Boston and he came round and stayed for lunch. We sent the steam train once—she went very well, and then we played with Tinker and sat in the greenhouse.

Horrible news! Germany has practically invaded Denmark and is invading Norway by sea. All her marines were on iron ore steamers disguised and in this way they captured Narvik. Oslo surrendered in the evening after being bombed. Naval engagements off the coast—but we can't know anything definite …

Wednesday 10th
I didn't go to Boston or ask him round as it is the last day here.

News is that a great deal of naval activity. Germans have lost 3 or + cruisers, 2 or + destroyers, 3 submarines, 10 or more supply ships and 5 transports. We have lost 2 destroyers, and [plus] *one badly damaged. Norwegians holding out on land …*

Packed after tea, also bought two films which Mommy had given me. News very good.

to Glatting

Thursday 11th
Filthy journey. Train started at 9 and we got to Petworth at about 2.15.

News of the sinking of two more of our destroyers. We have now lost HMS Hardy, HMS Hunter, HMS Glowworm and HMS Geurka [Gurkha].

Glatting very well. Andy and Flopsy [rabbits] *looking better than for a long time.*

Friday 12th
I cooked breakfast in my house—porridge and bacon. Spent most of the morning there, and made the coffee for my lunch. During the morning I spilt paraffin on my sweater, and had a row with Margaret, not a very long one.

We went for a walk in the afternoon: through Scotchers Bottom and along towards the willow herb patch [this was in a crater, probably caused by an off-target sea mine. We called it the willow herb patch as this plant had been quick to establish itself, as in London's bomb sites]. *Just before we got to the wood saw a stag! I just got in John's binoculars as … it leaped over a bush about three foot high. He was the most graceful creature I have ever seen. Coming back through the wood we went very quietly, and though I saw no deer, I saw a fox slinking along in the wood …*

Little news, except we have laid minefields in lots of places.

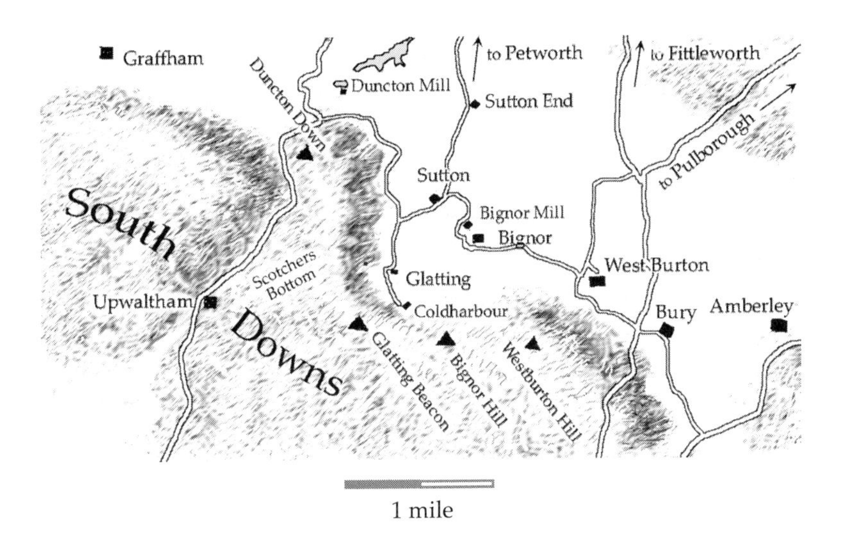

Saturday 13th

… Wonderful news. In Narvik Fjord we sank 7 German destroyers, losing two slightly damaged! …

Figures of losses which I quoted were taken from the news, and in time I realised that they were seldom accurate. Historical records show that there were two phases in the Norwegian naval engagements; in the first the British losses included 5 destroyers, in the second 8 German destroyers and two U-boats were sunk at little cost to the British.

Monday 15th

When I woke up (I was sleeping in my house) it was pouring with rain. It cleared up quite soon. After Margaret had drawn the fungus she found yesterday, we went down to Sutton and bought lots of things. There was a hunt, and they were all outside the pub. Even the Armstrongs were there—disgusting …

Fox hunting was not approved of in the family.

Tuesday 16th

… 2nd Lieutenant David Nash (Ex-Bombardier) came in time for tea. He is going to stay for a few days. He was all dressed up in his uniform [he had joined up in the ranks and then got a commission].

I have a chicken which lays just outside my house. I so far have two of its eggs, and I leave one in the nest so that it will go on laying. It is very convenient …

Wednesday 17th

An absolutely marvellous day. I was so warm in my house that I didn't wake up until about 4 mins. to eight. We have bombed Trondheim aerodrome for the 8th time, and bombarded it from the sea.

We all went for a long walk in the morning. I climbed two trees to investigate squirrels' nests. … Going down the path from the willow herb patch I got the surprise of my life to see a Hawker Hurricane just through the trees! There were 12 or 15 planes altogether, the aerodrome stretched right to Gumber Farm! I had never seen a real fighter before—they are lovely little things! They are making an enormous road there too.

I later realised that the 'Hurricanes' were plywood dummies intended, I imagine, to draw attacks from the RAF fighter base at Tangmere, a few miles to the south.

We saw the first swallow … by the sign post. Mommy came to supper in my house. Soup and omelette, quite successful.

B.E.F. [British Expeditionary Force] *in Norway.*

British, French and Polish troops were sent to Norway—a force which, combined with the Norwegian army, outnumbered the Germans, but lacked a clear, unified command. The eventual naval victory made it possible to evacuate them, leaving the Norwegian army with no choice but to surrender.

Thursday 18th
David, Nora and I went for a walk. After finding a few pieces of pottery, we walked along the path right at the top of the sheep track—toward Scotchers Bottom. Just before we got out of the wood, we heard a crackling noise on the right of the path (in the big field) and 'perceived that the vegetation was being devoured by flames'. With horrible war cries we lept up, and proceeded to beat it out. After about ten minutes arduous labour we succeeded in our object. I think it might quite possibly have burnt down the wood. Quite a lot of grass and several bushes were burnt …

Saturday 20th
… Margaret, David, his friend (Miss Shepard) and I went to the 'Roman Rubbish Dump' [an area in the woods where I had found a lot of bits of Romano-British pottery] *and found several pieces of pottery. Then we lay in the sun, except for Margaret who looked for lichen to dye the wool she's been spinning with. … I heard the cuckoo for the first time this year.*

to Cambridge

Tuesday 23rd
[Back to Cambridge for the rest of the holiday.] … *We arrived in London at 10.45 and shopped. At 11.15 we had a sandwich and an ice-cream soda on Selfridge's roof, then we shopped until 12.35, when we went to see Pinocchio. There was a very good film 'Babes of the World' showing several young animals, wonderful photography, then Pinocchio. It was wonderful; the music was not so good, but the drawing was much better than Snow White. Then we had tea lunch, and*

went and collected the luggage … We met Daddy at the station (Liverpool St.) and when we got back the family was complete. … John enters the navy on Monday.

The household now included Kenneth Richards, a cousin from Rhodesia, who had come to join the RAF, and a Spanish Republican refugee doctor (Henry Bassadone). Kenneth was convalescing after having his appendix out, and he and I greatly enjoyed playing together with my trains and canoeing on the Cam. He ended up in the Fleet Air Arm and, having requested a posting in East Africa, found himself on HMS Uganda off the Hebrides. He visited us once more on leave but I never knew what happened to him thereafter. HMS Uganda survived the war, serving in the Atlantic, the Mediterranean and the Far East. Henry Bassadone had been a doctor in the Republican army in Spain. In due course, his qualifications were recognised and he worked in hospitals in South London.

Saturday 27th
Not a very nice day, rather sultry and dark, but quite warm. … In the afternoon Margaret and Kenneth came on the river with me. They got some weed from ditches …

At 6.30 the others (except N and M) went to see a G.B. Shaw play. We had supper earlyish and listened to Garrison Theatre [a radio comedy series, broadcast by the BBC Forces Programme] …

We are not doing very well in Norway.

Monday 29th
A misty morning, rather murky all day …

After lunch Mommy and I did my clothes until 3.30, when we went and had tea, after which Dr. Bassadone, Kenneth and I went on the river. We had a naval battle and all got pretty wet. Good fun.

Nora was feeling ill or something, and was rather cross all day, and until he went on the river Dr. Bassadone was terribly mournful, and poor Mommy was rather desperate. She was OK in the evening though …

We are doing a little better in Norway.

to Norfolk

May

I spent three days sailing on the Norfolk Broads with 2 other boys in the charge of the geography teacher Mr. Bagnall Oakley.

Thursday 2nd
The following notes are rather brief, being written a long time after …

Friday 3rd
… S there already. E not coming, P instead. … Boat called Lullaby … P. Hunter and sons, near Potter Heigham. Went to Hickling Broad in the evening, spent the night. S and I sailed on the broads in the sailing dinghy. Mucked about with S's Webley air pistol. Good fun. P jolly decent …

Saturday 4th
An absolutely marvellous day. Before we started we scuttled two milk cartons with the air pistol. P and I started off first in the dinghy. Joined others when we reached the main river. We frightened two swans with the air pistol. While getting under a bridge, S fell in up to his waist. I took a few photos of the boat etc. We visited a heronry in very marshy ground, but found no inhabited nests …

Had crab for supper. Tried to get slugs for air pistol in town, couldn't get any as mangy old ironmonger had just closed and wouldn't let us have any. Last and very good Garrison Theatre.

Awful mess up over Norway, we've lost S. and Central. Due to [behaviour of the British] *Cabinet etc.*

Sunday 5th
I was very sick many times last night at about 12 o'clock onwards because of the crab. Began to feel better after a bit.

River beautifully clear, had quite a decent run when the wind got up. We ended the day at the Ferry Inn, where we had supper + sundry ginger beers.

Monday 6th
When we woke up it was a horrible cold grey day, and during breakfast it began to rain. We cruised about a bit. … We had tea at S. Walsham broad, after which I took 10 pictures of a grebe on its nest, with its crest up. Only one photo has been taken of this before, by Mr. Oakley and a friend of his. Mr. Oakley got some too, and said he wouldn't sell his reel for £5! …

In the evening we went to Yarmouth and saw 'Gulliver's Travels'. Jolly good.

to Holt

Wednesday 8th
Usual beginning of term muck. Hundreds of new boys. … I am in the Senior dorm …

Thursday 9th
News was that Gov. majority has dropped to 81!!! Rumours that Chamberlain may resign!!! … Hooray!!!!

May 1940

Friday 10th

1st Austria 2nd Czecho-Slovakia 3rd Memel etc. 4th Poland 5th Denmark 6th S. and Central Norway 7th Holland 8th Belgium 9th Luxemburg!!! And we have landed troops in Iceland—'protective arrest'. Chamberlain not yet resigned [in fact he resigned on this day]. *We are going to the help of Holland and Belgium. Parachute troops used not very successfully. Open towns bombed! … So WHAT???!!? We look more like losing the war every day. Why don't we do something? Why won't America come in? It wouldn't pay.*

We are going to have extensive ARP [Air Raid Protection] *Practice, one at night.*

Nothing further to report from Norway.

Saturday 11th

Quite a nice day, lessons were all right on the whole. In the afternoon there was a Dayboys vs. Boarders [cricket] *match. … After tea I played tennis, good fun.*

Monday 13th

… In double MT we had to make little things for being shot at by the Corps. Beastly fag …

Tuesday 14th

… In the afternoon I played cricket. I was on Birtles' side. Birtles used to play for Yorkshire, and also soccer professionally …

Birtles was the school 'pro'. Sport in those days, most notably cricket, was played by two distinct groups, public school and university amateurs on the one hand, and by professionals who were paid, on the other.

Wednesday 15th

Very boring day. Bad news. In view of increased German pressure, Holland's main army has recapitulated! However we are doing quite well elsewhere …

In Geography Mr. Bagnall Oakley told us about the war.

Mr. Bagnall Oakley was one of the minority of teachers who conveyed both a real interest in teaching and an awareness of the world which he felt we should share. In most cases school work and activities carried on as if, apart from some inconveniences, nothing abnormal was happening.

Friday 17th
Whoopee! My photos arrived by the morning post—the grebe ones are very successful indeed … I also got:—a good one of my train, a nice one of Mother, a nice one of the river, a windmill, and one of P up a tree …

Saturday 18th
… I was told that I had to have my photo taken for a passport photo in case I was going abroad because of the war. We tried the place twice but it was shut. … In the end Mr. Oakley took my photo, and I wrote a very worried letter asking what it was all about.

Monday 20th
More worries etc.—I got a letter which made things cheerfuller, then Frank told me something. Nora and Margaret are going [abroad] *definitely in about a fortnight, they wanted me to go. Did I want to? NO! But - - ?!? Miserable. Went about a little glum all day until after tea, when I rang up Mother and she explained it all. It would be pretty nasty here, but if I wanted I could definitely stay. … I did. Daddy was going to join the RAMC* [Royal Army Medical Corps], *Mother going to be a nurse, John still at Chatham, Martin at Swanage. Nora and Margaret shortly in S. Africa with W. Ernest* [uncle]. *… Me school.*
So all's well, as yet—until the bombing begins, if it does. News bad—Germans advancing into France via Belgium.

Martin was at the (euphemistically named) Telecommunications Research Establishment near Swanage, which was one of the main centres where radar was being developed. This, of course, was not public knowledge at the time. Radar research had begun in the 1930s in many countries, including Germany. My brother had graduated in Physics from Oxford in 1939 and was now part of a research group working on basic developments and applications of radar. As the Swanage area is virtually an island, it would have taken a very small group of Germans to kill or capture them all, and they were soon relocated to Malvern. Developments in radar allowed the accurate location of aircraft, ships and surfaced submarines, and played an important part in winning the Battle of Britain and the Battle of the Atlantic. My brother was involved in the development of airborne radar devices, and in the creation of an illusory invasion in the Eastern Channel at the time of the D-Day landings in 1944.

Tuesday 21st
News a little better, the Germans have been checked, and the Allies are attacking from opposite sides of the German-occupied bulge trying to cut them off. This is called the Battle of the Bulge. The German objective is the channel ports, as in the last war …

In the afternoon [in cricket] *I only made six, being out by a pretty good catch by H. I did quite a nice catch at cover point …*

Wednesday 22nd
News pretty bad, the Germans have got Arras and Amiens. Not far from the coast. Actually Amiens was recaptured later by French troops. The Germans are doing too well all the same.

My Supermarine Spitfire and F's Messerschmidt M.E.109 [construction kits] *came today, they are wizard …*

Thursday 23rd
Not much more news except we are a little more Nazified, i.e. the Govt has complete power. Had double art, I made a lousy mess out of oil-paint …

Friday 24th
Another nice day. I expect that we'll be bathing soon …

The news is pretty grim, they are pretty near Calais, and doing rather too well—actually at present being held back, but will it last? I hope so …

Saturday 25th
Bathing will begin this weekend!!! Headmaster announced this in Prayers. … We played the Upper School again … I made 27 caught slips—my average is now 20 5/7. I also caught the last man on the fourth ball of the last over …

I practically finished my S. Spitfire …

Sunday 26th
At first it was a very nice sunny day. In chapel we spent about 20 mins. praying, very tiring and boring. When I got back I wrote home. That afternoon I had been going to play tennis, but a torrential downpour made the ground too soft.

I finished my Spitfire (i.e. put aerial and wireless mast on) and then almost immediately bust it. I had a collision with F's unfinished Messerschmitt and mine dropped on the floor and the wing bust off. I had no glue left. I blamed F though it was actually just as much my fault. I was extremely annoyed.

15 French generals sacked, … Marcus Bauer [Jewish emigré] *went off to* [his home in] *the Argentine in the morning. Good luck!*

Tuesday 28th
Perfectly foul news. King Leopold of Belgium, as commander of the Belgian army, has capitulated—against the wishes of the government and without consulting us—and has left us with the possibility of being surrounded. SWINE! Actually half the army is still fighting, and the other half have capitulated. Things in the future look very gloomy. I didn't learn the news until the evening, rather depressed … a little cheerfuller later as we are sure to win in the end.

Wednesday 29th
For about 20 minutes in geography, Mr. Oakley told us about the war; pretty sticky in Belgium. After tea (for which we had wizard ice-creams!) we had nets [cricket practice], *during which a large flight of ancient biplanes flew overhead—I don't know what …*

Friday 31st
A letter from Daddy in the morning. Right at the last moment, the girls couldn't go [to South Africa] *as they couldn't get permits. Nora is going to learn to be a child's nurse (near Newcastle), and Margaret is going to do forestry with Uncle George (the bearded one) in S. Wales. Daddy as yet has failed to join the RAMC as they don't seem to want him or something. Mommy may be a nurse if he does get in. Surgeon-Lieutenant J. C. Ryle* [brother John] *is soon going to sea as surgeon to a flotilla of minesweepers.*

News foul. They've as good as got the Belgian channel ports, we are disembarking successfully leaving most of the tank corps and armoured units of the BEF behind. Street fighting continues in Calais. Three destroyers lost, several smaller boats and one transport. Pretty grim [this was the start of the Dunkirk evacuation].

My father did not get into the RAMC (Royal Army Medical Corps), probably because of his pre-war pacifist views and unwillingness to participate in research into poison gases. But he did leave Cambridge in order to work for the Emergency Medical Service, travelling the country to teach from his First World War experience, in particular about the management of chest injuries, and he returned to his beloved Guy's Hospital in London. Margaret, a shy 17–year old, went to work as a timber measurer for tough Canadian foresters in Wales, but later returned to school and went on to Oxford.

June

Sunday 2nd
The day began with a ! or two. We were told to go to Frank's study where he began by saying "You go home on Tuesday" (Cries and applause). Waffle concerning why … then "The summer holiday will be shorter" (groans). We will reassemble in about 2 weeks at "Somewhere in England". Pack. Awful rush etc. We got all we could done, and spent the afternoon playing rounders …

News:- The most wonderful rearguard action ever—withdrawing troops from Belgium via Dunkirk is nearly completed.

The re-definition of the catastrophic defeat and the Dunkirk evacuation as a great British victory was underway. Which is not to deny the real strength and heroism (or the fortunately calm weather) which allowed the evacuation of a considerable proportion of British troops and also of many French soldiers.

My diaries' record of these days is one of the few which does not entirely match my memory. I recall Frank (the housemaster) addressing all the boys in the junior house with passionate anger at our apparent unawareness of, or lack of interest in, the historical moment. Though I excused myself from this charge—unlike most of the boys I did follow the news in the papers made available to us—it is strange to read how we went on playing cricket and swimming even through those frightening days.

to Cambridge

Tuesday 4th
Woke up at about 5.40. … Station 6.40. … Very slow and boring journey. … Daddy home for lunch and Dr. Bassadone [and another Spanish refugee doctor]. *John came down all in uniform looking very smart for two days' leave. All the family had dinner at the Arts* [theatre] *and saw 'Little Review'. Went to bed about 11.30 exhausted.*

Wednesday 5th
Bathed in the morning [in the Cam]. *… Met boys from Kings College Choir School* [my old school] *there and was told there was an old boys match in the afternoon. I was asked to play. I did …*

Big new German offensive launched on Seine. 120 mile front.

Thursday 6th
… I got out of bed and found that I had a very tender patch on my left heel. Apparently there was a very small thorn in it which had all gone septic.

I gave my best pictures of the grebe and a heron to daddy to be enlarged. I am going to send the grebe one to the 'Field'.

I had a bathe, but when I got back Mommy put a much too hot fermentation on, and I was told to lie down all day …

Friday 7th
I had been aware of a noise which threatened to wake me up for some time, when Margaret came in and told me to get up as it was the air raid siren. We all went down to the passage outside the dining room and sat on the very concrete floor. We heard a few aeroplanes but nothing else, and after about an hour we went upstairs and lay on mattresses in that passage. All clear 30 minutes later.

Mommy and Nora went off early to Newcastle. … John rang up—arriving tomorrow afternoon for week-end leave.

Saturday 8th
… Mommy arrived at 8.30 having travelled all night. We had had two air raid warnings in the night, one for about ½ an hour at 11 o'clock, and one at about 2.30 for two hours, in the later part of which we slept. We heard altogether 1 rifle shot.

Mommy however had had only one warning in the train, and had later passed through Peterborough and seen one roof damaged by a small bomb. One row of incendiary bombs fell in a row down the middle of the street.

John arrived for tea, after which he and Daddy went for a bathe.

Sunday 9th
… John went off finally, at 10.30. He is going to the Indian Ocean or somewhere …

Monday 10th
… In the morning Dr. Laycock came, froze my heal, and cut off the dead skin. It oozed a lot and felt much better. I had to be in bed all day …

Mommy went off to see John for the last time before he goes off to the Mediterranean. … When she was in London she got me the Frog Penguin Gloster Gladiator set [this was the last biplane built for the RAF, and was already obsolete].

Margaret and I read aloud to each other out of the 'Sword in the Stone'. Very sultry, good sky but no storm.

Tuesday 11th
I stayed in bed all day and made the Gloster Gladiator. After tea, trying to make the Spitfire look better I ruined it, and so sandpapered it clean and wrote to Hamleys for some new transfers and paint …

I was told, to my great surprise, that Italy had declared war on us yesterday—I wasn't told then. Just as John goes to the Mediterranean. Got a good navy too …

Wednesday 12th
… The 'Gladiator' is finished and looks jolly good. I put a dashboard in yesterday …

Foul news, Germans advancing to Paris. French tiring …

Friday 14th
On the one o'clock news the Germans were in Paris. French line unbroken but exhausted. Italians have done nothing, we captured 60 men, two officers and 33 machine guns with no casualties! …

We heard where the school are going. … We go to Newquay in Cornwall, on or before June 26th …

Saturday 15th
… Dr. Hopkinson lent me two bird magazines. He showed me round his garden. It is a very nice one, but the rain has been so black— probably from smoke from the Great Battle— that lots of the flowers were black …

Monday 17th
… I spent the rest of the day reading 'Beau Geste' by P.C. Wren. Daddy had had him as a patient once, and had asked him what his profession was! He said that he was an ex-soldier, and the next day Daddy got a present of two or three of his books …

Everyone very depressed as France has stopped fighting. Will we go on?

Tuesday 18th
P and F came, and we took my canoe down on the trolley and went canoeing. We had a battle and all got soaked (the others v. me). I then sunk F by the edge, he went right in. When I got to the Mill Pond, P was there having come by the stream, and we had another battle. I beached, waded out and sank his canoe in about 1 ft. of water. F lost his shirt. Good fun.

Wednesday 19th
When I was woken up at 11.30 it was to hear a warbling note of varying pitch [the air raid warning siren]. *We went to Mommy's room first, but then we went back to sleep. When I next was woken again at about 12.15, I heard a big BANG and was told to go down to the pantry, which was the safest room. We heard anti-aircraft fire and then went to sleep. 'All Clear' at about 12.50. In the papers it said about 12 killed, and we knew that they were all here at Cambridge.*

… on the way [back from canoeing] *attacked by a tough. Argument, he loses temper, we laugh, I hit him on jaw, he hits me on ear. A man arrives and he flees.*

7 planes down last night out of 100.

Thursday 20th
… In the afternoon Margaret and I greased Martin's things. … Finished papering his windows [to black them out] *after tea (nearly all our crockery is in there) …*

France negotiating for Peace, but still fighting.

to Newquay

Monday 24th
Left for school by car with Mr. Candler, who had offered to drive me down to Newquay. He had stayed with us the previous night.

… we went and picked up his father and the woman who looked after him. His father was in his second childhood quite definitely, and grumbled the whole time. His chief difficulty was in remembering the

word 'honeysuckle'. He got terribly worried about everything, and sounded as if he were going to cry all the time.

We passed a cement lorry which had been burning for two hours, and had collapsed in the middle and was setting in the cement. … We stopped at a guest house in Glastonbury in Somerset.

Tuesday 25th

In the middle of the night they had their first air raid warning here. The guest house proprietors and several children (and a baby who screamed intermittently for the whole 3½ hours) ran about the house shouting "Air Raid! Air Raid!", and all the children got awfully excited. Got to sleep after about 3 hours.

We looked at the ruins of Glastonbury Abbey, a terrific building about 500 yards long. … We arrived for tea at Mawgan Porth where we had a bathe, then went to Newquay. The country is marvellous and the hotel very comfortable.

The school—much depleted—had re-assembled in two hotels in Newquay. The junior house, Kenwyn (where I was), and Woodlands (where I soon went) were in the Bay Hotel, 2 or 3 hundred yards from the sea and overlooking Fistral Bay (now a popular surfing centre). A cinder path led up to the Pentire Hotel, where three other senior houses—Old School House, Farfield and Howsons—had a floor each.

The hotel bedrooms became study bedrooms for three or four boys. The lounges and bars were adapted as classrooms in the Bay hotel, and as the Assembly Hall and laboratories in the Pentire. Games were played on the more level parts of the nearby golf course, and supervised swimming and surfing became available. The rock pools and cliffs and the tidal estuary of the river Gannel, as well as the more distant countryside, offered scope for biology, natural history—especially bird watching—and for exploration on bicycles. We were allowed unaccompanied access to these at weekends and on half days.

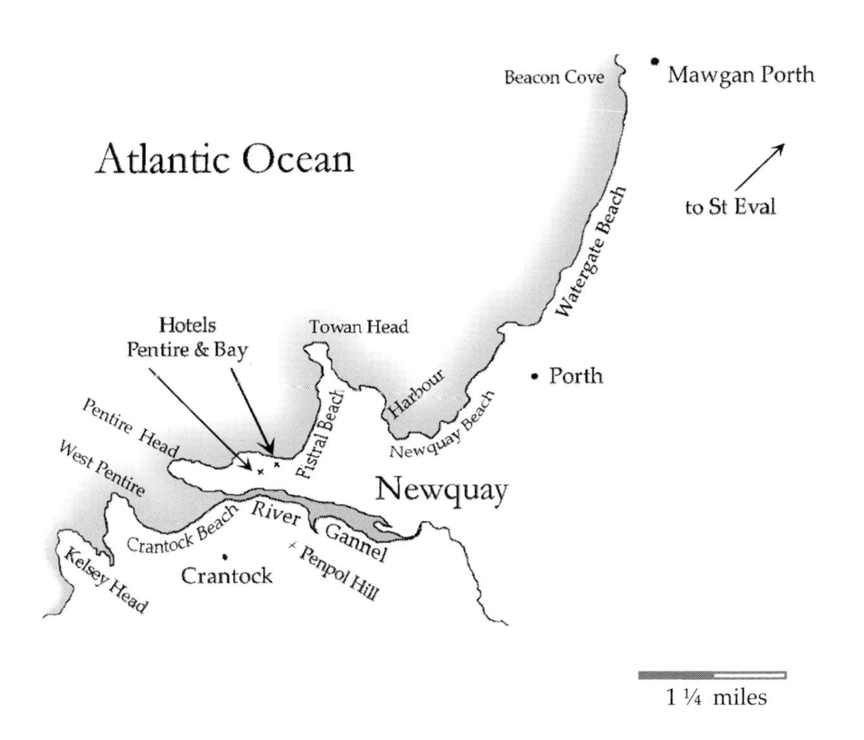

Wednesday 26th

... I went down onto the beach to look for sea-anemones, then I walked toward Pentire Head with Wood. After tea we got about half-way to the Point when we realised it was about 4 mins. to house prayers. We ran, but were two mins. late, with about 15 other people who had been on the beach. We were let off with a caution.

I don't have to have special milk as all the milk is pasteurised [I and another pupil had previously had our milk boiled].

RAF Initial Training Wing inspection on Newquay Beach, 1942

Friday 28th

… After afternoon lessons and tea … we all tidied up, and gathered valuable scrap iron, which we conveyed nail by nail to a heap by the petrol pump about 80 yards away …

Saturday 29th

The weather at first was horribly dull … but it cleared up and the afternoon was lovely. … We had a wizard bathe, with terrific waves.

Then after tea Wood and I walked right along to Pentire head. On the way back he investigated a seagull's nest, which entailed quite a difficult rock climb (which is absolutely forbidden). I funked it rather, but he has climbed in Austria. I did a very little very easy. There were two babies and an egg in the nest. We also saw a seal in the water.

Sunday 30th

A lovely day … I went to a NHS [Natural History Society] *meeting, concerning coming activities. … then Wood and I took surf-board and went to bathe. Lovely big rollers, and not too many people. … After lunch we took our cameras and some bread, and went along the cliffs. We photographed spray and seagulls. … we saw a seal again …*

July

Tuesday 2nd

In double biology we went down on the rocks and looked at the fauna and flora of the different level rock pools. Very interesting …

In French the Kestrel hovered outside the window for about 30 seconds.

Immediately after lunch Wood, F and I biked into town, we all bought surf boards and I got a film for my camera …

I got a letter from Daddy, all well.

Wednesday 3rd

… We were told that Treweeks possibly had an infectious disease, that the town was out of bounds, and that we had to gargle three times a day with salt water …

Thursday 4th
The French fleet has largely come over to our side. 1/3 has been sunk because they opposed us.

After the French surrender, the Vichy government had undertaken to remain neutral. But their promise was not trusted by Britain, and after the French naval force in Algeria rejected the offer of safe conduct to neutral places, it was attacked and several ships were sunk, with the loss of over 1,000 French sailors. This caused much resentment against Britain. The justification for the attack was the fear that, if strengthened by these ships, the Italian navy could pose a serious threat to the supply lines to North Africa. Later, in November 1942, as Germany occupied Vichy France, the French fleet which had docked at Toulon was scuttled.

Treweeks has not got sunstroke—but he hadn't got diphtheria or scarlet fever either—but, worst of all, Infantile Paralysis! So we're in quarantine with all sorts of restrictions.

Infantile paralysis was the name then used for polio—which was often fatal.

Friday 5th
We were isolated all day ... and had to do lessons by ourselves ...
Lunch early so we don't mix with Woodlands [house]. ... *Treweeks is rather worse. Both his lungs are slightly paralysed, and he is in an iron lung. No one else has it ...*
A Beaufort flew past very low ...

Beauforts were maritime patrol aircraft stationed at RAF St. Eval about 4 miles away.

Saturday 6th
... There were three air raid alarms in the morning, and I heard three 'huns' and AA [anti-aircraft] *fire. Quite exciting.*
In the afternoon Wood iii, A, F and self went along to Pentire Head. We climbed down and got some photos of the young gulls, which were lovely and fluffy and speckly ...

Sunday 7th
A beautifully slack day. A bathe at 10.15, lovely in, but there was a cold wind, and it was raining when we were dressing, which was horrid.

After lunch ... Wood and A and I went along to the Point again. We walked about and tried to take photos of ma and pa gull diving at us when we went near their nest. I don't expect that they'll work though. Then we were climbing down on the Fistral Bay side when I saw a plane above looking like this: I said "there's a Hun", half jokingly, then I said "actually I think it is really". They said "Yes, come on, let's go down". Then 5 Spitfires shot over the same way then 'whumph, whumph'.

We raced up to see several dots far off, and a large cloud of smoke about half a mile past the river Gannel. WIZARD! A Beaufort also came round lower than the cliffs, and a Spitfire.

We won two bob from Mr. Oakley, for catching a special sort of beetle. 8d each. They were six-spot burnets with the spots joined up.

On later reflection I wonder if the 'Beaufort' was a mis-identification and that it was in fact a German plane seeking to fly below our radar. If so, its presence was probably connected with the RAF base at St. Eval a few miles along the coast. In the ensuing weeks, there were large numbers of German attacks on coastal towns, ports and shipping. The raid on Cambridge and then the shooting down of the German plane were my first direct war experiences. But perhaps experience is the wrong word; it was more like theatre, and it generated excitement and no fear. Neither these events nor the news brought home to me the reality of Britain's military situation. Both the optimism I expressed as I chronicled the disasters of the previous months, and my willingness to believe our propaganda in the face of the catalogue of disasters, were quite irrational, but shared by most people.

Tuesday 9th
... Good news, a non-given up French battle ship badly damaged. Several planes brought down over England.

July 1940

I got a letter from Daddy asking me to write in ink legibly, also from Mommy. I'm sorry.

Wednesday 10th

... After rest I fished for Blenny and got a 5-inch one which I managed to put back. Up with bent pin and cotton! ...

News—naval engagement in Mediterranean. We sighted two battleships and several cruisers, fired two shots, hit a battleship, and they lay a smoke-screen and ran for it. We gave chase and are giving chase ...

Thursday 11th

... In double MT ... I made a Blenny fishing apparatus. In Biology we had Mr. Ramage, who talked all the period before break on the sea shore in general, very interesting. Then after break we went down on the rocks (of which there were few, as it was high tide) and looked at seaweeds ...

Saturday 13th

... In the afternoon we were going to go along to the Point, but before we went Frank said "You three have been reported to me by my intelligence service for climbing on rocks! I absolutely forbid it". Sneaks someone. After that we couldn't very well go down to the seagull's nest, so we didn't go very far. We Blenny fished a little, but I'm getting bored of doing that ...

Then BANG! Mr. Spencer told us that he was sending this circular to all masters concerned: "I think that this house is treating this term too like a summer holiday, therefore I propose to institute detention periods on Tuesday and Saturday afternoons. Offences are cheek, slackness and bad manners, late for meals and talking after lights out". Phew!

Monday 15th

... During 4th period (maths) we heard a big bang, saw a Heinkel or something having just made a low-flying attack on the [St. Eval] *'drome, and saw anti-aircraft fire. He escaped into cumulus clouds ...*

I heard from Mommy in the morning. I got the robin photos (quite good) and my Identity disc. All well and busy. Also Punch.

Thursday 18th
… In biology we … saw little transparent fish which we don't know what are. We saw a small crab changing its shell.

After singing, in which I sang as badly as I could or not at all, Mr. Hales said that I needn't have turned up, and that in future I could bring a book and read. Out of the choir!!! …

Sunday 21st
… In the afternoon, Wood and I went along to the Head, with the intention of stalking F and F. We didn't find them. We did find the signallers however, and I was able to read their messages. I was better than two of them, who couldn't read it at all (S and W), and A told me various things. I think I will join them when I'm in the Corps [school cadet force or JTC].

Monday 22nd
… In MT I made a box to keep the burnet moth caterpillars in, because they hatched this morning. They have nearly, if not all, come out and are about this size -- . We gave them some ragwort. We now have to wait about 5 weeks.

Tuesday 23rd
… Wood, A and I bicycled into Newquay for a rehearsal. The play is going to be the 'Merchant of Venice', and it is in the town theatre. We spent most of the afternoon watching, but in two scenes we had to stand absolutely still on the stage. Our only movement is one bow, and walking off the stage once. The actors are all jolly good …

The budget announced: 8/6 in the pound, everything 20% more govt. tax, luxuries up much more. Jolly good but pretty tough …

These were increases in income and purchase tax.

Friday 26th
… In MT we dug the beginning of an Air Raid shelter …

Tuesday 30th
… English, in which we discussed about whether we should declare our Peace Terms now …

After lunch we went to the rehearsal. During our bit I felt extremely sick and dizzy, and had to go outside. I think it was too much lunch and the fug in the theatre while standing on the stage. Then at 4.15 all those in the play went and bathed in the harbour. It was very clear and about 9ft deep. It was 14ft to the water, S and O dived, the others went by the steps. Jolly warm. Good sunny and no surf.

Wednesday ***31st***
… We were weighed in the evening, I weigh 7.7½ (up 2½). N has gone up 9 lbs! He is only half a pound less than me, so does Wood.

August

Friday 2nd
!!! Prayers outside, then "One of the maids at Pentire has a suspected case of Infantile Paralysis" …

A Telegram was sent home "Do you want your children home?" …

to Cambridge

Saturday 3rd
[6 boys] *etc. all going. And Wood. Its going to be foul here without him and nothing to do. (Written at 9.15).*

At 9.24, 6 mins. before the bus was due to leave for the station, I was told that I was going! I was in the middle of painting my name on my surf-board. I rushed off, bunged a few things in the suitcase, and got on the bus. Phew! … Cambridge about 9.40. Very tired. What a day, and what a term! The maid who got I.P. died.

The Cambridge house was being packed up as it was being given to the Army for the duration of the war. My father would be based in a small flat in London, while the rest of the household moved to Glatting.

Sunday 4th

I was rather tired all day. Harry [a friend of Martin's] *was there, he is going into the navy as a wireless operator, and has just got his uniform. … Harry went on the 2.5. We brought a woman RAF Sergeant who had missed the train back, the next train being at 5.4 …*

A Handley Page Hampden dived down over the house, pretty manoeuvrable …

No news really. Japan a bit uppish.

Monday 5th

I did several scale drawings for Mommy in the morning. They were of the different rooms in their new flat in London. Very wiggly in and out walls, about 20 corners per room. That is a not very slight exaggeration.

I did nothing most of the rest of the day, except … cook supper (omelette with fried potatoes and onions).

Wednesday 7th

… News—Ominous Quiet …

We heard from the Headmaster that it [the maid's fatal illness] *definitely was not I. Paralysis but angina or something. We aren't going back earlier all the same.*

I painted a kitchen table which is going to London.

Thursday 8th

… In the afternoon I painted the kitchen table, and had another bath.

News. Big [German] *attack on a convoy* [in the Channel] *with MTBs* [Motor Torpedo Boats] *and dive-bombers escorted by fighters. We lost some ships. Got one MTB and 53 aeroplanes! We lost 16 fighters.*

This was the beginning of the Battle of Britain, which started with attacks on shipping and coastal defences and then switched to attacks on airfields.

Friday 9th
We have now shot 60 not 53 down. 27 dive bombers. We lost 16, and three of our pilots are safe.
... went out to tea with Dr. Hopkinson. We went to the Bird Sanctuary before tea—it is quite dry, and about 5ft of nettles nearly everywhere.
Gladiators in Libya shot down 15 Italians, although outnumbered by 2–1, and only lost 2!

This, if true, must have involved equally obsolete Italian planes. In engagements with contemporary fighters, Gladiators suffered 100% losses.

Sunday 11th
... Another big airbattle, 60 down for 24. The FANYs left us for Dr. Hopkinson.

Women of the Field Army Nursing Yeomanry had been billeted at our house.

Tuesday 13th
In the morning B rang up, and as I could not think of an excuse in time, I went round. We had quite fun, all his points [in his railway set] *are electrically operated, so we could do quite exciting things.*
In the afternoon I read and let in the patients. Prof. and Mrs. and Mr. Cornford came to tea. After tea we began packing stores. Bassadone is again having his meals at the department, as he is a guinea-pig [this was work on a highly nutritious national loaf].
Several 'planes down, number not certain.

Wednesday 14th
'Hitler in London tomorrow!' (written in June). My foot!!! He said he would be, but yesterday we got 78 planes, lost 13, but 10 men are safe!

We began to pack …

The furniture was to be delivered to Glatting over the next week. In retrospect, it seems amazing that 4 or 5 pantechnicons could be employed as if the war was not happening. In fact, as events I witnessed suggested, this was the period when German plans to invade Britain were being prepared.

to Glatting

Friday 16th
Mommy drove Duddy, Tinker and me to the station. The journey to London was uneventful but crowded. … As we went out of Purley or somewhere, the air raid siren went, we pulled down the blinds but nothing happened. … We got to Glatting at 3 o'clock …

After tea I was upstairs when I heard rat-at-at-tat. Machine guns! We went out, and after many short bursts and zooms, heard a long burst and a dive bomber, smoke and flames pouring from its port engine, crashed down over by East Dean. We got 144 down yesterday.

Saturday 17th
Apparently there were some parachutists from the plane we saw; about 5 mins. after, they got three down at Petworth, all in the same field! 76 altogether …

Sunday 18th
In the morning we went for a long walk to look for the wreckage of the plane, which, we were told, was this side of the road between Littleton Farm and Upwaltham. We didn't find it, because it was on the other side. The RAF had taken the engines but left the rest. Several village children had bits. We came back by the Willow Herb patch, and heard the sirens. Several fighters about, but no Germans. Then we went to lunch with the Armstrongs, after which there was a lot of AA and/or bombs and machine gunfire, but we saw nothing. We couldn't find a place in the stream where there was enough water to cover ourselves with, so we lay in the garden.

About 560 planes down in a week.

Tuesday 20th
… We began removing [receiving furniture] *in the afternoon. A lorry plus van came, there are six more to come!*

Wednesday 21st
Two more loads in the drawing room. I helped a bit …

I went for a short walk in the afternoon with Tinker, I sat above the chalk pit. On the way back saw a Heinkel through a gap in the clouds. In the evening a man came from Bignor who said a "plane had been shot down by three Spitfires at about that time" (I had seen the Spitfires about ½ minute later) …

Actual losses in air battles were hard to estimate, and both sides made exaggerated claims. Post-war records suggest that over the whole Battle of Britain the Germans lost nearly 1900 fighters and bombers and the RAF a little over 1000 fighters.

Thursday 22nd
… I went for a walk in the morning with Tinker, up past [Col.] *Shiner's* [Cold Harbour farm], *along the top and down by the green slope. On the top a soldier asked me if I knew where the bomb which was dropped about a month ago fell. I said I didn't, but it wasn't in sight of the path …*

to London

Friday 23rd
My father had taken a small flat over a shop in Pilgrimage Street. This was near Guy's Hospital, in the area where Chaucer's Canterbury pilgrims had gathered. Over the next few days we were getting the flat ready, but sleeping with friends in North London. There were frequent air raid warnings and raids.

… After changing at East Croydon, we got in a crowded train, in a compartment with 2 soldiers and 3 others. Mommy had a long

argument with one of them about brass buttons; he had 130 pieces of brass on his equipment, not counting his uniform. He had been in the last war, and was in favour of plenty of 'spit and polish'. We arrived at the Mullaly's at 7.45, to find Daddy waiting for us, getting worried. After supper Daddy and I went to the Marshalls', where we are sleeping.

Saturday 24th
After breakfast Daddy and I went to the flat, as far as we could by bus, and found Mommy and the removers already there; Mommy blowing up the Harrods' linoleum layers for not doing their job properly, although they had had a week. The flat is awfully nice, very sunny, and very small. Rather a business getting the furniture in, they had to get the iron desk in through the window. They left before lunch, Mommy tipped them £5 for the team …

Sunday 25th
Breakfast at nine. News. Ramsgate heavily bombed. 47 down for 10.

We went to the flat and worked until lunch, after which we rested until tea. We then did an hour's work, and then went round to the Mallalier by bus. We arrived exactly on time, had supper and then went to the 'flicks: 'Fire over England' [with Vivien Leigh and Laurence Olivier, about the Spanish Armada]. *Very good. Just before the end Air Raid siren.*

Afterwards we walked a long way up to the Marylebone Road from Oxford Street, and found a tube. We saw the light of two flares. While we were in the tube, although we didn't know it, the All Clear went …

Monday 26th
… After the news Daddy and Mommy came up. I was still awake, and while we were looking out of the window the siren went. We went downstairs and then decided to go to bed.

After I had been asleep I woke up and heard AA fire and possibly bombs. Also I heard planes but I went to sleep again.

Tuesday 27th

A six hour air raid in the night. Nearly all the neighbours were in the shelters—we went to sleep. In the morning I went and bought some ironmongery in the Borough High Street—the man was very shocked to hear that we'd been asleep—and then I had great difficulty in finding my way back. I also went off to London Bridge to get some sausages, but took the wrong turning at the end of Pilgrimage Street, and found a butcher after I had gone about 15 yards.

We went out in the evening for supper, as the man who was laying the linoleum fused the power, and we had supper in Soho. A jolly good supper at a Restaurant where Mommy and Daddy had been before they were married. The managers were Italians, the present one being the old one's son. As soon as we got back the siren went.

Wednesday 28th

… there were two air raid warnings during the night, we slept all the time and I only heard the first warning.

After lunch Daddy and I … walked to where you get the boats in Regents Park. … At 3.30 we got a sailing punt and went out. There was not very much wind, but it was quite fun, and Daddy and I took it in turns. …We had tea in the park.

Air Raid warning at 9 o'clock—to bed …

Friday 30th

No air raids at all, so we all felt much better. I went sailing again. Just after I got there the siren went, but even so I had to wait hours. Actually I got the smallest boat after waiting ¾ of an hour. Quite good, but not quite enough wind.

Just as I came in the siren went again. All the [barrage] *balloons which were down shot up at a terrific rate. There was quite a good AA barrage to the North. Went back by bus. When the All Clear went our nearest siren did the warning by a mistake … Air Raid warning 9.15.*

Saturday 31st
We came downstairs at about 4. We heard two bombs—whistle bump!—they must have been about a mile away. The windows shook. Just as we were on our way back to bed the all clear went.

... to London Bridge where we met Mommy and Daddy, who had had a very noisy night. Glatting for lunch. Tinker very excited.

to Glatting

September

Monday 2nd
... sent 'Swallow' [steam launch] *which leaked. Martin rang up from Pulborough to say he was there, fetched him ...*

Tuesday 3rd
... I went for a long walk with Martin ...

I bicycled to Sutton in the morning to get some cheese. I saw a plane trying to shoot a stray barrage balloon down, but it didn't succeed.

Wednesday 4th
I sent 'Swallow' after mending the safety valve. She went much better, and Martin and me were quite exhausted from running after it ...

During lunch we heard machine gun fire. We saw quite a good battle, first a probable British one dived down on fire and landed near Amberley. Then a ? glided down and hit the hill beyond the hill beyond Bignor Hill. After both these two there was a big puff of smoke. Then later I saw two big ones shot down by two smaller ones, so I think they were Germans. Jolly exciting—Martin hated it.

In retrospect I can fully understand his reaction. He was by nature—and until the war by conviction—a pacifist. My spectator sport attitude to the air war must have jarred with his knowledge that falling planes could be ours as well as theirs—and had men on board.

Thursday 5th
... We went to Francis' house at about six. Francis was on duty as a special constable ... [these were civilian volunteers recruited to stand in for or supplement regular police]

Saturday 7th
... I took Bassadone up past the Rising [a spring in the woods] *and then on to where we could see the sea from. Tinker dug unsuccessfully for badgers. I caught him trying to run away twice.*

In the evening we went for a walk on the Downs. We could hear German planes overhead, and on the way back saw a large red glow to the north east. ?

Sunday 8th
News—big attack on London, dock on fire, which I suppose was what we saw last night. Daddy decided that he had better go back [to Guys] *to see the casualties, so both he and Harry* [Martin's friend who had been staying] *went off in the afternoon; I saw them off with Mommy and Martin.*

This was the start of the night raids on London and many other towns.

Monday 9th
On my way to Newquay, my mother and I stayed with friends in North London.

We caught the 10.30 train, leaving Martin to catch the 10.35 to Swanage. ... We ... got into another train, but the siren went, and we had to wait in the station for 1¼ hours until the all clear went. We left most of my luggage at Paddington, and then went on to the Marshalls' ... we spent the night in the Marshalls' dugout

The dugout was probably a mass-produced corrugated iron Anderson shelter. These were half buried in the garden, and offered significant safety and considerable discomfort.

to Newquay

Tuesday 10th
Daddy rang up in the morning to say that the shops below the flats had been blown in, but that he was alright. I went to the station, got there at 10 o'clock and my train didn't leave until 11.45. Awful train, very crowded, full of evacuating slums. One mother told her child "Behive yer bloody self". I luckily had a seat about ⅔ of the way. The Woods didn't get on. Arrived at Newquay at 6.50, where I sent a small boy whom I had been looking after all the way to his billet by taxi. Mr. Candler on the platform.

Went for a walk on the beach and to bed at ninish.

Wednesday 11th
I went on a trip by car before term started with Mr. Candler (physics teacher), Martin Wood, his brother Christopher and others.

…We had our first stop when we saw a stone circle, and soon after we left the car at a farm and began to walk towards a Quoit [Cornish megalithic tomb]. … *After that we left the car somewhere, and walked about 2 miles to the Leland Youth Hostel. We slept in little tin huts with 3 double decker beds.*

Thursday 12th
We went for a walk up the same hill as I had gone up with Christopher yesterday, and we could see both seas and the 3 rocks past Newquay, about 35–40 miles …

Last night Christopher Wood at about 10 o'clock, came and talked to me for about 2 hours. He came to warn me about not making friends older than yourself, and then we talked for about an hour on religion. It was much easier to talk seriously in the dark. He had quite good views, although he has been confirmed etc.

Friday 13th
Started off by car, and then walked about 3 miles to a coastguard station in sight of Lands End Lighthouse … Martin and I climbed a little, and then we all went back via almost Lands End. It was raining quite hard by now, and part of the way we were walking through a marsh …

Monday 16th
First whole school day. … After that I finished reading the 'First Hundred Thousand' [a novel by Ian Hay about the first volunteers to join the British army during the First World War; 1915].

Tuesday 17th
… in the afternoon there was Corps. I have joined. We marched, left and right wheeled, about turned etc.

Wednesday 18th
… We had a house run, in which we ran up the road, round the caves, walked to the Gannel, climbed along to the Fern Pit [quarry], *and ran to the Bay. Quite fun. I went on the rocks with Martin Wood after tea.*

Naval guns on the other side of Fistral Bay fired their practice shots in the afternoon. Hell of a bang.

Thursday 19th
… I got a letter from Daddy and Mommy some time lately. Daddy says you walk around picking up shrapnel; and Mommy's, which came later, said Guy's had been hit, all medical block stairs and landing removed; that no one was hurt, and all out in 23 mins, and Daddy had made an emergency escape plan. !

My mother's fuller account—which I was told later and have confirmed since from a letter she wrote to her parents at the time—described how, when my father had returned to Guy's, he had found very inadequate plans and preparations. He had mobilised the Works Department to remove the bars from a window providing an escape route from the wards, and had had walkways installed over the glass roofs, and it was these which medical students had used to evacuate the patients.

My partisan mother always protested that my father's contribution to the successful evacuation was never acknowledged, whereas the hospital superintendent, who had not been there, was photographed posing with a bandaged arm (which had been injured by a burst hot water bottle). Students were also recruited as firewatchers, and were stationed on the roof with buckets of water, sand and a stirrup pump—as firewatchers were on all large buildings—ready to deal with the hundreds of incendiary bombs that were scattered over the town.

Sunday 22nd
… A notice to the Home Guard. … 'A situation of acute alertness remains'. Several people were out all night …

Older boys in the school Officer Training Corps—soon to be democratically re-named the Junior Training Corps (JTC)—were incorporated in the Home Guard. The 'acute alertness' was presumably related to the fear of invasion.

Thursday 26th
… After Prayers I went up to Mr. Parsons' study, and he gave me a new boys' jaw [I had now moved to Woodlands House, where Max Parsons was the housemaster]. *I was there for 50 mins, 40 of which he discussed religion with me. He was quite broad minded and willing to see my point of view.*

Bomb damage, Guy's Hospital, 1941

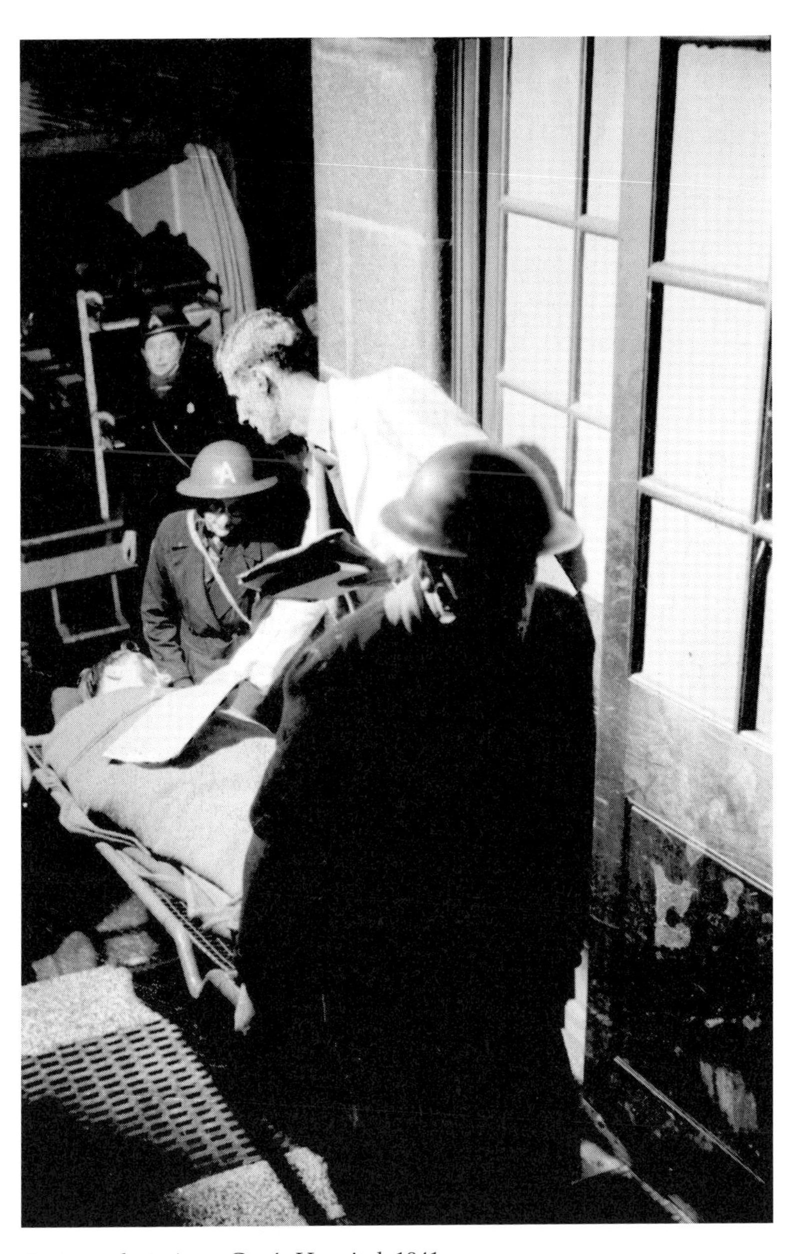

Patient admissions, Guy's Hospital, 1941

Sunday 29th
... In the evening the seniors were playing a game like this: on the ground they laid out straws, representing railway lines, with bottle tops for oil dumps, pennies for AA guns and a line for a secret weapon. Then they walked up with three darts and dropped them like bombs. They totally destroyed it ...

October

Wednesday 2nd
A letter from Mommy in the morning, shrapnel on flat's roof. She is now driving about London finding bombed people [people rendered homeless by the bombing needed clothing etc. and had to be dissuaded from entering their damaged homes]. *... After tea Wood and I went along the head. There was a lovely cave which the water rushed in with a lovely bang ...*

Thursday 3rd
... After lunch a notice went up saying FREE DAY !!! Wood and I went and explored the caves which we saw yesterday. A low Spring Tide, so they were about 18 ft. from sea level.

Then we went up into a cut-out of rock. There was a 20 ft. climb, which took us 25 minutes. At first it was easy up 9 ft. along, then you found you couldn't get back. Up to find rocky earth. Along. No hand holds, three foot holds, all of which eventually flaked off. I dug a hole in the earth, and after about 15 mins., got my chest on the ground and my foothold gave way. I got up, but it was even difficulter for Mart with fewer footholds. In the end I helped him up with my hand. Good fun!

Sunday 6th
When I woke up there was a terrific wind and quite a good sea. ... As soon as Wood got back from choir practice we put on our macs and went out. It was raining a little and there was still quite a good wind. First we went to Splash Point [our name for a blowhole not far from the hotel, where big waves sent water spouting 40 foot high], *and stood on a rock as low as we dared. Then an enormous wave came, and we*

were absolutely soaked. My pocket was even filled with water. Then we went higher and got soaked by an even bigger wave.

Tuesday 8th

In double Chemistry I was holding a test tube about half full of iron filings, sulphur and sulphuric over a bunsen burner, when somehow I spilt it all over my hand. I ran down to Woodlands and got some Tannofex put on it. Then it began to hurt like Hell for about three quarters of an hour. After that it slackened off, until after lunch it was quite all right.

… There were some quite good films, sailors dancing the hornpipe which was frightfully funny.

Wednesday 9th

I got a letter from Daddy in the morning. It began: no news, except that the flat was burgled on Thursday; they took the electric clock, two of Daddies suits, all Mother's stockings, an ornament, a suitcase and all daddies small [First World War] *war-medals. Also they dropped a molotov bread basket* [incendiaries] *at Glatting, and set a dry leaf on fire. No news!*

… In prep we heard a whine of an aeroplane and some machine-gun fire.

Wednesday 16th

… Wood and I went for a walk past Baker's Folly [a house built into the cliffs a few hundred yards from the school hotels] *and down on the rocks. On the way back there was a probably British plane machine-gunning out to sea …*

Tuesday 22nd

In Corps (JTC) we had rifles and learnt to Present and Order arms fairly efficiently. Then we took rifles to bits and saw how they worked.

Monday 28th

… Italy has invaded Greece, who is fighting pretty well.

Devastation close to Pilgrimage Street, Southwark, 1941

Tuesday 29th
... In Corps we nearly all had rifles; first we went down by the road to the Bay, then we Ordered, sloped and presented arms in the Gym. I had to stand to attention most of the time, while one of the five without rifles had mine. We marched back up the path.

In the evening I had another long talk with Mr. Parsons, 8.35–9.40, about religion etc. I showed him Daddies 'On Death and Dying'. He gave me a book about it to read also.

'Of Death and Dying' was an essay published in the *Lancet*, arguing that death should not be feared, and that modern medicine can alleviate any pain accompanying it. 'Those ... whose lives are compounded of action and a faith in mutual aid need know no death, and ... they will find, in all probability, that the phase of passing is quite different from all imagined experience, from all that ignorance, fiction and superstition have made it.' It was shortly to be published in a collection of essays *Fears may be Liars*.

Thursday 31st
... I am now 7 [stone] *8½* [pounds], *up 1½ pounds since the beginning of term ...*

I got a typewritten letter from Mommy, she says she had decided to become a Communist as then she won't have to remember names, only Comrade. All the same she won't have anything to do with other Communists.

November

Saturday 2nd
... At 8 o'clock I met Mart. and we went up to the [school] *Debate. We were sitting in the front but one row, but got shoved out and separated. The motion was that 'In the opinion of this house Woman's finest contribution to the World is in the Home'. Mrs. Spencer and F* [a prefect] *made very good speeches. The motion was carried by 104 votes to 77. I voted for.*

November 1940

Sunday 3rd
… In the evening I went to a camera club meeting. Mr. Oakley showed us how to touch up prints, and how to project negatives on to paper and shade them in. He did two very good drawings. Very easy …

Tuesday 5th
… In Corps we had a lecture on a Browning machine gun …

Saturday 9th
At 4.0 we went to Mr. Hales—quite a good tea, he was very polite etc.; the idea being, I suppose, that we can't rag him so easily …

Sunday 10th
… After Rest I went and found Martin, and we went off in gym shoes; first down to the edge of the Gannel. Then we went and climbed in the quarry, Martin did quite a difficult climb. Then we went right along the Head and clambered about. Then Martin went absolutely mad. He said it was due to strong marmalade which he had had at breakfast. It was extremely funny, and very extraordinary …

Tuesday 12th
… In Divinity I had an argument with Habershon on Mohamedonism v. Christianity. I never knew what it was before …

Saturday 16th
… During rest we heard a zooming above the clouds, and rushed to the window. A Spitfire did an almost vertical power dive to about 600ft, when it flattened out, circled once, and did a power dive straight into the sea. Ugh! It must have been going quite 500 mph.

I found later that he had dived onto a Hun, his engine stalled and he had got out of control, poor chap!

This is an image which has stayed with me all my life—remembered not as a sports spectacle but as my witnessing the moment of a man's death. I did not record that thought in the diary, and it may be that I experienced but did not record similar feelings when describing other events.

In the Session Woodlands match we beat Howsons [another senior house], *despite the efforts of Mr. Candler (the referee), who gave them at least 20 penalties. Everytime he awarded them one, Martin Wood and I just roared with laughter …*

Wednesday 20th
… Quite a good rugger game, but it went on too long. As I was changing there was a hell of a bang the other side of the golf course (about a quarter of a mile away). Two people had been blown up by a mine; a small evacuee had got under the barbed wire, and a man had gone to fetch her back. Feet and entrails lying about, people flocked to see them and proceeded to be sick. Ugh! Lots of people got bits of metal, P was disgusting enough to take some bone.

The sand dunes above all the beaches were mined, the mined area being surrounded by barbed wire with warning notices.

Sunday 24th
… Martin came back from choir practice. I met him and we went out. First we went down to the Gannel, then along to the quarry. We were climbing there when A appeared and told us (1) We couldn't climb in leather or rubber walking shoes and (2) the climb Martin was trying was impossible. As he had done it the last time it was bad luck. We went on. Good fun, the first time I've really seen him to talk to for a fortnight. … He almost definitely is coming up next term [from Kenwyn to Woodlands; he was very slightly younger than me], *which is just wizard. … The more I know him, the more I like him …*

During the term Martin Wood had become my best friend and we spent most free time together. Another day's entry includes: *I don't know why I refer to him as Martin, I never call him anything except when there others about, when I call him Wood. I do usually think of him as Martin.*

Monday 25th
A terrific sunrise. Stubs of cloud of all colours from pink and orange to deep purple surmounted by a light turquoise sky. … Immediately after rest I biked to town and was innoculated. Didn't hurt at the time, but rather stiff afterwards …

Tuesday 26th
… In the evening I had a Winter [senior prefect] *jaw, he accused me of being lonely. I said I wasn't, which is true, and also that I would like to share a study with Wood next term …*

Wednesday 27th
… After third prep came up [to the dormitory]; *T and R had filled my bed with bits of wood. I lost my temper with T, pulled his bed to bits, and threw a sponge at him. I went out of the room for a minute, and when I got back my bed was full of water. Miserable night, until I took one of T's blankets.*

Thursday 28th
… I began to feel a bit queer. I did not eat much lunch, and then there was Corps. We learnt how to shoot from Mr. Oakley, as we are going on the Range next week. I discovered that my left eye is much better than my right, so I am going to shoot left-handed.

I felt pretty sick after Corps, but went up to periods [classes]. *I had to go out in the middle of French, and was sick on the way down to the Bay. Had diorhhea all day. San at 6.15.*

Friday 29th
… dozed until about 8.10, when I had one charcoal pill and about a table spoonful of pepperminty medicine. The doctor came at about nine, then I

had 'breakfast' consisting of half a small soup plate full of arrowroot and stewed apple. Read Jamaica Inn and dozed until 1.30, when charcoal and medicine repeated. More arrowroot and apple at 2 o'clock. … Ravenous … I am very annoyed about being in the San. This is my first whole day off school for over a year …

December

Sunday 1st
Two pieces of buttered toast for breakfast. Feel quite better but very bored. Nothing to read, so count number of separate days on which Martin Wood's name occurs [in my diary] *since he came. 88! + 3 before he came. He's been here 289 days …*

Looking back it is clear that my preoccupation with this relationship was a powerful experience like falling in love. My feelings were, however, non-sexual, and I remained uninterested in homosexual relations throughout my time at school—in which I was, I think, a minority.

Tuesday 3rd
Woke up about 8.10. Breakfast came, in widely separated and wrongly ordered instalments, then I finished reading 'the Yearling'—a lovely book. At 11.30 Mr. Candler came and saw me, and then I got up. I was told that I would go tomorrow soon after breakfast! Perfect! … Looked at innumerable magazines, relating chiefly to the invasion of Czechoslovakia and the Finnish war …

Friday 6th
Gale and rain. … Heard this from one Irish Station on radio: "Calling No. 1 Tory Isle. I call your attention to S.S. [blank] *on the lee shore of Tory Isle". Then he asked all stations in Donegal to keep ready to receive distress messages.*

Monday 9th
… Beggar's Opera rehearsals in full swing, performances on Thursday and Friday.

Wednesday 11th
... After tea I took up the height measuring machine to the Pentire. Weighed and measured: 7 stones 7 lb (down!) and 5ft 6¾ (Up!).

Thursday 12th
... I read in my room. Chris [Martin Wood's brother] *came in and asked me a question which I was to answer lately—Martin was going to ask me for part of next holidays, and would I rather he was there or not? (because of what people say about Juniors and Seniors being friends etc.) I am frightfully glad that they are going to ask me. I like Martin an awful lot ...*

We went to the Beggar's Opera at 6.55. It began at 7.34 and was very good indeed. H was frightfully good. Martin as woman, I can't think why his dress stayed on. Jolly good tunes etc.—well done. Collection for minesweepers—I gave 6d.

Saturday 14th
In Chemistry the teacher (Mr. Hughes) told us about his experiences in Germany in the Munich riots.

Sunday 15th
... I packed my trunk in the morning, then T, R and I went along the Headland with a rubber glove puppet—Archibald, the Bishop of Truro—who having been stuffed with paper and soaked in oil, was lit in a cave; he burnt beautifully.

... Chris Wood came and I told him I would rather he was there. We talked about his [and Martin's elder] *brother and John (in the Mediterranean). His brother is anti-submarine officer on a destroyer which has sunk 7 submarines this war ...*

At 7.30 'the Housemaster', frightfully good and very funny. Very well acted. Everyone loved it. Kenwyn came but no other house [this was part of the end-of-term celebrations].

to London

Tuesday 17th
Up at 5 o'clock, and after breakfast we got on the bus at 5.35. Two buses (Kenwyn and Woodlands) pretty full. A lovely moonlight morning. When we got there the train wasn't in; when it came I didn't get a seat, nor did the Woods at first. We started fairly punctually; I looked out of the window for the first hour or so—absolutely still, frost on the fields, and looking back round a corner you could see the smoke curved back in the moonlight. At 8.30 I got a seat … I eventually got to London at 5.45, 2½ hours late. Mommy met me, Daddy examining at Cambridge. Supper in the [Pilgrimage Street] *flat at 6.45, then* [we slept in a] *room under Hospital* [Guy's]. *Room full of noises caused by water pipes and Mr. Entwhistle (a cricket).*

A man from the Works Department showed me several bits of shrapnel etc. and took me up on the roof. Unfortunately no blitz. Bed 9.40.

to Glatting

Wednesday 18th
… I went to the dentist, who found a small hole in the back molar of my left lower jaw. He drilled and filled it. Horrid feelings—but doesn't actually hurt …

Off at 2.20. V. cold, quite a lot of bomb damage, but less than I'd expect. Glatting at about 4.45. Lovely. Tea and supper, bath and bed by 9.30.

Thursday 19th
We didn't get up until 9.25. After breakfast we went by car to Petworth to register ration books and buy Christmas presents …

After supper we heard four or five planes go over, the gun over the other side of Farm Hill fired five rounds rapid. Bed at nine because Mommy thinks that I'm too thin.

Friday 20th

...The AA fire which we heard was two bombs near Petworth station. ... After supper we played Beggar's Opera and Gilbert and Sullivan records on the gramophone. Heard a few bangs and planes etc.

Monday 23rd

... In the morning Franics, Tinker and I went and fetched two christmas trees and some holly. It took us about two hours, most of which was spent in looking for holly berries, of which we found 9. Very cold.

Mommy went shopping in the afternoon, I played darts (I found 2 good 3s of darts) and read Gilbert and Sullivan operas. Mommy, Bassadone, and Daddy arrived at about 4 o'clock, and we had tea. Supper at 6.30. 6 Big Bangs over Bury direction. Bed 9.40.

Wednesday 25th

... Mommy and Daddy had given me a beautiful bicycle, I had hoped awfully that I would get one, but hadn't dared expect it. ... Didn't hear any planes in the evening.

Thursday 26th

... No planes in evening.

Friday 27th

... Several planes—London. In the afternoon we went for a walk on Farm Hill. Saw a Bren gun.

The Bren gun was a Czech-designed light machine gun widely used by infantry and also mounted on a tracked vehicle such as the Bren carrier.

Sunday 29th

... I spent the afternoon in my house. Good fire. Several planes and bangs to N.E.

At this time there was no effective night defence and one went to sleep at Glatting to the constant drone of German planes on their way to London.

Monday 30th
Up early because of Daddies train … [In the evening] *Daddy rang up. Every block in Guy's hit, and he had to walk back from Victoria. Few casualties.*

No planes in the evening.

Tuesday 31st
… I read most of the day. In the morning I biked to the village and got the week's rations.

End of the year—and what a year! …

Chapter 3: 1941

World events: 1941

At the start of the year it had been possible to follow the main events of the war on a map of Europe and the Mediterranean; by the end one needed a globe, thanks to the German invasion of Russia and the Japanese attacks on US bases in the Far East. Early in the year the British were fighting and eventually defeating the Italians in North Africa, but the arrival of German troops altered the balance. The British decision to transfer troops to go to the aid of Greece against the invading Italians weakened the force in North Africa and was a disaster. After the costly withdrawal from Greece and Crete, there were no British troops on European soil apart from Gibraltar.

The German attack on Russia on June 22nd provoked massive confusion, and the Red Army had to retreat on all fronts. But the German assumption that blitzkrieg tactics would bring a speedy victory as they had in the West was proved wrong, and the Germans were unprepared for the Russian winter. The Russians lost a vast amount of territory and millions of troops, but Leningrad and Moscow were held, and much of their industrial equipment was evacuated to beyond the Urals to provide the industrial base for the later crushing victories of the Red Army.

Over the previous decade Japan had been at war with China, occupying much of Manchuria and many of China's industrial coastal towns. At the end of the year the Japanese attacked the US naval base at Pearl Harbour. This was the start of an offensive aiming to secure supplies, especially oil; by chance the American aircraft carriers were out at sea and escaped destruction. Attacks on Malaya, Burma and the Philippines followed.

Diary for 1941

at Glatting

January

Wednesday 1st
… I had to go to lunch with the Armstrongs. … After that I had to go for a walk with Joan up Farm Hill and back via Glatting. Found a burnt-out incendiary bomb; she got the fin, but I got some melted middle. Otherwise very boring, hardly talking at all …

Slept in Martin's room, with nasty sore throat.

The 'had to' betrays that this was the idea of parents rather than the participants, and we never established any rapport. Joan was the step-daughter of a writer living nearby. Her father was the American poet Conrad Aiken. She became a well-known author of children's books.

Saturday 4th
… I finished making a meccano wind vane for my house, and after lunch I fixed it up—it worked. … After tea I designed the perfect (??!) sailing dinghy (as I'd like it).

After supper we sorted out nails and screws. Long job …

Monday 6th
… I took Tinker for a walk up on the Downs. We went up the Green Slope, at the top of which Tinker disappeared. After I had called him for some time he came back, sounding like a pack of wolves in the leaves. I sat quite still on Glatting covered way, and could hear hardly anything—a distant train, and the blackbirds. I could only see about ½ a mile …

Lovely news, Bardia [a port in eastern Libya] *has been captured, with 25,000 prisoners. Our casualties are between 400 and 500! Now 1/3 of the Libyan* [Italian] *army has been killed or captured.*

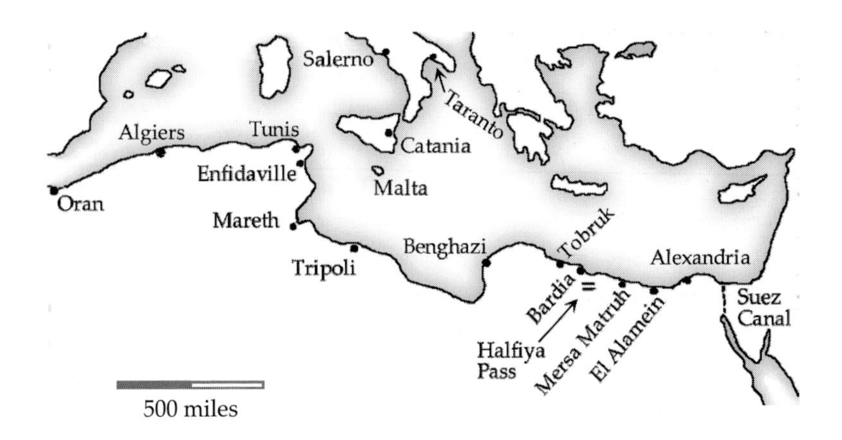

Tuesday 7th
... the mist cleared, and all the trees above a certain well-defined height appeared a lovely silver-grey. It was very beautiful ...

The news wasn't much except that our mechanised forces are at Tobruk [a Libyan port]. *Quick work! ...*

Friday 10th
... I took Tinker up on the downs for a walk. ... There was an icy wind and brilliant sunshine—you could see as far as Chanctonbury ring ...

News—40 miles past Tobruk, and several successful land and air raids on Libya, Naples and Germany, including a midday one today. The Greeks have got one of the key towns for the capture of Valona [an important Albanian town which the Italians were defending]. *I should think they'll have it by February. Lovely.*

Saturday 11th
... I read 'The Ragged-Trousered Philanthropists' ... The Tuppers arrived at 7.15, and we had supper. After that they just talked, chiefly about bomb-damage in London (of which Miss Wilkinson [our cousin] *had some marvellous photos) ...*

Sunday 12th

… At 11.5 Daddy, Miss Wilkinson, Tinker and I went for a walk. We went up the shepherds path, and at the bottom of Farm Hill we turned right and went round until we got to the Chichester road. Then we went up through the piggeries, and onto the Bishop's ring hill. Just then the old pig man came up, to see who we were, and he had a long conversation with Daddy in very broad Sussex, most of which I couldn't understand.

After we had been to Bishop ring, we re-crossed the road and went up Duncton Hill. Here we saw a buzzard, quite close to, flying very slowly with his head on one side, and his wing tips bending upwards. This is the first definite buzzard which I have seen. We passed the deserted searchlight post, which was in a pretty good mess …

Mrs. Francis came up in the evening to thank Mommy for the chicken which she had given her, she has 3 people extra from Portsmouth, who became—because of a bad raid—without any food.

Little news.

My last day at home. It will be nice to know that Mommy at least is down here and safe.

Monday 13th

I got up early [for a visit to Martin Wood near Oxford], *and after breakfast I filled and started the car. While Mommy was taking Daddy to the station, I got ready, washed up etc. We got off at 9.30; there was a mist which froze on the windscreen, and for about 15 miles, beginning at Cowdray, we had to have the windscreen open …*

[At the Woods'] *A large batch of evacuees came to tea. After which there were 'Felix' etc. films …*

Wednesday 15th

… After breakfast Mart and I went out and got four blankets from the [Women's] *Institute … still snowing fairly hard. When we got back, we scraped anti-splinter paint off a window …*

After tea we took several games and the cinema [equipment] *down to a party for choir boys …*

Thursday 16th

... we packed up the car with skis and sledges, and at 12.30 started off to the hills, via the house ... of some friends of the family called B-R ... we had lunch and went off. A simply lovely place, crowds of the people came, all staying with the B-Rs ...

Mart was pretty good on skis, Chris [his brother] *tried a jump turn, landed on a tin, and cut his knee to the bone. Went to the First Aid Post and came back and skied. I tobogganed terribly fast ...*

I'm afraid that Martin is going to be confirmed, it seems a pity; he is otherwise so frightfully nice and pretty sensible.

to Newquay

Martin (MFW) and Roger Cruickshank (RJC) were my study mates this term. Encouraged by RJC, I became a better-informed bird watcher.

Saturday 18th

... I told Cruickshank that I was an Atheist, Mart heard and apparently didn't know before. He seemed to mind rather a lot. Later on when he was getting into bed after having a drink, I asked him if he hated me for it. He said No.   ?

Sunday 19th

... Headmaster preached a boring sermon telling us to give all our money to charity. Said he thought all hospitals should be supported by public donations. Does not seem to realise that this means that they are all stony broke and unable to buy decent apparatus. Poor fool.

Friday 24th

... We had Mr. Aldiss for Geography. Talked about space. I had one of my brighter thoughts:

Space, as everyone admits, is limitless. But it stands to reason that everything (e.g. Space) must go on for ever (and ever). Therefore I come to the conclusion that there is absolutely no reason to suppose that it hasn't been going on for ever (and ever). Therefore one of the needs for the existence of a God is unnecessary (e.g. as a Creator). This could be worded much better. [Later addition:] *On looking back on this I think it's a lousy thought.*

Sunday 26th

… At 10.30 Cruickshank, G and I went to the Gannel bird-watching. We saw snow-bunting?, a black-headed gull (not black-headed) scrabbling in the mud with his feet and catching the small fish it stirred up, a grey wagtail, and my first goldcrest. Quite fun. Also a bren gun carrier in the Gannel (running around) …

Martin Wood and Cruickshank and I all joined the marionette business. Ought to be quite fun. Toad of Toad Hall …

Monday 27th

… I was playing in the Woodlands first game, and made a pretty good fool of myself …

… Don't seem to be on very good terms with Martin Wood, I don't know if its because I'm an Atheist or what. ?

Tuesday 28th

… Only two preps, Martin Wood and Cruickshank both had baths. We talked about Space and then about the feeling and experiences when you die and about what happens afterwards.

Friday 31st

… In the 12–1 [an hour of variable activities at mid-day] *Martin Wood, Cruickshank and I went and saw Brooke* [Peter Brook] *about our*

parts in Toad of Toad Hall. I may be Rat, rather a big part, but it ought to be quite fun …

MW had a 50 min. Winter jaw in the evening.

Peter Brook, who has since had a distinguished career in the theatre, was a rather older pupil. He left to work in films very soon after this.

February

Saturday 1st

… I tried to make marionettes' bodies.

I went and had a talk with Winter 8.50. He said that when talking to Martin last night, it had come up that Martin thought that our friendship could not continue because I was an atheist and he was C. of E. I was afraid it must be that. Winter asked me to discuss it with him, and said that Mart wanted to discuss it also. I will always be very grateful to Winter if it helps … Winter said he explained to Martin that differences of opinion were often the basis of friendship.

Sunday 2nd

I broached the subject to MF [Wood], *but he was very sleepy and didn't say anything. Either it means he won't go on or else he was too sleepy …*

After tea the marionette club came and we read through the play.

Monday 3rd

… I still haven't really discussed things with Mart, it's going to be awfully awkward. He does seem more friendly now?

Tuesday 4th

…We saw a Whirlwind showing a Spitfire (Mk. III?) how to go up and round corners. Astounding, absolutely vertical climb for 1,000 feet. Down and up like this: U while the Spitfire went V! …

The Whirlwind was introduced in late 1940 but saw little active service due to technical problems and high landing speeds. Some were stationed at St. Eval.

Friday 7th
Benghazi captured. Italians running very fast …

Played a pretty lousy game of hockey. I hit Aldridge's bottom very hard with a hockey stick. He hit mine quite hard enough! …

Saturday 8th
… I had to go and see Winter. He asked me if I had spoken to Wood yet, I had to say no. Then he asked if it would help if he said something to Wood. I said it would, and told him about my views about an Atheist and a C. of E. being friends. He said he would speak to Wood, and that we must discuss it. He saw him as soon as he'd finished with me. When MF came back, Cruickshank asked him if he'd had a nice time. Mart said "Yes, very". ?

Sunday 9th
… After lunch MF and I played darts, and bust one of Cruickshank's, and then we walked up to Church. I asked him what he thought of my atheism etc., and if he felt we could be friends. He asked why I was one and I told him, but didn't finish the conversation very satisfactorily …

Then at 9.0 we listened to a very good speech by the Prime Minister …

Tuesday 11th
I was awake for about 1 hour from midnight because of my sore throat. A lovely night—full moon …

There was a frightfully good lecture in the evening. 'Nature in the Wild' by -- Hoskin. He told several very good stories with wonderful slides. First he showed us several photos which he took from a hide of a buzzard on its nest. There were two young ones, and both parents came. He had sat quite still for 7½ hours while photographing them, and his legs and voice were quite gone.

Next he showed us wood pigeons, pied tree-creepers, greater spotted woodpeckers, a kingfisher, and some frightfully good flashlight photos of little owls. Lastly he told how a tawny owl had clawed his eye when he was going to the hide, and how he had very nearly died from loss of blood. He lost his left eye, and two days after the operation he went to get another photo. He didn't get it until the following year, and he showed them to us, and while he was taking the last the tawny owl dashed at the hide and knocked the camera over! …

Wednesday 12th

… I gave MFW a list of reasons for being an Atheist, we [he?] *didn't say anything about it. We read through part of the play. After callover* [roll call] *I sat outside the window looking at a perfect sky.*

Thursday 13th

A fine morning, but windy and clouded by 4 o'clock …

JTC—we did a tactical exercise which constituted getting fairly muddy and wet crawling about the headland. Not bad fun …

Friday 14th

… A fairly wettish day. No hockey, instead we went out in sections of seven and had to get back to the Bay untouched by the defenders. Very good fun. I got caught 10 yds. from the door. We had another voluntary go. I was about ten yards ahead being chased by W and did an almighty slide for about 10 ft. on my bottom, rather painful, and I was caught.

Saturday 15th

… Cruickshank asked me to take up bird watching seriously, as after the summer all the experts will have left. I decided I would, and Wood said he would too. It will be very good fun.

Sunday 16th

… off to Mr. Candler for Breakfast … A terrific head-on offshore wind, I had to walk a lot, and there was driving rain … good breakfast, then B and I shot at starlings with an antiquated air-gun. He killed one, I removed a few tail feathers. We then pruned an apple tree and I cut a dead one down. Quite fun …

After tea I went along to Baker's Folly with Cruickshank where he had seen some Gannets. Rather fun, they dived into the water from flying with a terrific splash, like the Spitfire last term.

Monday 17th
… we went to a voluntary religious Passion play, by the Pilgrim Players, called 'the Way of the Cross'. I hadn't meant to go, but forgot to give my name in, and I enjoyed it when I was there. Mr. Trevor was acting. It was with practically no scenery, with wonderful acting. I do not understand what people see in that sort of thing though …

I've also got my first boil, on the back of my neck—painful, a bit.

Sunday 23rd
… A stray barrage balloon was shot down about 6 miles away.

A lovely day. At 10.15 Cruickshank, G and I went off to the Gannel. We saw a Whirlwind doing its stuff on the way. We saw when we got there: about 12 ringed-plovers, two partridges, redshank, a good flock of gulls which two fools (D and someone) scared before we could have a good look. Then we saw our first notable bird—a buzzard. Shortly after I put up a Jack Snipe from under my feet.

We got back, and found that G had two oiled up live Guillemots (we had seen a dead one). During rest we saw about 12 on the beach, rocks and in the sea, some dead. After lunch I photographed them—good light as there were few clouds all day. Cruickshank went to the Gannel and almost caught an oiled Razor-bill, and B found a Black Guillemot's corpse. MFW saw a kingfisher on the Gannel. Rather a wonderful day! [Later I] *watched the Guillemots being fed, only one ate anything. … Saw guillemots being washed in soap and later ether.*

Over the next few days other oiled-up sea birds were found. I made no comment on where the oil came from, but post-war records show that the German Battle Cruiser *Admiral Hipper*, based at Brest, sank 7 ships in a slow convoy west of Gibraltar on February 12th. Six other sinkings were recorded between February 7th and 11th, 2 from submarines, four from aircraft, location not recorded.

Thursday 27th
… In JTC we had an indoor parade, Frank talked to us. We had some cake after that.

There is an oiled up red-throated diver here now, but 3 guillemots and a razor bill have all died. When I came up from 3rd prep, Winter was in the room, he had a magazine with a picture of Daddy in—about his 'On Death and Dying'.

March

Saturday 1st
In Biology we cut up cockroaches, very good fun indeed—looking at the bits under a microscope …

Wood spent the afternoon on the Gannel, and brought back a gull with a broken wing. After tea B, G, Cruickshank and I went down, we saw B stalking a Red Throated Diver, and catching it although it could swim well. We put it back as it wasn't badly oiled, and could dive for 15 secs. … We rather crudely set the gull's wing, with the help of B (who nearly fainted, poor chap) and T.

We had a tough after supper, Cruickshank not feeling well and did not come. I was sat on by P+ and dragged along the floor on my forehead. Rather painful. Quite fun …

Sunday 2nd
My birthday! I opened the parcel from Daddy, a very nice compass, and a notebook from Margaret for bird notes, and a film from Nora. Mommy is giving me the [photographic] *developing things for Glatting. Lovely presents.*

RJC, G and Wood and I went to the Gannel; I photographed a red-throated diver, and saw a coal tit. I am not going to put down what I saw fully as it is in my bird notes …

We were read to in the evening—rather a horrid Edgar Allen Poe.

A good birthday, but I can't help comparing it with the ones at home.

Wednesday 5th

… I began to feel pretty sick.

Thursday 6th

I woke up feeling better, but felt a very little sick later. Apparently I looked worse than I felt …

We had a rather good talk on tactics by Major Kerridge in JTC re: infiltration and then deploying …

Friday 7th

I read 'Wuthering Heights' in the 12–1 [the hour before lunch was sometimes free time]. *Wood unsuccessfully sand-eel hunted with T for the gull, whose wing B had bound with adhesive tape.*

… the 'Chinese Magician' gave his show. I got a good seat fairly near the front between a radiator and B. Wood was with Smith—although he's usually quite friendly, he never seems to want to do anything or go anywhere with me. He did some quite clever conjuring tricks …

Sunday 9th

… My boils were anti-floed [treated with anti-phlogiston] *after breakfast, and the little one squeezed. The big one is still rather painful, and not ready to be squeezed. That will be nasty …*

I got some fresh bramble leaves for Cruickshank's caterpillar …

I read after tea 'Pride and Prejudice'.

Wednesday 12th

… Gas mask inspection tomorrow, which follows well on a story M told me the other day about gas at Falmouth …

Officially one carried gasmasks at all times. I don't think this applied when cycling about on the North Cornish coast.

Friday 14th
... They were firing the guns on Trevose Head at a target. A lot of talk about invasion; there will certainly be a hellish lot of air raids. We did the biggest [raid] *on Hamburg and got 11 of theirs down. 3 by 'other means'.*

I walked back by myself from games—so did Wood—sometimes he's friendly and others not at all. I dunno at all.

I got a letter from Mommy—the flat is blown up badly; they've got the furniture at Glatting ...

I went to see Max [Mr. Parsons] *in the evening, for making an unnecessary noise while going downstairs to see Miss Macrae* [matron] *during 3rd Prep. He also talked to me for about 20 mins. about various other subjects—I had a small streak of insolence which was a bad thing, and about Wood. A nice jaw for me, on the whole.*

Sunday 16th
... I read the 'Good Companions' [J.B. Priestley] *until church. ... An invasion scare in the evening—the weather about perfect, I think the* HG [Home Guard] *are going out all night.*

Monday 17th
HG only had to sleep in uniforms, and then go on patrol with fixed bayonets! Scare practically over ...

Tuesday 18th
... Went to see Winter—he asked if I was feeling argumentative. Then he began to discuss religion with me. First he said that until recently he had really been an atheist, but now he was a Christian—but a much better sort than most, for instance he does not really believe in the future life, and agrees that people who now call themselves Christians are not. He concluded that the chief difference was that what he called God, I called conscience. He is going to have another discussion; this lasted over an hour and we could have gone on.

Wednesday 19th
… Winter gave me a notebook with extracts from a book called 'The imitation of Christ' by Thomas Kempis, with his comments as they applied to me in particular. I did not have time to read it thoroughly today—there are pages and pages. Very interesting to have someone trying to 'convert' me—it enlarges my ideas etc.

It seems odd that a prefect was encouraged to do this. He was essentially kind and probably ended up as a benign clergyman.

Thursday 20th
In double MT Cruickshank and I both started to make 1/72 scale models of a Heinkel 70a. By the evening I had finished both wings and the fuselage—RJC had practically finished but slightly split one wing …

Thursday 27th
I got on a lot with the Heinkel 70a, and left it for someone else to finish.
… In JTC we were to have had a Tactical exercise, but having been forced to shelter twice by showers, we went and had the usual jaw from the Major. Before French B gave me the plans of a Beaufort, which I had asked him for; he had done them very nicely—rather a good chap.
We went to Howson's play in the evening, called 'Rope'. A horrific murder story, frightfully good, and very well acted …

Friday 28th
… Read a lot—'Gone with the Wind'. A very good book …
After discussion with Cruickshank I've at last realised what, and how foul, the school definition of 'tarting' is. Another appalling thing is how widespread it is, even among people whom you would expect to have more self control.

There was a considerable homosexual culture in the school, with younger boys who were sought after by older ones being known as 'tarts'.

Sunday 30th
… H and Smith went to St. Evell and between them got about 120 rounds of m.g. ammo, 6 Verey lights and a few bits. Good hunting!

Monday 31st
My trunk went off in the morning. … several people went on the Norfolk bus at 4 o'clock. … I read 'The Ragged-trousered Philanthropists' all the afternoon …

Breaking news. 5-7 Italian ships (2 or 3 cruisers) sunk, with no casualties at all except for two planes! Biggest battle in the Mediterranean.

to Glatting

April

Tuesday 1st
Up at 4.50 … I didn't travel with Wood, as I still feel awkward and did not know whether he wanted to or not. … We saw surprisingly little damage along the coast …

Glatting is much the same, except for a great gash in the wood above Glatting lake which has been cut for an electric cable [a line of pylons] …

My mother was now at Glatting with two new evacuees.

Wednesday 2nd
My first day home. After breakfast I fed the rabbits (Flopsy has four lovely little uns, two black and two like pa, black and white) and the goats.

The rabbits were reared for eating, and were kept in movable hutches which had to be moved on daily; the goats were intended to provide milk and cheese, but were so destructive that they were eventually disposed of.

... After lunch I tidied up and arranged my dark room ... the dark room lamp Mommy has got me is lovely, but has only a yellow filter so I can't develop yet ...

On [a] *walk ... I got several pieces of bomb, and we visited the land mine hole where there were several pieces of parachute. A longish walk, rather tired when I got back ...*

This was the willow herb patch we had visited before.

Thursday 3rd
... all went for a walk. We went up the green slope, round in the woods and down by the new gash. Martin [my brother who was on leave] *is always very tired and rather depressed ...*

This was true throughout the war, attributable in retrospect to his working under pressure in the development of radar, and to his knowing too much to allow any complacency.

We had tea early and then Martin left—rather depressed and making Mommy depressed also. I began making the model Beaufort. ... Two more Italian destroyers sunk, other news all good.

Saturday 5th
... Someone rang up saying "I have been told officially to tell you to take 3 days food and hide it". Mommy said "Is there an invasion?". "That's all I'm to tell you, you know best what to do", and rang off. Mommy, as the person gave no name, rang up people and the ARP (actually she got the police by mistake) and found that the order was about 3 months old. Some silly fool to put it like that ...

Tuesday 8th
... Several planes, bangs and searchlights in the evening. The planes were leaving clearish white tracks.

Last night we did a very devastating raid on Kiel, but the Germans are doing quite (too) well in the Balkans.

Wednesday 9th
… I did a little homework, fed the animals, and then got on with the Beaufort—quite well.

After lunch we did some gardening, first planting potatoes where Margaret's and my gardens used to be, and then burning …

The raid last night was very heavy, on Coventry. We again did Kiel.

This was the most devastating raid on the UK so far. Coventry was an important engineering city which had already been badly damaged in a raid in November. Much was made of the destruction of the cathedral and the 1,000 casualties. This should be remembered in the context of our far more devastating raids on Germany in the subsequent years.

Thursday 10th
… I took two photos of rabbits, finishing the film. … I developed the film, quite successful, a lovely one of Glatting.

After lunch I read and tried to print with the dark room lamp. It took 20 mins., but then Mommy suggested the Aladdin, which is obviously the thing to use.

I read Eileen Bigland's 'Laughing Odyssey' about Russia, rather funny.

Friday 11th
… We saw the first bluebells out and some anemones.

After lunch I set my camera on top of the large hawthorn hedge with the ball and socket 'tripod', and tied a bit of string onto the shutter release hoping to photograph a sparrow. I lay down about 12 ft. away reading 'Lawrence, by his friends'. One came between me and the camera, otherwise I had no luck at all …

Tuesday 15th
Up earlier than usual as we are going to London. … Our train did not arrive until 11 o'clock, so we arrived about 10 mins. late at Fry's [dentist], *and had to wait one hour, during which I had a hair-cut. He said that my teeth were very good, and didn't do anything.*

I went to Daddy's room, and waited until he came at 12.40. Margaret arrived at about one o'clock, with a painful front tooth. We had lunch in a very crowded restaurant, no food shortage! and then bussed to D.H. Evans. The only damage I saw was round Guy's, behind St. Pauls, and John Lewis. When we had shopped we walked with Daddy to Victoria, via St. James Park. We caught the 3.48 [to Sussex]. *... Not a bad day. It's nice to see Daddy again.*

Wednesday 16th

A lovely day, despite a brilliant orange sunset last night. Kenneth [my cousin], *Margaret and I (and Tinker) went for a hot walk in the morning. First we went up Farm Hill, on the top of which we lay cooling for about ½ hour, while we watched planes making trails in the sky at about 20,000 feet. Then we went down and round to the Ordnance survey beacon, and down to the tumulus to see the Isle of Wight ... We didn't because of the haze. Kenneth discovered an aerodrome about 7 miles off, it took me about 15 mins. to find it—Good camouflage! (or bad eyes?).*

I finished the Beaufort and hung it in my house; after lunch I went to see it, was readjusting it, when it fell on its back on the floor. Only the propeller was broken. I mended it with cold solder ...

A horrible lot of planes in the evening, more than I've ever heard before. I heard machine gun and cannon fire.

Thursday 17th

Daddy rang up earlyish, to say he was unhurt etc., but that they had had the worst raid ever, and that every block of the hospital not in use was demolished, and none of those in use were hit!

The day began misty, but cleared. While it was still misty, Kenneth and I started on a walk, without Tinker as he had run away. We went past Coldharbour [farm] *straight over the top, from where we could see the sea, the puff of exploding bombs (which we also heard) and the barrage of AA fire (which we did not hear). Then we moved on, went round Scotchers bottom, down and up the valley, and back through the woods via the rising. I saw the first swallow ...*

The windows shook a lot in the evening, and we saw a glare towards Portsmouth and Chichester, saw AA shells bursting and heard a few bombs (not nearly as many as we felt).

Sunday 20th
… while I was investigating an old nest in one of the fir trees at the orchard end, I found what a marvellous smell it had, so took several sprigs and hung them in my house.

Tuesday 22nd
A perfect day, bright sunshine all the time and only a very slight breeze. In the morning I cleaned out the big father rabbit's cage, and then we put the other five outside in a run made by Margaret to fit against a hen coop. After that I built up stands for a bench on which to place the father rabbit outside, in the third pigsty …

After lunch I puttied and pitched the roof of my house, getting my legs, hands, face, chest, and my right arm very pitchy. I had three baths, which anyway spread the pitch evenly all over me and the bath. Then I cleaned the bath. Then we had tea …

Green patches are becoming more and more frequent in the woods, and all the blossom is coming out.

Thursday 24th
… I went down to the stream above the lake, and was following a water vole's course under water, when, as it disappeared, I heard a big splash behind. I looked, and saw Tinker with his head under water. I thought he slipped, but he reappeared with a real water-vole in his mouth! He took it up the bank, and, looking as if he wasn't sure what to do, half-heartedly shook it. He then proceeded to play with it like a cat, so I went to get a stone to finish it off. Before I got there Tinker had. He was immensely proud all day.

When I got back I mixed up fat and sugar for cakes …

I learnt many years later that airedales had been trained to catch otters and then voles—T had clearly reconnected with his heritage.

Friday 25th
... After lunch I lit a fire in my house, and read the 'Dark Invader' there all the afternoon. Daddy read theoretically, actually sleeping most of the time.

We are (as a country) just completing another 'brilliant rearguard action' in Greece; to come, is our evacuation of Iraq when Germany enters via Turkey, our evacuation of Africa (perhaps) and finally a brilliant action in which we will leave Iceland to the Germans. Then we will proceed to win the war.

Europe now will consist of 4 countries, soon perhaps 2 or only 1. At present they are Germany, Italy, Turkey in Europe and part of Greece, and part of Russia. I've forgotten England; that makes five.

This sardonic tone is new to my diary. It was probably an expression of anxiety.

Saturday 26th
... Up Bignor Hill, just onto West Burton Hill, and then down the loveliest wildest valley I've ever seen—chalk screes with yews, beeches, wild cherries, hawthorn, blackthorn, ash + growing on them. A marvellous place for birds. We went round, and up a more wooded but very lovely valley, to come out about 300 yds. from Bignor chalk pit ...

Sunday 27th
... Churchill spoke at 9 o'clock. A very good, cheering speech, telling nothing at all.

Monday 28th
... The evacuation of Greece has begun. Athens is in German hands, so is the isthmus of Corinth.

Tuesday 29th
... A lovely sunset. A 5lb tin of butter arrived from S. Africa [from relatives]. *We dissected a shrew in the morning.*

Tinned butter always tasted slightly rancid. An earlier tin had been called 'party butter' by Clara and Lorna (evacuees), who at home probably only replaced margarine with (unrefrigerated) butter on special occasions. By this time food rationing was an accepted part of life and we never suffered serious shortages. The average weight and height and general health of British children improved significantly during the years of rationing, an indication of the widespread deprivation of the pre-war years. In addition we were helped by vegetables, eggs, fruit and honey from Glatting.

May

Thursday 1st

... Great excitement before breakfast when I saw a (supposedly) migrant pair of ring-ouzels. I tidied up my house in the morning and locked it up—it's an awfully nice little house.

Mummy, Daddy, Margaret, Tinker and I went for a lovely walk to the wild valleys. On the way back I scraped off part of my nose while climbing a beech to investigate a nest ...

The news is not, to say the least, exhilarating. We have anyway got 80% (48,000 men) of our Greek force away; the Iraqi army are being a nuisance to our troops, and threatening one of our big 'dromes; the enemy has penetrated into Tobruk, where there is fierce fighting. I got a nice letter (March 10) from John in the morning—written in a Libyan harbour. His ship was half lifted out of the water by two bombs, and the Germans or Italians claimed in [their] *English bulletin to have sunk them!*

Last day of a lovely holiday.

to Newquay

Friday 2nd

... Daddy came to Paddington and we had some coffee—he stayed till about two mins. before the train went. I was a little miserable but being in a crowd it was all right. ... The journey was uneventful until after Exeter, when we shot up North on the west side of Dartmoor using a

single line Southern [i.e. not Great Western main line] *track. Saltash bridge had received a near miss …*

The country round Dartmoor—vast undulating stretches of dead bracken, with occasional stone cottages accompanied by stone hedged fields. Here and there tough, scraggy little sheep ran loose, otherwise there were no living things but birds. Further on, as we approached Wadebridge, the country was more hilly, with drum-shaped stone hills, and instead of stretches of bracken the plains were walled in; a few grass fields, but the rest the usual bracken. This view was rather depressing, as with the slight mist everything seemed grey.

After Wadebridge we got to Par (by a very strange and devious route), but as we left Par and returned twice, we got to know it well. Now it was blackout time, but the lights would not work, so I suggested a sing song, which went on to Newquay …

I have a four, Cruickshank, Wood and Smith, the same room …

Saturday 3rd

… Wood heard that his brother's ship had been sunk, with heavy casualties [survivors were later picked up by another destroyer], *and then re-sunk—poor devil.*

Sunday 4th

… 50 survivors from about 1000 were picked up from the two destroyers, so there is one chance in about 10 of Wood's brother being alive (some got to Greece). Even so he was strangely cheerful, refusing to believe, I think, that he could be dead …

Double summer time. No blackout for us.

Tuesday 6th

… Wood heard that there were only about 20 ratings saved from the 'Diamond', so the only chance of his brother being safe is that he swum or was in the only boat to Greece—rotten luck.

HMS Diamond had been involved in evacuating troops from Greece. She was sunk by dive bombers.

Thursday 8th

I was isolated in the San because my mother had German measles, but I was not ill. Teachers brought me work, and I could go out on my own.

... PSN [the headmaster, Philip Newell] *came to see me. ... Pointed out that it was all very silly, but if I wasn't isolated I'd be sure to get it.*

After lunch I went off to the buzzard's nest, leaving about 3.15 to let the bird get back to the nest. I put a note on what I'd seen in a pre-arranged place for Wood or RJC. Had to [go by] *ferry back as the tide was up. Miserable feeling going back into the San. 2 WEEKS! Ugh! And some people would love it. After tea I read the paper, wrote more* [of a] *letter etc. until 7 o'clock. Sister heard on the wireless that we got 23 last night! 23! Not, thank goodness, on London. I listened to the 9 o'clock news—24 now—20 fighters, 3 AA, 1 balloons. We attacked Brest, Scharnhorst Gneiseinau (as usual). Today we got 10 for 1 over S. Coast. 2nd Battle of Britain? (We've got over 70 in 7 nights).*

Sunday 11th

After tea Max came—stayed about 10 mins. He brought two letters—Mommy and Daddy. He said re: the AA fire put up by ships the other night, that it had been lovely fun to watch, and that they'd had a stirrup pump practice since. RJC's version was that a trifle windy little man had rushed round with a stirrup pump and bucket on the night, saying "Hah! Hah! Don't get excited! Hah! Only a practice! Hah! Hah!".

Other news: that Wood's brother Charles is 'Missing believed killed'. They've taken it jolly well. ... Bad raid on London, but 33 down!!

I have never really understood how my friend went on in daily activities with no evident change; whether it was denial, courage, British inexpressiveness or acceptance. But from May 8th I was not around, being in isolation in the school sanatorium. I had never met the brother, but saw a pre-war photograph of him tranquilly steering a dinghy with one hand on the tiller and the other supporting his chin. Throughout my life, when enjoying small boat sailing, I often found myself aware of being in the same posture and remembering the image. A kind of memorial.

Tuesday 13th
… Strange news—Rudolph Hess, 3rd Nazi chief, has arrived in England, by ME 110 [a German fighter] *and parachute, of his own accord. He was taken by a Scottish peasant, to whom he said how lucky he was. The Nazis say he is mad—our doctors say that he only has a broken ankle. I hope it is Hess, not a substitute to fool us.*

Wednesday 14th
… Everyone hero worshipping Hess—I hope they're beastly to him …

Saturday 17th
… I read 'The old century and seven years more' by Siegfried Sassoon—nice.

… John has given me his Webley air pistol—won't Margaret be furious! In bed I wrote a poem—'Early Memories', didn't finish it—I felt 'inspired'.

HG and band marched through Newquay—looked v.g.—band in cricket clothes.

Sunday 18th
Soon after breakfast I walked off to West Pentire Headland. The weather was almost sultry, with big black clouds blowing over, and a halo round the sun. Quite a nice walk there but lonely.

On the way back I passed some soldiers and two navvies building a Home Guard post. They asked if I'd like a job and I answered "sure, if you want help". "Go and get 40 more and tell the blokes with the bloody bugles [the school band was practising] *to stop blowing—our men keep thinking it's dinner time". I went back via Penpol creek; in one of the stone walls a cast iron cooking pot had been built in—about 2′ 6″ across …*

It rained all the afternoon. I wrote a poem re: the closing of Sunday theatres, which I'm going to send (anonymously as the School (capital S) wouldn't approve) to P[icture] *Post …* [a skit on A.P Herbert].

The other poem I wrote turned out 34 lines long—it's quite fun writing them when they come out nicely. I might put that (anonymously) in the Grasshopper [the school's literary magazine].

Nice news, 20 Germans down in East, Duke of Aosta asks for terms, as Amba Arlagi (spelling?) is surrounded with 7000 men inside. Doing well with German prisoners round Tobruk and Fort Capuzzo. They played the Abyssinian national anthem. Petty-Officer (and proud of it) A.P. Herbert gave the postscript [a weekly radio broadcast]*—better than usual, or anyhow not so bad.*

Amba Alagi (a mountain in northern Ethiopia) was the last battle of a long campaign between the Italians, who had invaded British Somaliland, and a mixed force of British, Indian, Rhodesian and other Commonwealth troops and Ethiopian irregulars.

Tuesday 20th
… During tea about five Blenheims played about, a few times going along the Gannel valley lower than me. … Hales came in (as usual), explaining how tired he was, and we discussed politics. When talking to him about school I always want to put my tongue in my cheek.

News—airborne troops in NZ battledress (about 1500) attack Crete—held under so far.

Wednesday 21st
… I packed mostly before tea. Last day [in the San]*! I don't like the news much—still more* [German] *troops in Crete 'mostly accounted for'—they've had enormous losses. We got 18,000 men* [prisoners] *at Amba Arlagi.*

Friday 23rd
… There was JTC after tea; we did a sort of tactical exercise—crawling, sliding on rocks—quite fun …

Not very nice news—RAF gone from Crete, Germans very heavy casualties but still lots there. I'm afraid we'll probably evacuate it.

Sunday 25th
… Fearful news—HMS Hood sunk off Greenland—magazine hit and few survivors.

Hood, the Royal Navy's largest fighting ship, had been sunk by the German battleship Bismarck. There were in fact only 3 survivors.

Tuesday 27th
… Beautiful news, after hours of chasing we've got the 'Bismarck'. Crete rather bad.

Bismarck would have been a serious danger to our Atlantic convoys if it had got away. The German invasion of Crete was the first major assault from the air. The Germans suffered very heavy casualties in the first 2 days, many inflicted by Greek civilians because the German weapons were dropped separately from the men; but they were much better equipped than the mixture of Greek Army, civilian and New Zealand forces.

Wednesday 28th
… In corps we did Ceremonial—marching past and eyes right etc. There were uniforms available, but Sergt. Gale didn't have time to fit me. I hope I do get one.

After tea I rolled the tennis court and had a haircut. I prepared my bike for tomorrow, Field day—when we (No. 5 platoon) are going to be on bicycles—wizard …

Thursday 29th
Field day. …I changed into my own uniform in the rest (I'd got one in break). … Then we took our bikes up, and biked to the headland—I had a rifle, but only H had blanks—20 .303 rounds (mine was .22). We did one glorious charge, losing half our men, from the first seat [public bench] *on Pentire headland, down by the chemistry lab right past the Pentire Bay path. It rained a little. I was killed on the charge to Fistral Bay (knocked off my bike by Wood), but went on and was blown up by a hand grenade soon after. It was raining, so I had to collect all uniforms for the drying room.*

Field Days were supposedly training exercises, with referees posted around to declare who was dead etc. It was obviously fun, but cannot have been a great learning experience! I managed to get killed in every one. I seem to have made no connection in my mind between the Field Day and the events in the world of the previous few days.

Friday 30th

… In the 12–1, RJC and I biked to the gulls' nest, and I photoed the chick just emerging (its foot was through).

After tea we changed, and did the same as yesterday, only better and more fun. Pretty warm work. We 'mopped up' the Bay [hotel] *yard on the way to the Fistral. There was no enemy today …*

June

Monday 2nd

… Wrote for English essay 'How to ensure lasting peace after the war'.

Smith ii [the middle brother] *showed what 'Who's Who' said about RJC's father—he got the MC in the last war—cavalry, galloping and rescuing two wounded on his horse.*

I think RJC is probably my best friend. Wood is not particularly friendly, rather shallow, and he doesn't show signs of liking me much. If he did it would be different.

The news is just foul; we got 15,000 men from Crete, with very considerable losses, the Huns had complete air superiority. This whole war is just awful.

Friday 6th

… *The* [JTC exercise] *plan didn't work according to schedule, so it was good fun. Only about 12 men of our platoon reached the chemi-lab.*

I lay down behind some cinders at the top of the B-P path, a small evacuee asked why I was—"so I won't be shot". He soon collected all his friends, all of whom asked the 'College boy' if he was going to be shot. Smith ma[jor] *(temporary section leader) was also asked. He said "Because I'll be shot by a machine gun if I don't". Terrible excitement, and warnings not to give the 'College boys' away …*

Saturday 7th

A warm, sunny day. After chemistry, RJC and I photographed Trinder (the lab boy). He bust some flasks, and with Nitric acid and zinc got some goodish fumes of smoke. I also photographed him pouring some liquid into a measuring cylinder. Hope they come out …

After tea I developed films, successful. 2 of gull chick emerging from egg, two of buzzard's nest, one of young greenfinch in hand. There was a good Camera club meeting in the evening on Photoflood use—several people did things.

Sunday 8th

… *After lunch I cleaned* [my] *bicycle and khaki-blancoed my JTC belt and read* [blanco was a cleaning paste used on belts and straps] …

The first House bathe at 4 o'clock in the Gannel, lovely. I lost my temper with Cruickshank—he's always so boring and funny ha ha that I got tired of it. All the same I shouldn't have lost it.

Monday 9th

… *Had to see Max … standard jaw—Hah! no community spirit! self centred! Hah! object to criticism! Hah, selfish! Have done nothing for the House! If there's no improvement you'll have no free time Hah!*

Ugh! Most of what he said was untrue, I haven't done much for the house, but haven't had much chance; by 'objections to criticism' I suppose he means looking bored (Hah! arrogant air!) when told to point my shoulder at the ball, or brush my hair. Hah! The jaw lasted about 10 minutes.

News—we're advancing into Syria, with those swinish French opposing us.

Thursday 12th

... General inspection. There was a frantic polishing of uniforms ... then we rushed to the Pentire [hotel] *and fell in. By now the weather was clear with a good cool breeze, so it wasn't too bad standing being inspected at attention. He* [Major Hoplack, the inspecting officer] *peered up at my tunic-collar and said "Ah, poor fellow—reduced to a safety pin". Then we did battle drill and watched a very good camouflage demonstration.*

Fall in at 2.15—the usual Field Day programme with modifications. We left our bikes at the chemi lab and walked to the Bay, above which we destroyed an ambush with grenades. Then it was time; Major Hoplack gave us a long, not particularly instructive or complimentary talk, and it was over. Quite fun.

A lovely fresh evening.

Saturday 14th

... [At cricket] *I made one (3 according to the scorer) and was caught. I then read 'North West Passage' ...*

After tea went to town. ... I then went and was mesmerised by the sea—a lovely breeze so I felt all funny and happy inside, watched RJC, CMGS, MFW and T ring young oyster catchers, and then went back ...

Sunday 15th

As per pre-arranged plan, H woke us up at 5.30 and, creeping silently out of the house, H, Smith ii, N, RJC, Smith iii, R, B, H and I congregated in the bike sheds and set off for St. Evell. We wore games clothes, and got there in under an hour. We weren't allowed in (although the sentry was very decent), so we got boring bits of Blenheim to show we'd been. From Porth, RJC, S and I raced, as we thought G might come and wake Wood for H[oly] Communion. We got back about 5 mins. before them, all getting in successfully, and got into bed. Good fun, and we never expected that we'd not be caught …

Monday 16th
A grey morning, clearing at about 11 o'clock to a lovely sunny day. During the afternoon some very dense patches of mist formed and drifted inland—the foghorn blared all the time …

I'm not getting on particularly well with Wood, in fact I'm almost beginning to give up trying …

Sunday 22nd
Astounding news; Germany is invading Russia. PM spoke in the evening. I didn't like his speech much as he was very frank about his dislike of Russia. We are allies however. I don't like the rest of the news. Germany will probably beat the Russians eventually—the Russians have 160 divisions on a front from the Black to the White sea. Finland and Romania are helping Germany …

After lunch I went to a demonstration of the new enlarger, passed a test so I can use it, and visited the oyster-catchers which T tried to photograph from under a rug. They came very near but behind rocks etc. Then I bathed again.

Tuesday 24th
Field Day. We fell in at 9.10 and marched for an hour to Kelsey head (Cubert Common). Very hot. Then we split up into sections. Our section was on the extreme flank, and I was on its flank. Before lunch nothing happened except I lost my lunch and water and gas mask container, to find it in the stream 20 mins. later with the water gone, and the food and box dissolving. Very hot.

About 2.40, B and R came past, having killed off a section and being dead themselves, and they gave Smith ii and me their rifle and 6 blanks. Then the enemy appeared and began to fire at us. I replied while Smith reported to Platoon HQ. They advanced along the skyline, under fire from two brens (tins and stones) and about 3 rifles. Then they charged down a field and huddled in a hollow. I stalked up—wizard fun—and chucked two grenades in the middle, then I ran. Frank reported the whole section out.

Then we went and joined the remnants of the platoon in the wood; went to tell Winter the news, and came back to find two survivors—mortar fire. The reserve platoon also attacked. Then the finish went.

Frank said both sides had won, and mentioned my 'magnificent bombing attack, in which I was certainly killed'. We then marched back, I with a very empty tummy, but having had 6 mouthfuls of water. We had a bath before tea to cool and de-sweat us. Good fun.

Thursday 26th

… I had a four page essay on disobedience for B [prefect], *because H and me dropped the mustard pot in the water jug during lunch.*

We were photographed for the house record in Rest, a photo to be called 'Study'.

… a rather poor voluntary game of basket ball after tea.

July

Tuesday 1st

… Began a weather notebook in the evening.

Wednesday 2nd

… We did squad drill by cadets, quite fun. Everyone laughed at my marching because I lifted my feet up and swung the wrong arm …

Saturday 5th

… The Russians are still retreating, killing thousands of Germans and busting lots of German tanks.

Thursday 10th

… We drew veronica flowers in Biology. I had shooting and I shot 50 rounds. My first score (the first in my life) was 20; I managed to get

a second try and got 31 which was better—quite fun. I found it difficult to close the right (i.e. left) eye at first.

Sunday 13th
… A good sermon, chiefly about the need for doctors and education in India—very well put across.

The compulsory church services on Sundays were something I resented, but sermons such as this, delivered by people from outside the school, were often a breath of fresh air.

Sunday 20th
… There was the NHS exhibition. I showed the grasshoppers and my young herring gull photo. The exhibition was very good. A gave an interesting lecture on bees. Daddies 'Fears may be Liars' has been put in the Biology Lab …

Donald Soper was preaching—the best I've ever heard, he seemed very sure but didn't convince me about anything new—I still don't believe in a God who guides, and I still certainly don't think Prayer works—and I am convinced that I'll not change my opinions. I'm also convinced that if people were real Christians the world would be better.

Soper was a prominent Methodist minister and socialist, who was famous for his outdoor preaching.

Saturday 26th
A hot day. Also a field day. We started off and crossed the Gannel under fire from a perfectly visible sniper, who fired a three-round burst, and then roared along with people other sides of walls and things. … eventually we had a wizard battle, all being killed and killing all the enemy …

The Lord Lieutenant of Cornwall came to give prizes, he made the speech prophesied by Max— i.e. he was honoured, he had been a dud at school (he looked it!), he advised us to work and play hard, and (UGH!) said that the old school tie was a damn good thing, that the other people were jealous; there! UGH !!! I felt quite sick. The headmaster made a pathetic speech too …

I am sharing with Cruickshank next term NOT Wood or Smith iii. … I will be relieved now to be away from Wood, I am now at the stage when the sooner I'm away from him the happier I'll be.

… I got a letter from Margaret, a good plan for Ecological survey of the wild valley.

The wild valley was the one near Glatting we had discovered in April.

to Glatting

Tuesday 29th
The leaving prefects raided all the juniors at 4.28 with glasses of water, 2 mins. before the bell went, when we had intended to do it to them. We retaliated—I scored a direct hit on B.

Off by bus early … I had a good breakfast on the train. … The train arrived on time, I caught the underground, and arrived just before the train left for Pulborough. In the compartment were two brothers with a young tame jay, two downy white sparrowhawks and a young ? owl. They fed the jay on rabbit, and were just going to feed the hawks on a young pigeon which they killed on the spot, when the carriage was invaded by elderly gentleman and wife. Birds were all hurriedly bundled away, but jay contrived to knock on the box. The man opposite me was asleep, and dribbled down his waistcoat periodically. I changed successfully at Three Bridges.

When I got to Pulborough I rang up—no answer. I began to walk and rang up from the box near Stopham bridge—no answer; so I rang the Armstrongs and asked them to find [my mother]. *I went on walking, but no car appeared. I arrived at Francis' house after nearly two hours, to learn that she was at a concert, so I went and stayed at the Armstrongs till she came back—I met her in the village—she was surprised! She had the young evacuee with her, Eric, or Little by Little, known as her 'April shower' as he wets his bed most nights. Funny little boy …*

'Eric, or Little by Little' was the title of a moralistic Victorian novel about a boy at boarding school.

Wednesday 30th

Home! After getting up, having breakfast, moving on the thirteen rabbits and putting out the goats … we spent the morning getting out … John's fishing rod (for catching fish with next term) and then we went to Petworth to get a beehive …

Margaret arrived from Fittleworth à la bicyclette—also very wet.

Thursday 31st

… After lunch we went off in the car to Sutton end, where we spent over an hour cutting reeds to thatch the haystack. Rather fun, but the sickles blistered our hands. We got the back of the little car full of bundles. … I saw Archibald (one of the large grasshoppers bequeathed to me by C) eat a housefly in less than two minutes.

August

Friday 1st

… I read 'The Uniqueness of Man' and dozed until 3.15, when we all went to the village, calling at the Neals' [farm] *to say that we'll help at the harvest if they want us …*

Saturday 2nd

Daddy arrived at about 12 o'clock. Before that I put new hinges and a new lock on my house door.

We had lunch early, and after it Margaret, Daddy, Tinker and I went for a walk. We went slowly up the shepherds path along, partly through woods, and back via the deserted orchard. I caught several butterflies, Margaret found two broad leaved helleborenes and some fungi. The weather cleared and there was a lovely sunny evening. After tea Bassadone arrived and I set all the butterflies.

Monday 4th

... we posted a parcel and collected some foxglove leaves to make a drug with (the government have asked for them). When we got back we went and spent the morning mending leaks in [the dam of] *Glatting lake ...*

Mommy got furious with the telephone in the evening, as the porter rang up [from Guy's] *for Daddy, who wasn't in. She nearly wasted much more money by breaking her spectacles. Mrs. Francis went to hospital, with query (?) appendicitis.*

Tuesday 5th

I spent the first part of the morning in my house, modernising the model 'spitfire' (by adding shell guns) and the 'Beaufort' (by adding backward firing turret under the nose).

Evidently the model planes I had were updated as were the real ones. The modification to the Beaufort was, I believe, because German fighters had found that the most successful way to attack involved approaching from behind and below.

... I went and ate about ¾ lb of dewberries (hog!) [bilberries] *and saw a comma butterfly. After lunch I helped cut the lavender, and then read in my house until tea. I went for a stroll at about 6 o'clock, it rained quite hard but I sheltered under a hedge.*

Wednesday 6th

... I spent the first part of the morning separating foxglove seeds for the government (for the drug digitalis) ... went for a stroll. I stalked rabbits, getting 14 yds. from one, which was then scared by Tinker; and within 2 yards of another, which was sitting on its hind legs facing the other way ...

Friday 8th

... I played a little with Eric and T, as they were dressed up as Indians. Then I cooked until Dr. and Mrs. and a small East arrived (he is an Indian), when we had supper.

Mr. East was a surgeon in one of the south London hospitals linked with Guy's, and he had spent periods on duty at Guy's. When the staff were sleeping in the basement during the night raids, the matron would bring round an evening cup of cocoa to the common room, and would conspicuously not serve Mr. East; so my mother would accept hers and then equally conspicuously take it to him.

Saturday 9th
Quite a nice day. After breakfast I showed Mr. East round the garden and gave him an archery lesson. Mommy gave me the air pistol, and I played about with that until lunch time …

After tea I went and tried to shoot a rabbit—I tried, but from too far off.

News—Germans doing big Ukrainian drive.

Sunday 10th
… I failed to shoot a rabbit—missing at ten yards, but I know the place, and there is often one there. Rabbits don't mind the noise of shooting much. After lunch Margaret and I shot with the pistol and bows.

After tea we all except Mrs. East (spelt?) went for a walk to the Willow Herb patch. We went beyond, and on the way back found where a plane had crashed—British, we found an air ministry crown and hundreds of identification numbers e.g. Sc/7973015. Brought lots of bits back.

Tuesday 12th
… During the morning Margaret, Isabel [East], *Tinker and I went for a walk, towards the Wild valley, but not getting there. We picked lots and lots of mushrooms, mostly horse. When we got back we cooked them and had them for lunch—very good …*

Wednesday 13th
… At 3 o'clock we caught all the chickens and put them in the chicken house; the door blew open so we had to catch them again. Two people came to see us [about the chickens], *saying that we've 10 old, and*

7 pullets worth keeping. They dissected (tore apart!) one which died recently—either a parasite or avian TB.

Thursday 14th

… At 3 o'clock I listened to an important announcement by Attlee—it was a statement of our Peace aims, which seem pretty good …

Smolensk has been evacuated by the Russians, who are also withdrawing in the Ukraine.

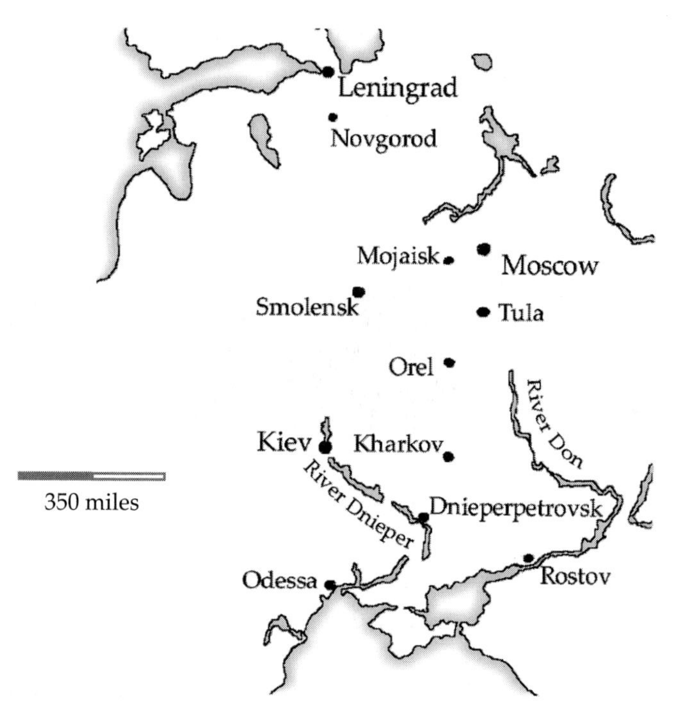

Sunday 17th

We spent the morning dissecting Archibald [the grasshopper] *who passed away during the night. Mommy made a lovely coffin, and Daddy wrote a beautiful epitaph* [see 31st Dec.]. *It was very interesting dissecting the creature.*

After lunch we were going to go for a walk, but when we got as far as my house we decided to stay there. We lit a fire, and chiefly Daddy and Joe [a visiting friend] *had a discussion: is there any purpose in Nature? …*

Tuesday 19th

[In London] … *We saw Daddy in his rooms—he was going to leave for Redhill soon; and then went to Fry* [dentist]. *My teeth were all alright.*

We had lunch and then went to see Disney's 'Fantasia'. It was pictorial impressions of music—very very clever and most of it very nice. We tried to get tea at Victoria, Mommy got furious with a rude waitress and left the first tearoom, and was pretty angry at the next, where we were not given clean plates. Arrived at Glatting at about 8 o'clock—but Margaret stayed in London with Mrs. Mapother to see the tailor tomorrow.

Wednesday 20th

After breakfast I went to see Mr. Fawkes, to ask if I could help with the harvest. He said not today, you can come if you like later. In fact nobody really wants me to help. When I got back I mended one of the orchard gates.

During the afternoon I read in my house, and practised with the air pistol. I find that I'm much more accurate when standing than when lying down using two hands …

Thursday 21st

… The news is worrying—the Russians are withdrawing behind the Dneiper, and are holding Odessa, and there is fierce fighting around Leningrad.

Two good remarks—a Russian spokesman said "Odessa is neither another Tobruk or another Dunkirk, it is Odessa, one of the fiercest battles of the war". And a conversation between two fighter pilots returning from France:

"Do you realise that practically all that matters about your tail is missing?"

"Crikey! There must be a war on."

Sunday 24th
... I typed part of an 'airgraph' letter to John, hard and slow work. Churchill spoke at 9 o'clock—not as good as usual I thought, and so mean to the Russians. The Americans are vile! The Russians are holding the Germans all along the line. Losses according to Moscow—Russians 700,000 men, Germans 2,000,000. Probable, but how awful!

In fact Russian losses were far higher.

Monday 25th
... Good news, we and Russia have entered Iran (ex-Persia) and the Russians are holding the Germans.

Tuesday 26th
... The Russians have evacuated Novgorod—Leningrad sector. Germans claim Dneiperpetrovsk (??), the 'City of Steel'. Little resistance in Iran, both we and the Russians are advancing.

Wednesday 27th
... I got some beautiful new shoes. ... After elevenses I went out and cooked lunch in my house—thick potato soup and cocoa—Mommy came. At 3.30 I went rabbiting with Tinker—missed once ...

News: Darlan shot and badly wounded by young French man who slightly wounded another French traitor (Déat). Poor devil now (meaning the young Frenchman).

In fact it was Pierre Laval, recently and later head of the Vichy administration, but now out of power, who was shot. Marcel Déat was a Fascist journalist. The young Frenchman, a Communist, was arrested on the spot.

Saturday 30th
A lovely day. I spent most of the morning cementing up part of the wall on the south side of the drawing room above the window, where the rain comes in ...

We had parsnip wine at supper to drink John's health, it being his birthday.

Sunday 31st
A real summer day. We left Glatting at about 10.30 and picked blackberries. When we got back I read in the sun, Mommy bottled 29 lbs of blackberries.

Another of Margaret's fellow timber measurers came to supper, with two New Zealand foresters. … A lovely evening.

September

Wednesday 3rd
… I spent the morning clipping the green parts of potato plants off, as we have got blight. Very tiring job as your back is bent the whole time.

… After tea I failed to shoot rabbits.

Two years of war.

Friday 5th
… Mommy and Daddy arrived [back from London] *with two books for learning Russian with, and a loose leaf note book for birds.*

Saturday 6th
… In the morning I learnt Russian (part of the alphabet) and did my bird note-book …

Sunday 7th
… In the morning I did my Russian with Daddy—I now know the alphabet. After that I and Margaret strung beans while Daddy read us a book about Russia—'Country with a Plan' by Pat Sloane.

I spent the afternoon doing bird notes. After tea we set off on a family blackberrying, which Margaret ruined by marching on miles ahead looking glum, and later sitting in a mood and yelling to us in a furious temper to come and see some long-tailed tits. Of course they flew away. She may do lots of work but she's damn disagreeable to live with …

My father's bringing home Russian books was a sign of a new identification with the USSR. My diary did not record any discussion concerning how this came about but, as the subsequent diary entries show, it persisted. This may now seem hard to understand, and some explanation may be helpful.

During the period between the World Wars, reports of life in the USSR had been polarised. Some conveyed the image of a country which—despite foreign intervention, a harsh civil war and many cruelties—was overcoming the inequalities and injustices of the past. Others reported the facts, if not the extent, of famine, repression and the Gulag. Since the war these negative aspects have become the whole received truth, and how I and millions of others could have ignored or discounted the evidence for them is difficult to understand. I believe there are three main explanations.

First, many critics of the USSR were suspect witnesses, paying little attention to abuses committed by the European colonial powers, and being complacent in the face of the gross inequalities and widespread poverty in the capitalist world.

Secondly, there was widespread disillusion with the years of appeasement of Germany, Italy and Japan, and with Britain's failure to support the government in Spain where, for the first time, there had been active military resistance to the spread of Fascism. The Spanish war had mobilised anti-Fascist public opinion in Britain, and in France the Popular Front, a socialist-communist alliance, had won the 1936 parliamentary elections. But Spain had not been saved, and then Czechoslovakia had been abandoned.

Thirdly, by the end of 1940, Europe was largely allied with, or occupied by, Germany, and it was not easy—and certainly not rational—to believe in the survival of Britain. In this precarious situation the German invasion of the USSR, despite the early chaos and massive losses suffered, brought us a credible military ally. We needed to believe in the Red Army, and in the possibility of peace and of a different future.

My diary shows that I realised how this need might blind me to the realities of the system, and records how I tested my enthusiasm by reading books that were critical of or hostile to it. But as the war progressed, the Soviet Union, despite horrific civilian and military losses, proved to be a remarkably resilient military ally, whose victory offered the main basis for our hope of peace.

The hostile British press now recorded Soviet achievements and Stalin became Uncle Joe, and sober critics began to feel hopeful that the pre-war oppression would yield in the face of the shared sense of suffering and achievement. In the end I continued to link my socialist and egalitarian ideals to a largely fictitious version of Soviet society. I was not alone in doing this. Also, Communists, inspired by the achievements of the Soviet Union, and by the historical theory and traditions on which they were seen to be based, played a leading role in the resistance movements in occupied Europe. As their contribution became known, I found further justification for my beliefs.

Tuesday 9th
Daddy, Bindeman [a friend staying for the week] *and I spent most of the morning carting wood in the trailer from by the pylon to the woodpile. Quite tiring. Then I read. After lunch I did Russian, and after tea we picked and de-stalked elderberries.*

News: we've landed a large force in Spitzbergen to counteract German aims—cool place. Also good Russian counter attacks in centre.

Wednesday 10th
… I spent the afternoon russianising—getting the rules for gender of nouns taped. After tea Sydney [Binderman], *Tinker and I went for a walk. We came back through the wood east of the chalk road, and at the bottom found a badgers' earth—3 entrances, and bedding strewn about. … There was a fresh hazel nut in the entrance to one hole, and a smashed snail shell on the path …*

After the news Mommy and I strolled to meet Daddy—we met him quite soon, very tired and dripping from the ride on his heavy bike with the dynamo.

Monday 15th
… I learnt Russian in the afternoon and read the life of Madame Curie. Miss Quintrell came to supper, which we had at 6.30. Shaw's 'Joan of Arc' on the wireless—a frightfully good play.

Thursday 18th
I spent the first part of the morning puttying my house up, and most of the rest lying under a groundsheet waiting to photograph a cole-tit … when he went in the right place the first time the string stretched and did not work the shutter, so I moved the 'hide' (a groundsheet over a camera-tripod) under the tree, and took two photos of the tit and one of a robin. Good.

Packed after tea—depressing, very.

to Newquay

Saturday 20th
… Tired and feeling a little down in the evening, but it's no good not accepting school life.

Monday 22nd
… Sometimes I feel rather frightened when I think of the invasion if it should come; chiefly selfishly afraid about Mommy and Daddy, but when I read of what the Russian people do behind the lines and by Leningrad, Odessa, and now in Kiev, I feel rather ashamed. I wish we could help them more; why not risk sending most of our tank output?

Propaganda accounts of Russian valour were at odds with the military debacle; but as the war progressed, both the high cost borne, and the courage and skill of the Red Army, were indisputable.

Tuesday 23rd
… JTC in the afternoon. Rifle drill (without rifles) and 'drill' by cadets; T told us to wheel half right when we weren't moving, Ha Ha. I'm sure being able to form platoon at the halt on the left is awfully useful when one's being a guerrilla—no doubt the Russian peasants all learn it …

Wednesday 24th
… I'm in the school routine coma now …

Thursday 25th
Instead of MT we had to dig potatoes; the machine didn't arrive so we did it with forks, and got a jaw from PSN for clod throwing …

The school had cultivated a potato field.

Friday 26th
… lecture on Rec. patrols and army ritual in JTC. … I have nearly finished learning my Russian nouns—slow but I hope quite sure. Да, Нет? *(Yes, no?)*

October

Wednesday 1st
More school—what a monotonous life this is; one thinks largely of food—there are no other excitements. … What a life and what a world this is. But how nice we're going to make it.

Thursday 2nd
Had a good dream before waking up—I was biking and saw 3 other blokes fall off (actually saw this on Gannel yesterday), and then went to meeting, where I sat next to Goering who got up and said he'd murdered Hitler (this was in Germany). Cries of "long live the German republic", which when I remembered I changed to the 'united soviet of socialist Germany' (for 'Germany' put 'world' and I'm right) …

Saturday 4th
[beach rugger] *… no ball having appeared, we played a very poor and silly game with a tennis ball, which amounted to a rather poor free fight. I played not very hard—I can never run so well as most people, I don't know why. RJC got very mashed up—bits of tongue and lip missing.*
After tea we went to the Gannel, and biked through it as the tide was over the road. We saw little …

Thursday 9th
News none too good. Germans have Orel, 200 miles S. of Moscow, and an important railway junction. Russian position precarious. … Letter

from Daddy and Soviet War Newses [a newspaper-format weekly issued by the Soviet embassy in London].

Friday 10th
News rather depressing—[Germans] *120 miles to Moscow, decision a matter of weeks or months. I get nasty feelings in my stomach when I think of it. I wish I could help somehow, and I wish England could do something useful …*

Tuesday 14th
Russians have evacuated Vyazma—130 miles west of Moscow; advance slowed up. Awful fighting. Both sides exhausted and shoving in reserves …

Thursday 16th
Position round Moscow deteriorated. … Nothing interesting as usual, apart from the news.

Friday 17th
… News as usual depressing. Rumours of Odessa falling, and fighting on Moscow's outer defences. I am going to write about 20 sides ahead what the date today is, and what I think is going to have happened by then [see 15th Dec.].

Sunday 19th
… Fierce fighting, Germans held round Moscow.
Made a [£5] *bet with Smith i (MG)* [that there would be no more wars in our lifetime] *see inside last cover* [31st Dec.].

Another example of the triumph of hope and belief over reason! He never collected.

Wednesday 22nd
… Max jaw in evening—he says I'm getting better as I get less shy, and that I must adopt more humble attitudes in periods.

Thursday 23rd
… A practice and then a short very fierce game on the beach—my training's a little better, but certainly isn't good. I got a letter and some Soviet War News from Mommy. News—more evacuation—slowly falling back, but the army remains fairly intact (i.e. not cut off).

Friday 24th
… RJC and I went for a lovely bike ride in the afternoon, just the right temperature if you keep moving. We went round by Trenance to West Pentire and back by the Gannel. A gentleman farmer, good accent, unshaved, thought we'd left his gate open—we hadn't. He'd already lost 3 cows over the cliffs through others' carelessness—he asked us to be very careful, as it was hard on 'us folk'. He struck me as the sort of man who might well be the central figure in a novel. I unfortunately didn't hear the news, but I think that there wasn't much.

Saturday 25th
… I did works—burning damp grass and brambles in a very cold wind. Then I had to get the ½ week's potatoes from the Pentire—one sack burst just before we got to the shed.

After tea I went to the ornithological section meeting, and then to a nice music recital—H and T playing a Mozart concerto. After supper we had quite a good general rag.

News—bad weather in Russia—it will be a relief, to put it mildly, when all this is over. Actually most people here don't care much about the war.

Monday 27th
… News: held round Moscow, not too good in Donetz area, Kharkov claimed by Germans. Voroshilov and Budenny are organizing new armies behind the front—may those armies be successful.

Tuesday 28th
Very windy. I went along to Splash Point in the break—lovely, I just got hit once, the spray was very beautiful. We had a lecture on 3-in. mortars in the afternoon—interesting ...
War fierce, but weather slowing up the Germans.

Friday 31st
... Blitz in latin—I just got over half marks.

November

Saturday 1st
... After supper I played ping-pong and darts, and then dissected a tommy gun in Wood i's room with his brother and RJC (and him). I doubt if it will ever work again. There was a debate, 'This house prefers to know the worst', which I did not attend, as it seems such a silly subject.

Sunday 2nd
... A very very good sermon by an Indian, Mr. Singha, calling for no more party politics, real planning with minding the cost, and for colour equality (see Russia, though he did not).

Monday 3rd
Grey, rather cold day. Great excitement during first 2 periods—a sloop anchored beyond Towan Head, and signalled. I got part of the message, but missed about 10% of the letters. I got this RAET LTCAINE IEPS CTPNEIEEI EN DGRE LCIU EIE or IEEN NE.—Some sort of repetition, allowing for mistakes—it was hard to see the light in the bright sun ...
After 2 30 min. preps there was a flick—propaganda for the bible, the good samaritan etc. on the screen. Father moralising to son who wasn't going to take bible when joining RAF ...

Tuesday 4th
Cold. A good JTC thing—a demonstration of a platoon in battle order. They [visiting soldiers] *unpacked the plat*[oon] *truck etc. and went to positions, then they formed up and all came forward, saying what their respective jobs were. One poor fellow was terribly nervous, with his legs shaking, and besides that he could not speak loudly enough …*

Wednesday 5th
Guy Fawkes. Ha-Ha …
News—Germans right down in Crimea, 5th Moscow battle on—mud frozen up. Depressing. A letter from Mommy at last, she's well but harried with evacuees and rabbits …

Tuesday 11th
All the house but 5 have Pentire plague—acute diorihea. I went twice before 7 o'clock and 3 times in the morning—general squoogly tummy.
In JTC Capt. Shand [probably an old boy] … *told us about his experiences in the French business '40. He was attached to 51st Div*[ision]*—4,000 odd survivors from 22,000. He was on motor bikes part of the time, out of 50 cyclists 7 survived; he went into the square of one town to find two lost bren carriers—he found some, but they were German. He got out quick.*

The 51st (Highland) Infantry division had escaped encirclement as the Germans advanced to Dunkirk, and withdrew to Normandy with part of the French army. The survivors eventually surrendered at St. Valery en Caux. The division had to be reconstituted from scratch.

During silence [5 minutes for prayers every evening, when I normally wrote my diary] *Max came in and told me to stop writing this, as it disturbed the others. I had to see him afterwards—he said it was a very selfish thing to do—even if I was an atheist, I ought to let the others pray in silence. Also I'm not humble enough, and he thinks it's hard for me to be without being a Christian. Silly twerp—Cruickshank and P both said they never heard the pen.*

Saturday 15th

I got a parcel from Mommy containing badger books—I am lecturing next Saturday evening …

After tea we went to the music recital. We heard a warning siren in one interval, and a little later a plane roared over towards Newquay, followed closely by a whistle. I was just going to whisper "ah! Spitfire" when there was a loud bang, and everyone sat on the floor—a bit late I thought as the plane had gone over, and the bomb was on the same side of us as the plane [i.e. it had been dropped after the plane had passed us].

Then C began whistling, D (so efficient!) shouted "Down!" and everyone did—4 times—very silly. I suppose they thought more planes were coming. When Hales had steadied his hand the recital proceeded …

News—Russians holding, 10 miles from Rostov; Tula - - Leningrad. Crimea rather bad.

Sunday 16th

… RJC and I biked ½ a mile to the bomb [crater left by the raid the day before], *which was this side of the Gannel, just above the farm Trethellen, in a ploughed field. like this:*

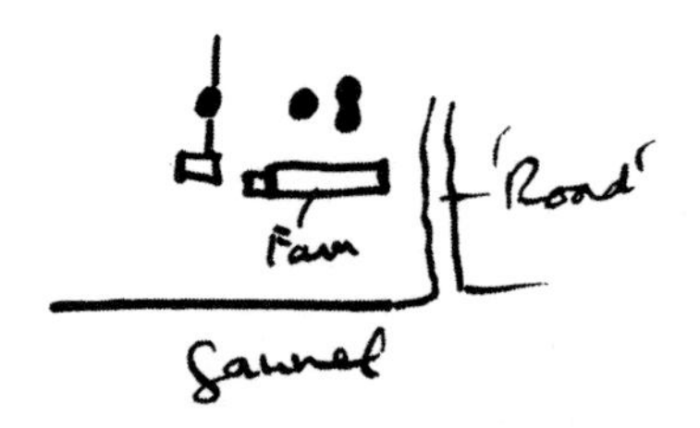

One double crater, one single, one on a wall. I got two pieces of bomb. The craters were 10–12 ft. deep, and about 15 ft. across.

When I got back, I painted toys for bombed children and prepared my [badger] *lecture …*

Thursday 20th

Double MT—I made toys for bombed children—tanks because they are easy to make—it's a pity to make them war minded though.

News—we are launching an offensive in N. Africa, which I hope may divert a few Germans from Russia. Army, RAF, Navy, commanded by Cunningham, Conningham, and Cunningham! Good luck to us. I smashed stones with a hammer all the afternoon—good fun.

Two brothers, Adml. Sir Andrew and Gen. Sir John Cunningham, and AVM Sir Arthur Coningham were simultaneously in command of sea, land and air operations.

Friday 21st
... News—fierce fighting in Russia. We are 10 miles from Tobruk's defences, to the S.E. [News]*papers are rather losing their senses of proportion I think, they hide the Russian news away and have 2-inch headlines about some small German retreat ...*

A 3-mile-away bomb in prep.

Sunday 23rd
... A good sermon by Max—one of the 3 best I've heard ...

After prep ... we got PB [Pentire bar, i.e. the school hall] *ready for the meeting. I gave my lecture* [on badgers] *first—it went off OK, and seemed to me to last 5 minutes, though I believe it lasted 20 ...*

Monday 24th
We've got lots of Germans surrounded in a line from Fort Capuzzo (which we've got) to Jarabub to Tobruk. Tobruk forces made a sally. Australians in Badia, took 15,000 prisoners. Big tank battles, we're using transport planes plus gliders. Russia: counter-attack in Rostov, very fierce fighting in Moscow area.

The story about gliders does not seem to have any basis in fact.

Tuesday 25th
... In JTC we did air dispersal—walking along in sections and spreading out fanwise when the whistle goes to lie on our faces.

A lecture in the evening on Russia by Sir Bernard Pares. V. good. He told the history of the Revolution—Trotsky being shoved out by Stalin, v. successful present system—collective farms, industry, education etc., but most people won't take it in ...

Sir Bernard Pares was a distinguished Slavonic scholar who had known Russia before the revolution. He was an admirer of the Russians and their culture as a whole, regardless of any regime, and had remained a firm but non-political advocate of the importance of continuing good relations.

While he insisted on the repressive nature of Stalin's government, he saw it as a return to Russia's tradition of autocratic nationalism after the Bolsheviks' earlier excesses of internationalist revolutionary fervour. His discussions of the potential benefits of Stalin's modernisation could reasonably be seen as a defence of the aims, if not the methods, of the Communist Party.

His lecture may have encouraged me in my writing of a eulogy of the Soviet Union (see 28th Nov.).

Thursday 27th

... News—still ok. Another big tank battle in Libya—we may just about encircle Cyrenaica. Russia—fierce fighting—casualties up to day: Germans 5-6 million, Russian 2-3.

Friday 28th

We did message writing in JTC ...

At 3 o'clock there was the confirmation service [induction into the Anglican Church]—*RJC being confirmed ... all walking up, and having their hairs ruffled in pairs by the bish.*

Felt a bit depressed in the evening—dunno why. There's an awful lot to do in this world before it's decent place to live in—I think the solution is a form of government like in Russia. When you look at the facts it beats me how anyone can be against it:-

No-one gets money with out work (no landlords); everyone works, but for the good of the state and not for the good of owner and shareholders; goods are manufactured for efficiency—not for profit; workmen work better and get better pay and housing (much better) as state cares for welfare of everyone ...

All have equal chances in education, all can have any ambition. Colour equality by law (practical christianity). No-one profits by war (nobody will want war then). Sex equality. 7 hour working day, 1 day in 5 free. 2 weeks paid holiday (more rec. time for coalminers etc). Free and efficient medical service for all. Representatives of the people are from the people, working men are not represented by old boys of public schools who cannot see their points of view, as in England. And what are the disadvantages? Max says they are spiritual or something—too low an ideal, no God to help them. Surely it's a better ideal … to work for a better world for the next generation than to spend one's life preparing for … a future life, which may not exist …

I described all the advantages (not one of which was an established fact) which together presented a vision of a Utopian, anti-capitalist world. Even after 70 years I find my level of certainty and my dismissal of others as *duped and self satisfied* too embarrassing to quote!

This was not a triumph of Soviet propaganda, however, so much as a distillation of what I hoped for. Many of the features were established in Britain by the post-war Labour Government, for example a free medical service for all, two weeks paid holiday, improved education, some moves towards colour and sex equality, and the State being concerned with the welfare of all. These were the widely-held hopes for a different society which determined the results of the 1945 election.

I contrasted the ideal society with the pre-war situation:

where very many live in filthy conditions, with their children stunted … where men have no hope of realising any ambition because they were born poor …

Saturday 29th
… at 4.45 C, R, T … and I … had a gut (cram, hog) in our study. We ate from 5.45 -> 6.45. It was one of Max's contributions to the confirmed. RJC did a wizard nose trick with quite hot tea.

December

Monday 1st
... Nice news, a Russian victory has recaptured Rostov, and the Germans have fled right back to Mariupol—about 100 miles. We've cut the Tripoli road in Libya (Tripoli-Benghazi) and we're just out to destroy the armoured forces of the enemy first ...

Max talk in evening, telling me that I ought to write an article for some paper, as I hold definite views on things (I'd thought of it but never dared). He said that he'd type them for me—jolly decent of him.

Saturday 6th
Wet and windy. The house match was v. Howsons. ... The ground was four inches deep in liquid mud, which made fast running impossible. ... In the first half I banged my chin on someone's head, and loosened two teeth, breaking part off one. It was quite painful for a bit, and I got re-hit once or twice. ... It was cool if one stopped at all, because you were always coated in liquid evaporating mud. We won 12–0, thanks to the weather. Tiring ...

Max has typed out my article for the New Statesman—it's on the future and Russia.

Monday 8th
Japan has bombed American islands, heavy casualties [this was Pearl Harbour, Hawaii]. *Big naval battle, Japan v. America, they've (USA) lost an aircraft carrier, but are doing well.* [Japanese] *landing in Malaya—thin bit. We are bloody fools to sit and watch their convoys pass, and now this. At any rate it will jip up America. ... Frank with all sorts of bloody but optimistic prophecies. Libyan battle not going too well. Russians doing fine ...*

At this point Japan formally joined the Axis—Germany and Italy—and the USA declared war and joined the Allies.

Wednesday 10th
HMS Prince of Wales and Repulse [British capital ships] *have been lost! Depressing—POW brand new, best out. Japs doing OK. All round …*

Friday 12th
News a bit better—Luzon landing party smashed, most of P.O. Wales and Repulse crews saved. Americans have sunk a Jap. battleship, a cruiser and more. The Russians are advancing all along the line.

Very near the end of term. Lovely. A letter from Mommy—a Belgian pancaked [landed without his wheels down] *a petrol-less Spitfire in Shiner's field right by Glatting—no wireless—he was lost. He stayed to supper and tea. Francis guarded the plane until the military arrived. It would happen while I wasn't there.*

Sunday 14th
… As I was fairly tired, and as the Headmaster was preaching, and as variety is the spice of life, I cut chapel. I lay under my bed and snoozed—Miss Milner came in twice and put my circulation rate up a bit …

Monday 15th
… Crawshaw read to us from 'The good soldier Schweik' [a satire on army life] *and he drew a picture of Schweik on the board. In the break PSN came in and* [taking it to be a picture of him] *said "How Young we are—rub it out at once before I get annoyed—go on—hurry up". The form, in unison, said "Mr. Crawshaw did it, Sir" and PSN went out quickly, amid cheers, clapping and hoots of laughter …*

[Prediction] *Written on Oct 17. Odessa may be taken. Fighting on Moscow's outskirts. What is happening on this page? Has Germany cracked or has Russia? Is America in? Has the winter suspended operations or has it helped the Russians? Have Moscow and the Donetz basin fallen? Have we started an offensive in the East? Is there a stalemate? I don't know on Oct 17 and I wish I did.*

Dec. 16. [Answering the question "what is happening?"] *Odessa is taken—few Russian casualties. The Russians are doing a grand general offensive. America and Japan are in—and Japan is doing too well—as must be expected.*

The attempt to remain optimistic through the disastrous year is still evident!

to Glatting

Tuesday 16th
Up at 4.30—rush, crush etc. and we didn't get a compartment. We were in a crowded corridor, and several thugs [seniors] … *came and tried to drag me off. I got quite annoyed, and wrecked two noses and tummies (L, C) and gave G a black eye (he nearly bust my thumb off). Then they left me. G later apologised and said he deserved what he got. Journey otherwise as usual …*

… We had tea at Vic … trained to Glatting. Mommy has a very good idea—wake up village youth—girls knit [clothes for Russian refugees], *boys guerrilla band. Nora and Margaret are both home, and two 9½ yrs.-old evacuees. 1st time I've seen Nora for two years!*

Thursday 18th
… After lunch I biked to the village to post some parcels, and to leave some mittens at Mrs. Powell for the Russians.

At 4 o'clock five boys arrived, and after tea we explained all about the Ordnance Survey maps, and got them very successfully to understand contours by giving them plasticine models, and cutting slices.

Friday 19th
… I took Tinker for a short run and brought the car up. We first went to Petworth station, where we collected lots of luggage … Mommy went on to Petworth, and Nora and I began walking back. Mommy caught us up about ½ a mile before Sutton end, and squeezed Nora in while I stood on the running board …

After lunch I biked in to Petworth, to fetch shoes from the cobbler (a good Red), and to get an emergency ration card for Nora. When I got back I helped finish the de-husking of corn.

Sunday 21st
A dense mist all day. … we all, except Mommy and Nora, went for a holly-picking walk. It was a lovely surprise when, half way up the green slope, we came into brilliant sunshine, and it was very beautiful indeed to look across the flat, stationary sea of mist, with the rise by Petworth sticking through, and the bottom parts of the hills cut off. When we got to the top I took three photographs. We got lots of holly (which the goats, who had come too, tried hard to eat) and then we went home to tea.

News—Russian pushing bulge before Moscow—line shortening excuse liquidated, Hitler, because of inner tuition [i.e. intuition], *takes command of German army. Cracking?*

Monday 22nd
… The boys came up at 3.30 and we went for a walk with [compass] *bearings, taken before we started. The first time we just missed, and we went along a path to the wrong crossroads, which were further than the right ones. Thus the next bearing did not work either. Then we practised 'scramming'—scattering and hiding quickly. Except for two of them, they all did it properly …*

I imagine I was passing on some things learned in the JTC at school. It was also my first contact with the boys in the village.

The attempt to involve my contemporaries in war-related activities was probably a bit romantic. What I did not know at the time was that we were only a mile away from a house where, since mid-October, some of the most heroic acts of the war were in process.

I only discovered this when I read *French Resistance in Sussex* (Pulborough, Barnworks Publishing, 1995, reprinted 2012), written by Barbara Bertram who lived in Bignor (3/4 mile away). I remember that my mother disapproved of her because she stopped accepting evacuees, and had too many handsome men, and some women, staying for short periods in her house. They were passed off in the village as convalescent French soldiers but were, in fact, French agents, her house being a staging post for those just flown back from France, or about to be taken there from RAF Tangmere. They were flown in slow, low flying Lysanders, navigating by moonlight to find—provided there was no mist—fields indicated by the French resistance by three torches, where people and equipment were rapidly unloaded or loaded.

Some 200 agents passed through her house in Bignor—some, delayed by the weather, staying long enough to take on the local darts teams in the White Horse in Sutton. Several crossed over and returned many times, knowing each time that they would be tortured and shot if caught, as some were.

Although at the time Barbara Bertram could know no details, from what she remembered and from what she learned after the war, she wrote in her small book a movingly understated and loving account of the incredibly brave guests who passed through her house, and of the pilots who transported them. The last view the agents would have had as they left her house would have been the line of the South Downs which was so familiar to me from Glatting.

Tuesday 23rd

... After lunch, I saw a sparrow-hawk pounce on a sparrow in the barnyard, which was kind of it, as I happened to be looking at the time.

... at 4 o'clock three girls came to knit. In the evening I started a child's mitten, doing about 2" of ribbing.

Wednesday 24th

Daddy and Henry Bassadone arrived at about 2 o'clock, and a bit later we went out for a short walk, getting a Christmas tree, which we decorated after supper. We are not having (m)any presents this year.

Thursday 25th

Christmas day—although we are having no presents, I got 3 pencils, a rubber, 2 prs. shoelaces (Nora), woollen garters, socks, a magnifying glass, butterfly net, 3d notebook, comb, 3 [collar] *studs (Margaret and Mommy) and two books (Miss Wade, Daddy).*

We went for a short walk before dinner—warm and sunny. I spent the afternoon knitting, and reading. A nice peaceful sort of Christmas.

News. Russians still advancing, Benghazi captured.

I finished knitting a pair of children's mittens for Russian refugees.

Monday 29th

Mommy went off early to London, taking the two evacuees who are going home for a week …

The [village] *boys arrived at 2.30, when we had shooting, and then went for a walk, in which we had a stalking game—in which they didn't stalk, but only said 'Got yer George' etc. …*

Tuesday 30th

…we went with the [car and] *trailer to Sutton to collect scrap iron, taking one load from us, and collecting two loads from a dump collected by the boys in Bignor.*

Wednesday 31st

… I went to Petworth to see Henry [Bassadone] *off, we found a still warm rabbit—killed by a stoat, which we brought back. Only two girls turned up to knit, presumably they don't like the afternoon.*

Good news—Russians in Kerch and Feodosia. Far East is an inefficient muddle apparently. Thus ends 1941. What does next year hold for us? Invasion? Victory?

December 1941

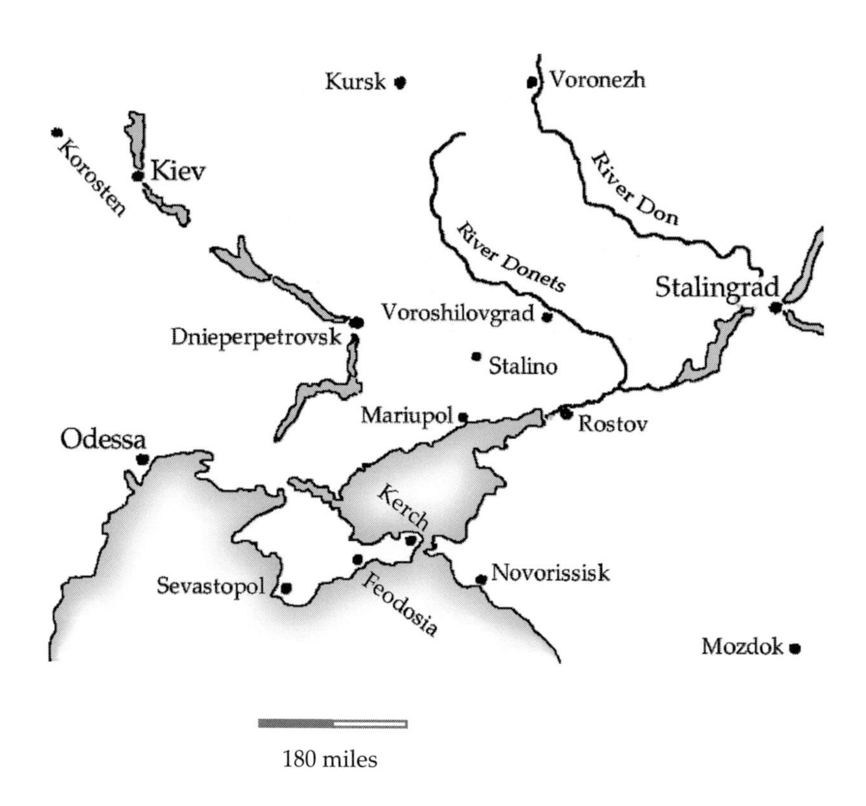

[Written inside the back cover of the 1941 volume]

In Memoriam—Archibald—Obiit 17/8/41

Here lie I—a green grass-hopper.
My wants were few, my conduct proper.
Born in a field, I came to pass
My latter days 'twixt walls of glass.
They gave me flies, though rather few;
I gazed upon the lovely view
From Glatting windows. Wrapt in thought
I dwelt alone. In vain I sought
To steel my limbs for one great leap
To the far hills and browsing sheep,
But lost at last the will to hop,
And fell asleep. Good-bye. Full-stop.

Oct 19. 1941 *At tea I made following bet with M.G. Smith (major). In the event of his decease before mine, if in the intervening period no more wars have arisen, he leaves me £5. In the event of my dying, the money goes to my next-of-kin.*
Should any war break out, I send him £5.
In the event of crises, reminders to be sent.

A. Ryle

Chapter 4: 1942

World events: 1942

Russia followed up their successful defence of Moscow with a major counter-attack, but it was finally stopped with heavy losses. The Germans then switched to attack in the direction of Stalingrad, and by the end of the year were engaged in bitter fighting there.

Japan quickly occupied Malaya, and entered Burma, cutting the supply route to China. A large British force in Singapore surrendered. The Philippines and Dutch East Indies were taken and Port Darwin in Australia was in range of aerial attacks. Naval battles were costly to both Japan and the US, but a decisive US win at Midway—where four Japanese carriers were sunk for the loss of one American one—weakened the Japanese position.

North Africa: major advances and retreats left the situation unstable, until an important victory was won in October at El Alamein. The German and Italian troops retreated to Tunisia, where they had good air support; opposing French, British and inexperienced American troops embarked on a long and difficult campaign. Germany occupied Vichy France.

Britain was increasingly involved in heavy bombing of German cities. In the Atlantic, German U-boats were sinking increasing numbers of the merchant ships bringing supplies to Britain.

Europe: The planned mass extermination of the Jews was under way. This was not widely reported in the British press.

Diary for 1942

at Glatting

January

Friday 2nd
At 12.30, Mommy, Margaret and I drove to Rapleys [cycle shop on the Chichester road], *where we caught the 1.15 bus to Chichester. We arrived there at 2 o'clock, and went straight to a flick. Not bad—last half 'Bombay Clipper' (complex), News, trailers; and Charles Laughton, Deanna Durbin, in 'It started with Eve'—quite funny and some nice singing. After a tea (Margaret too hot and looking furious) we walked to the station, and after a wait caught the 6.7 bus back. A nice outing, and a change …*

Monday 5th
Only Raymond Hedges [from the village] *and George Ward* [evacuee] *turned up to the meeting, and at 11 o'clock we set off morsing to each other. We stopped for lunch just before Whiteways Lodge and lit a fire …*

They were uprooting many thorn bushes by the signpost—for ploughing.

Up to this time the Downs—chalk hills a few hundred feet above sea level—were unfenced, dotted with hawthorn, yew and other small trees, and were grazed by unfenced Southdown sheep. The clearance was part of the major national expansion of agriculture, aimed at reducing dependence on imports.

Tuesday 6th
[London, to the dentist] ... *I had one hole to be filled and drilled—Margaret had a dead tooth ...*

Having shopped unsuccessfully (they had nothing practically which we wanted) ... we met Daddy and had tea. We picked up the small boys [evacuees who had been away since Christmas] *at London Bridge and had a very fast train back.*

Wednesday 7th
... only two knitters arrived. Even if they don't still come we've got about 11 little sweaters, a few mittens etc.

Saturday 10th
Daddy and another Austrian Professor called Winkenstein (spelling?) arrived at 7.30. Wink is awful strange—not a very good English speaker, keeps on saying "I mean" and "it's tolerable" meaning intolerable.

Sunday 11th
... Witkinstein spent the morning with the evacuees—he thinks we're terribly cruel to them [they were given their meals separately during weekends while my father was there]. *We spent the afternoon arguing—he's an impossible person, every time you say anything he says "No no, that's not the point". It probably isn't his point but it is ours. A tiring person to listen to.*

After tea I showed him round the grounds and he entreated me to be kind to the miserable little children—he goes far too much to the other extreme—Mommy wants them to be good citizens, he wants them to be happy. He caught the 6.18.

I was not, of course, the first to identify this issue! According to Dodds, in *The Greeks and the Irrational* (p. 211), Plato in the *Laws* saw the common man as being concerned with happiness while the legislator wants him to be good, in pursuit of which he tries to persuade him that happiness and goodness go together. This places Wittgenstein, who was one of the century's most distinguished philosophers, on the side of the common man and my mother on the side of the legislators!

At this time Wittgenstein was working as the pharmacy porter at Guy's hospital, something arranged by my father at the request of my philosopher uncle Gilbert, in response to Wittgenstein's wish to do something useful. It is said that he did his best to persuade patients that their medicines were more likely to do harm than good—which may well have been true!

Monday 12th

... Awful near the end of the holidays. Margaret goes on the 16th too, poor Mommy being here all alone. And [talk of] *invasion in the air (and by it too—ha ha) which makes it WUSS. I personally don't think it'll come off, but if it does, I'd far rather be here, where I could scout and guide, than at school—which makes it WUSSER going back. Still, we're all alive now.*

Tuesday 13th

... It began to snow at breakfast time, and it snowed hard, with a south wind, all day. ... Margaret and I took Tinker and the toboggans to Sodgers Bottom [our term for 'Scotchers bottom'] *to see if it was a good run. On the way back along the crest of the downs, there was a biting gale, and the flying snow cut into your face. It felt just like an arctic expedition. On the exposed parts there was only a thin covering of hard icy snow, and in the hollows there were drifts up to 3½ feet deep. We got Tinker to pull a toboggan a short way. We had a glorious slide back, tobogganing from the top of the downs down through the woods and down the green slope.*

News: Libya—Far East more withdrawals, except in Philippines where [Japanese] *attack repulsed, Russia very good indeed.*

Wednesday 14th

... At 3.45 several of the boys arrived, and we went tobogganing—first on the green slope and then in Shiner's field. They got very cold hands and knees, as none had long trousers and few had gloves. They came back, had tea, and went home, having decided to continue the meetings while Margaret and I were away—Morse, 1st Aid, knitting even, tracking games, exploration etc., and, of course, shooting.

Last evening but one—misery.

Thursday 15th
The last day at home. ... I could not help crying a bit in the evening—it's so awfully lovely here, and at school it's all the same, with the loud, unsympathetic, uninterested people, and never anything exciting. The next generation must have good, co-educational day schools—as it will (if) when we go socialist.

to Newquay

Friday 16th
Absolute, unmitigated misery. We got up at 6.15, Mommy had been naughty and got us a really slap-up breakfast—porridge, bacon and eggs, coffee. ...Then we [Margaret was returning to Oxford where she was now reading Biology] *went off in the car, leaving Mommy in the snow having kissed her goodbye in the dark ...*

I wish I could stop being homesick ... each term recently it's been worse, because school life becomes more stereotyped and detached from the world, and home life means more and more.

Saturday 17th
I slept quite well and didn't feel nearly as homesick as I'd expected. ... breakfast was at 9 o'clock. Awful familiar smells in the dining room. ... I am sharing with RJC and AG Smith in the corner room (two windowed) on the top floor ...

News—Halfaya captured [a pass over the Egyptian/Libyan border]; *5,522 prisoners.*

Sunday 18th
... During the afternoon I messed around chatting and knitting. ... I am writing a diary letter home—a good idea, and find that it relieves homesickness ...

Max 'jaw' in the evening. Re—my propaganda article—rejected politely by New Statesman . ... 71 days

Tuesday 20th
... In JTC we did standing and lying loads ...

... Germans trying to disappear in Mojaisk sector—complaining that the Russians are unfair—roar around on dog sledges with MGs [machine guns]*, and disappear before there's time to wake up.*

My height is 5ft 10½ inches and I weigh 9 stone 3lb. 1 case scarlet fever.

Wednesday 21st

Mojaisk is in Russian hands. Hooray! Few people here know where Mojaisk is, fewer care ...

Grey and clear in patches, occasional rain. I was doing works in the afternoon, carting slates from the quarry to the pigsty site [the school was going to rear a pig]. *We took 6 sacks (sandbags) each—good exercise. When we got back I changed, ate Horlicks powder, wrote a bit of letter and began knitting the second glove. Settling in to the old routine.*

Mozhaisk is 70 miles west of Moscow.

Thursday 22nd

... In MT I nearly finished a model destroyer to be sold in warships week for National savings.

The game was on the beach—'biff'—a ruleless rugger: not my opinion of fun being kicked in the face, hands frozen, hands and knees sandpapered. I had a nice hot bath after it, with some illegally study brewed (by Smith on a 'stovette') tea ...

I got a letter from Mommy—lonely for her. Awful lucky that Daddy does get most week-ends. I wish she was more healthy too, it would make it easier for her ...

Sunday 25th

... A minesweeper patrol boat L96 was in the bay all day, steaming to and fro past an anchored merchant vessel [this was not a normal anchorage] ...

Chapel was in school dress ... we did [not] *attend the service. Instead we ate our fill, spilt tea on the floor, and filled a bath with tea leaves. ... I ate very little at tea—causing comment.*

Monday 26th
... A tug came and took away the cargo boat, which had I believe a bust propeller ...

In chem at the end RJC was looking down a piece of glass tubing when Smith accidentally knocked the other end ... RJC had his eye bashed hard, and as it turned out he cut the cornea, luckily not quite through. ... After lunch he taxied to Dr. Richard, and then to Truro where he saw a specialist—three readless days. Taxi'll cost some! ...

Wednesday 28th
... News: 3 day parliamentary debate opened by W. Churchill. Much criticism of govt.—deserved ...

Rommel slowing up a bit. Russians OK. Jap convoy well mashed, we retreat in Libya.

In the afternoon we had to make paper flowers to decorate the window of the shop to be used for selling the toys which the school are (?) going to make ...

Another attack of homesickness. Wizard political argument [with] *Mullins.*

Friday 30th
... Making toys in the afternoon. Smith went into town and bought me a 2½d loaf—I always get ravenous at odd times of day ...

February

Sunday 1st
... We went down to the Gannel (RJC against rules because of his eye) and had quite a successful morning, seeing a peregrine, pochard, tufted duck, grey wagtail, ringed plover, sanderling etc.

I spent the afternoon drawing birds from a book 'How to draw birds'—I got two quite successful tufted duck. Then I changed for chapel, and at the last moment decided not to go, so I got under the bed, blocked up entrances and read. I'm there now. RJC is in the room, being off chapel for his eye.

I hope Mommy and Daddy are having a nice weekend.

Wow! Enter Max inquisitive. Asks after RJC's eye, kicks part of my barricade—the tuck box, and half stoops to look (from RJC). Exit Max, thank heaven. Wowch! another alert. Enter G, for 30 mins., during which Max comes twice, once to give G a magazine, once to fetch RJC to do some sweeping. Now G's left, and I'm alone. Better than chapel this. After that all went well—but for some awkward questions at tea time from Max.

Monday 2nd

... I did a better duck picture—a pochard. I'm determined to learn to draw birds—Margaret'll be pleased ...

Little news, American Navy raided Jap naval vessels—only sunk auxiliaries and damaged shore installations—no big Jap ships there.

Tuesday 3rd

... In JTC we did musketry—rather boring.

Otherwise nothing—News: we've withdrawn to Singapore Island, losing in Libya; Russians have lost half Feodosia but otherwise are doing OK.

Wednesday 4th

... I had to go and sell Vs [vouchers] *in the town, the proceeds to be given to the Newquay hospital endowment fund to be invested during warship week. I did not enjoy squeezing money from the people who haven't got much anyhow. One old man said he thought it was a silly idea—I told him I agreed. He gave 2d for the hospital. Another old lady told us how sad she was she could give nothing, so we gave her the shop's address. She was a kind old soul, that filthy wart L roared with laughter while we were talking.*

... we had a very good lecture by some retired Colonel on 'Understanding Animals'. He used to correct naughty dogs (no corporal punishment).

Newquay Warship Week parade, 1942

Warship Weeks were held in many towns as part of an official war-savings campaign. Towns pledged a certain amount of money and adopted a ship.

Saturday 7th

... A free afternoon for warships week, in which I went to town, had a hair-cut, saw the march past, looked at the school toy shop (awful high prices!), bought a book 'How to draw birds' (2/6d) and also a loaf (3½d) ...

In the evening there was a debate—'In the opinion of this house the British character is fundamentally hypocritical'. I was going to speak, but someone else got in first. Pretty funny speeches. ... We, the motion, won 33–20.

Monday 9th

... Saw Max in evening ... discussed means of getting interested people to talk to—as I feel annoyed at smallness of views of people here.

Wednesday 11th

Clear morning, later grey, no rain. ... RJC saw flashes, and heard a plane, St. Evell.

Saturday 14th

... After tea, Toad of Toad Hall was performed—rather poor, I thought—scenes too cut, puppets too unmanageable.

Sunday 15th

... After tidying the room I went along the headland with RJC to the big cave, where he smoked a cigarette. I also had one, but sucked too fast so it lasted only 2 mins. Thank goodness I don't like it enough to want to ...

After lunch I went up the Gannel with C, I and B—too many homo 'sapiens' about—no birds. We were nearly blown up (slight hyperbole) by a 'malteser' bag, which had been tied to a stick, lit with a match, and thrown down into the mud. Luckily it went out, and I took it back. It contained a grey crystalline substance ...

New World symphony in Music club.

I'm still on good terms with RJC, and I expect am outwardly still much the same, but I find myself sometimes being a little lonely, and often rather melancholy, because nobody here shares my interests—those in politics and the future of the world. Everyone here is so self-centred, and all look at the world with microscopes centered round their little bit of it. If only I could find a companion who shared my views and hopes, with whom I might talk and plan, life would be easier and much more fun, and together we might help a great deal to change and improve this muddled earth. Perhaps someday I'll find that, or those, companions—I hope so.

Monday 16th

... I woke up with diorhhea (spelling?) and a throat cough, which wasn't improved by chlorine in chemistry ...

News—Singapore has (as was inevitable) fallen, Sumatra's great oil centre going—I should say that we'll lose all the East Indies—then a hell of a fight in Australia. Thank goodness Russia's alive and KICKING.

Tuesday 17th

Light machine guns in JTC. 16-year olds are getting battle dress—no hope for me yet.

The Junior Training Corps uniform was First World War, including puttees and many bits of brass. Battle dress was the basic uniform worn by the army and the Home Guard—I clearly saw it as a badge of maturity.

Saturday 21st

Still beastly cold. In the afternoon I was collecting seaweed [for fertilizer] *from Fistral rocks, which was quite fun. R, B and I found a short cut through the wire (barbed) and carried six loads each, the others, six of them, also got 18 loads.*

Then I had a hot bath and read 'Gone with the Wind'—what a lovely book—the only trouble being that no other novel will be so satisfying to read.

Debate at 8.15—'This house looks forward with dismay, distrust to conditions in post war England'. Candler moved—rather useless to look forward with dismay I think—rather hope about communism coming at last. Opposing (4th) was an army officer, who gave a hate talk. Lots of horrible speeches—Mullins on hope because of our glorious Throne—Ugh!! I began to whistle 'God save the king'. I had not the courage to speak, and anyhow both sides were awful. I voted against; the motion was lost 63–24 …

The school debates did not attract big audiences and my unusually whole-hearted endorsement of the war and interest in its course was not generally shared, a fact which generated a (self-righteous? appropriate?) irritation in me. The school debates were often on interesting topics and were enlivened by speakers from local RAF and Army units, in whose contributions the changing mood in Britain was often evident. The theme of this one assumed the existence of a post-war England (together with Wales, Scotland and Northern Ireland, presumably) despite the precarious military situation.

Tuesday 24th
... cleaned my uniform. ... The parade was awful—simple foot and arms drill, bloody cold. Otherwise nout.

Good news—The Russians have cut the Vyazma-Smolensk road. Timor, battle bad, Bali bad. Soon Australia ?

Saturday 28th
... News. Big parachute and commando raid on France—Radio location station wrecked. ... success for MacArthur (American) in Luzon (Philippines). Burma lull, battle of Bali etc. has inflicted sizeable naval losses on Japs.

March

Monday 2nd
My fifteenth birthday. I didn't expect anything, but I got a packet of pounds of food—cake, biscuits, sweets and cheese (S. Africa) and also £1—which was very naughty of Mommy. In the evening I got a wire from Margaret—'nearly forgot, parcel follows' …

There was a film show by Rev. Finnis in the evening—3 films; (1) quite good propaganda film about Seamen's rest homes, (2) good torpedoing and then U-boat sinking, (3) Popeye.

I have lived 131,504 hours—not much.

Thursday 5th
Boring MT. I will give it up.

House game in the afternoon. I've been chucked out of the Junior House team—so I'm not so keen and enjoy it less …

News—Java being overrun, Russia doing well.

Friday 6th
Aircraft recognition in JTC by G—quite interesting ...

Lecture on India by Mr. Shoran Singha in the evening—v. good. Quite hopeful, and Red when referring to vested interests and the Princes. As a reason for lack of assistance of native population in the Far East he gave this example: outside a British club in Singapore was the notice 'No dogs or Chinese here'. Ugh!!! British officers in the Indian Army are still instructed in ways of keeping up prestige …

Saturday 7th
… House film in the evening—'Downhill'—all about sinking of public school boy after he had been expelled for immoralities of his friend—the 5th reel of the film was accidentally left out, which wasn't an improvement on an anyhow rather poor film.

Tuesday 10th
... Great excitement (this should be yesterday, but I forgot)—a card from Michael Adams, a prisoner of war in Germany Stalag 111e, to whom, in a fit of boredom, we wrote last term, having seen a request for letters in the Times. A nice letter—ours made him laugh—captured last July after floating in the N. Sea for a week. I wrote back—nice to get up a correspondence. He lives in Egypt.

Friday 13th
News of last few days: Far East—Java gone, New Guinea threatened, Rangoon evacuated; our forces having had to fight their way out, with both sides suffering heavily. Chinese troops arriving—they've been fighting years, with little support from us, or America, except bombs which came via Japan and exploded on arrival, and now we're relying on them to help us out in Burma. And they are—good for them.*

*This may be an allusion to a brief thaw in US-Japanese relations in 1940 which allowed the Japanese to obtain some military material from America.

Middle East—complete silence. Russia; slow difficult advance all along the front. Encircled [German] *16th army being slowly destroyed, and now defence is weakening. Good.*

The encircled Germans were sustained by an air-lift and broke out in April.

Tuesday 17th
Wizard JTC parade—a bren-carrier platoon came over, we had a lecture, demonstration, and then a ride. Grand—30hp Ford engines, 2–5 miles per gallon (2 on rough ground), and wizard up and down bumps. It felt like this

We bumped, jerked, swayed and it was grand fun. No. 5 platoon's driver was the best as far as speed was concerned, which was lucky.

Letter from Mommy and article by Daddy on State medicine—very good.

My father was a vocal advocate for a National Health Service. Many of his consultant colleagues angrily criticised him, suggesting he was pulling up the ladder up which he had climbed—an attitude conveying the commercial assumptions of private medicine. Younger colleagues and the doctors then in the Forces, on the other hand, were enthusiastic supporters of a National Health Service.

The patients treated at Guy's Hospital came from the region of the Docks, a densely populated area where poverty and unemployment were widespread, and my father had never forgotten the contrast between his work there and the private practice on which he depended for his income. It was some satisfaction to him that the NHS was founded, and I qualified as a doctor, shortly before he died.

Thursday 19th
A lovely spring day. I was working in a garden at the far end of the town—not too arduous and quite good fun; Miss Milner [matron] *had put me off games for my cough, which went two days ago.*

A good mowage of the Jap fleet by Yankees—tonic after our great defeat in Java invasion.

Friday 20th
Lovely day. I was collecting seaweed from the Gannel bank, we only took two sackfuls each, spending much time sunbathing (me without shirt—lovely). Lots of violets. The first narcissus in the Lyle's golden syrup tin on our windowsill came out—the other ought to tomorrow …

Saturday 21st
… I volunteered to go and build the Pentire pigsty after tea, but did not have to go. I finished Cronin's 'The stars look down'—a very clever and

good book [a novel about a mining community in the north of England]—*he can make people hate his characters.*

A debate—'This House distrusts freedom of speech'. A lot of pointless drivel, below the usual standard, but just worth attending.

Sunday 22nd

This was about the happiest day so far this term, the weather was good.

… After doing the boiler room coke fetching, RJC and I walked off to Kelsey Head … we cut up to the top, and collected lots of rabbit bones for school certificate identification purposes. We then walked round the hill tops, looking down into clear green water with a rock-studded sandy bottom, and seeing the deserted sand hills behind Ellenglaze …

The first wheatears I've seen flew across when we were on the headland. On the ridge the N. Wind was pretty cold, despite the sun …

I went to chapel … during an incredibly boring sermon, I read a good book on architecture …

Tuesday 24th

... In JTC we had a tactical scheme—The senior Coy. [company] + *recruits, constituting invading troops of 'Depravia', were advancing from the headland where they had landed by parachute. Battle expected between us and them W. of Pentire. ... No. 4 platoon engaged them in a line through the Pentire, destroying the recruits and suffering heavily. I was in advance of our main lines, being just W. of the Pentire Hill in a well concealed nest, armed with six grenades. H and J (Depravians), armed with a bren and rifle, crawled along the bottom of the 'spies house' in the gutter. I fetched an Umpire, and when they had been shot, and grenaded by me, they became casualties.*

I then got a rifle from one of our casualties and rejoined R, my section leader. We dashed across the road in front of the Bay, and crawled through the barbed wire, intending to get back through the wire near Splash Point and be a nuisance from the rear. Unfortunately an indubitably pro-Depravian umpire killed us by some hypothetical enemy, and we missed the main attack on that sector. Muscott and section attacked our place, but were repelled by remnants of No. 4 and

R's section, so they withdrew to the Pentire and were advancing down Pentire avenue when the bugle blew.

Result so far unknown, but their plan was upset by recruits' liquidation, and our line being further back than was expected. Quite good fun, but as always, too few umpires.

Wednesday 25th
… I weigh 9 st. 8 lb and am 5ft 10⅞" high …

to Glatting

Tuesday 31st
… Uneventful journey … an army lorry had bust down half one side of Stopham bridge, and was lying on its back in the water—minus driver.

Home, supper, and then talking in front of the drawing room fire. Bed after the news. Home at last.

April

Wednesday 1st
… In the afternoon I walked down to the village with Mommy, who had a Women's Institute meeting. … The 'Norton scouts' arrived, and we went on the downs to have tea. The fire did not light as everything was wet, and generally it was not a great success.

They played a game in which everyone 'got' everyone else (shot him as soon as they saw him, whatever position they were in, and whatever the distance, and always before he got them). Not much good either. The goats were an added complication, as the boys liked teasing them, and they liked eating yew [poisonous to goats] …

Thursday 2nd
After doing the rabbits and goats, I read a bit—Cole's 'Europe, Russia and the future' …

After lunch I walked to the village with Mommy—she went on to buy for a Red Cross lecture, I went and Solignumed [a creosote-derived preservative] *the chicken house of some new arrivals in the village—the*

Wolfes (spelling?). The family consists of a mother, a son (at Eton!) my own age, and an awful French woman who writes novels with Mrs. Wolfe.

The son didn't seem as bad as he might be—which of course is not saying much. Actually we didn't talk much as we were usually on opposite sides of the chicken house ...

Mrs. Wolfe, the new arrival, was a chain-smoking, much made-up divorcee—likely to evoke my mother's prejudices— but she was intelligent and entertaining, and in fact they got on well. David and I became friends and spent time together during the school holidays.

Lovely news when Daddy rang up—John is definitely relieved, will be home probably in 5 months to a job at a hospital in Gloucester.

Went to a funny film at the Women's Institute in the evening—Gordon Harker in 'Beauty on the Barge'.

Friday 3rd

Daddy arrived at Petworth. ... I did not meet him, as if my luggage were to have come there would not have been room [in the car] *(in Latin—imp*[erfect] *subj*[unctive] *in both halves).*

Having done the jobs, I visited George (the evacuee—the two pests went early in March and he came instead—more help) and some friends of his who had a camp by Glatting lake—they had the Indian wigwam and their lunches and were very happy. We spent the morning largely in talking about various things, chiefly political.

After lunch we carred to Hawton (Houghton?) to visit the nearest Communist, whose name Daddy had got from Harry Pollitt. We talked for a long time about that sort of thing, and she is going to send tired out communists to Glatting to recuperate. She seemed quite nice, and knew a lot, having been associated with the Party since 1917. Now she works in Collets (again, spelling?) bookshop. We stayed for tea and had quite an interesting afternoon ...

Saturday 4th

After elevenses Daddy, Mommy and me went out with lunch. We lit a very successful fire in the quarry (flint) on the far side of Sodgers bottom, where we ate our sandwiches and drank our tea. Then we were peaceful for a bit, and having thoroughly extinguished the fire, walked back by the green slope—a nice afternoon.

Everyone strangely tired and mournful after supper, but we cheered up a bit before going to bed. Just as we were getting into bed Margaret rang up from Pulborough, having travelled from Yorkshire by lorry etc. to London and thence to Pulborough by a non-existent [probably freight] *train. She's been at a Youth Hostel having political discussions—lucky devil!*

Mommy rushed off to fetch her, and Daddy and me prepared supper and relit the copper fire to give her a bath (we're economising in coal and doing without the boiler) …

Coppers were large containers under which a small coal or wood fire could be lit on washing or bathing days.

Sunday 5th

… Daddy and I went for a walk—deserted orchard, beech swing branches, home through the woods. … We brought back a bunch of wood anemones, white and purple violets, and some sprays of pussywillow …

George Ward's parents were there when we arrived. George returned from his church service (poor boy) during tea—they didn't seem very interested.

Tuesday 7th

… Mommy and I took the car to Petworth, collecting animal food and my trunk from the station. We got back from the station at 7 mins. to 1, so I leapt on my bike and raced to the village, arriving for lunch at the Wolfes' at 1 minute to …

After a goodish lunch, we sat and talked for a bit and then David and I went for a windy bicycle ride—I was on Nora's "bike". … We investigated a deserted group of cast iron huts and a boathouse, and we were following a duckboard (pre-war) path through some marshes when

I saw 2 legs and a dog ahead. We withdrew strategically. … we began to bike back, but stopped to see how wavy it was at the top of various pine trees. It was, very, and we descended with haste. We then returned, and I biked on home—he seems quite nice really, despite Eton.

Wednesday 8th

Mommy asked David Wolfe up for the morning to help collect wood ... we got two full trailer loads. After that we went down to the lake and sunk eggshells and paper boats with my air pistol …

His mother stayed to lunch, and afterwards we had quite an interesting discussion on various topics. After doing a little more boat sinking (destructive tendencies!) we returned, and Raymond and George came to the Norton Scout meeting—the others did not. We had a jolly good meeting learning various knots ... David knew a lot of them and helped teach …

Friday 10th

… Mrs. Wolfe … wants David to stay with us—while not with other relations—as she's joining up. She'll pay etc., but Mommy doesn't relish the idea of more school clothes. Anyhow, fate hangs in the balance, Daddy is going to be the final weight. The disruptive influence on home life, and the extra work for Mommy, are points against. Besides, we hardly know what he's like. He went off to stay with his father at Whitton (Yorks.) today, for about a week.

Saturday 11th

Indians have rejected proposals, total washout. 'Cripps orders his plane' (News Chronicle). General history is this—proposals in main accepted, but no agreement reached concerning (a) defence minister and (b) self gov. now. Muslims and Hindus both objected. I can see no defence for our attitude in (a)—Cripps lamely says it would mean a terrible lot of re-organisation, but in (b) I think we are partially justified. However, British diplomacy being what it is, I can quite see the Indians' point—if not now, ever? So what. Japs are at the gate, Ind. Imp. remains on the pennies and everything in the garden's awful.

Still, there's nought to be done but work hard for the final victory not of the British Empire, but of Communism—a fight for a new, real civilisation, without our present systems, where selfish exploitation with its resultant poverty walks hand in hand with mealy mouthed expressions of Christianity. The church is a useful shield and a wondrous refuge for the hypocritical self-righteous ones!

Stafford Cripps, a member of the government, was on a mission to India—seeking to gain support for the war against the Axis powers with an offer of increased Indian participation in government.

The fight for Indian independence during the years before the war had made little progress despite the widespread support for Gandhi's policy of non-violence. Churchill was contemptuous of Indians and remained an unrepentant imperialist, resisting any compromise; he was one of the influences which sustained my political convictions. Support in India for the British in the war against Japan was far from universal; the wish to get rid of the British was seen by many as of equal or greater importance. An Indian National Army fought with the Japanese in Burma. However, 2.5 million volunteers fought with the British in North Africa, Burma and Europe, and India was a major producer of war-related industrial goods.

Wednesday 15th

... I spent 11–12.30 sorting the village's waste paper [part of the wartime scrap-collecting campaign]*—a revolting job. Mommy and I stood in a small room 2 ft deep in paper—dirty or clean, mixed with filthy rags. OOF! ...*

Saturday 18th

Last night bombs were dropped at a place in the S. of England. Damage was slight, but there were some casualties, including some people killed. One enemy aircraft was destroyed. We heard the bombs, and the whole house shook—under 8 miles I should say ...

Daddy and I went for a bird walk along Rhinehurst Bottom. We saw or heard whitethroat, blackcap, chiff chaff, willow wren. Also a possible nuthatch …

News. 12 Lancasters made daylight raid on submarine engine factory in S. Germany. 4 lost S. of Paris, 3 after dropping the bombs. On the evening of the sweep (about 5, I think) I saw six 4-engined bombers fly off low down, like Halifaxes but quite possibly Lancasters. The time tallies I think. They flew at 30 ft. the whole way, what a journey!

This was the Augsburg raid. Two groups of six Lancasters converged over Selsey (15 miles from where I saw the six) and flew very low all the way; all but five were shot down. To this day I know exactly where I was when the six planes flew over, and recall my distinct awareness of the men flying them and of the fact that they knew that not all of them would come back.

Wednesday 22nd

… Mommy went off and collected the week's shopping from Mrs. Hare's, and some photographs of Russian life, for the talk and exhibition in the Institute hut on Friday (Mrs. Reckitt is going to talk) [my mother had organised a speaker on Russia to give a talk at the Women's Institute in Sutton].

Margaret and I biked to the village and did the paper sorting—which wasn't too bad—¾ of an hour. Nice surprise for Mommy.

The boys [from the village] *came and learnt Morse in the garden.*

Friday 24th

… At 4 o'clock we arrived at the Hut and with various helpers pinned up all the pictures. ... After supper (hurried) they carred and I biked down to the Hut, and I received the 3d [at the door]. *About 40 people turned up, the takings were 11/3 (Children 1d).*

The talk was good and the questions after very intelligent, I think the audience (most of whom were women) hold more realistic views on Russia today …

Saturday 25th

… We all went out soon after breakfast except Miss Reckitt, who slept late [the speaker had stayed over]. *We heard my first nightingale by the white bridge. ... We spent the rest of the morning discussing in the garden. I take little part in these sort of discussions, but I absorb much, which comes out at suitable intervals. Nice to hear live conversation—in a week I'll have left it behind for the land of the living dead—however, the picture isn't all that gloomy. Second front seems, with luck, imminent (Germany, not us, we've got about 5 already).*

Popular support for Russia's demand that a second front should be opened in western Europe (by an invasion from Britain) was widespread in the UK, where the enormous losses suffered by Soviet soldiers and civilians were recognised. The motives of the UK government in delaying it were suspected of representing a deliberate policy—based on the calculation that Russia would bleed to death, or at least emerge weakened at the end of the war.

However, the military reality was that preparation of an invasion force in the UK depended on winning the battle of the Atlantic, and accumulating US troops and armaments. This was only achieved with radar, sonar and effective air cover in 1943-4. Russia bore the full brunt of the European war for three years—over the whole war, three-quarters of German land and air losses were incurred on the Eastern front.

Supporting our Soviet ally: the audience at one of the nation-wide celebrations of Red Army Day, 1943

Sunday 26th

... We took lunch up on the downs, and had it near the keeper's hut at the bottom of Farm Hill. This is possibly going to be purchased (£10) for a lab for Margaret.

While the 3rd cup of soup was being poured out a piece of string appeared in the thermos. On being pulled, it turned out to be attached to a mouse. We kept the soup for Tinker—and found a second mouse later—'Terrible food shortage—reduced to mouse soup.' A pity, for the soup was up to Mommy's usual standard ...

We fetched [a loaned] *bike from Fittleworth, and brought it back in the car. Saw a very pretty girl there too—my sexual urges are now fully developed—and I know no one of the opposite sex nearer my age than*

Margaret [four years older]*—and above that the only females I know are over 20. Co-education, however, will make schoolboys' lives more normal.*

Living either in a boy's school or at Glatting meant that there were no occasions on which it was normal to meet girls and they remained an unknown species.

Monday 27th
… after talking to Raymond, Nelson and George in the village, I went in to lunch at the Wolfe's. Before lunch we sent (he was when I arrived) his steam engine—trying to churn milk …

After tea, we biked to Black Pond with some of the sailing boats, only mine went well and that ended up 12 ft. out in some reeds—George fetched it. Then we were going to stalk the deer, but Tinker was attacked by one of the late Major C's daughter's dogs. She remarked that he should have been on a lead—anyhow, we did not deer stalk but went home.

Wednesday 29th
Last day at Glatting. In the morning we put up Margaret's lab. hut in the orchard by the three pine trees with the help of Mr. Thurmore (late occupier) and Francis. After 11 o'clock I biked to the village where I shopped and sorted paper for 50 minutes …

David Wolfe came round, and after I'd finished drying up … we sent the steam engine burning wood (not very successfully). When the boys came we tested knots and morse (1 cigarette card for each letter more than five known) and then did 1st aid. George and Nelson (not at all discouraged by David) played the fool …

Thursday 30th
[To London with my mother, en route to school, and staying over]
… We caught a bus and after a quick look at Bumpus' books, queued up for the film of 'How green was my valley' [a 1941 US film about a Welsh mining family at the turn of the 20th century]. ... *It was one of the loveliest films I've ever seen, and even Mommy cried in it—what*

Daddy would have been like I do not know. The book was lovely, the film was as lovely and tragic as the book. Both Anghared (lovely name) and Bronwen were very beautiful, and Bronwen was acted terribly well—after her husband's death her "There's lonely I am" was impossible to hear without crying. Films are wonderful things …

After this we failed to get tea at the theatre café and went and chose our books—Daddy having given me a 21/- book token and Mommy 2 21/- ones. I got 'Bird Flight' (200 action photos) and 'Frenchman's Creek'. I took these and the Red Dean's 'Socialist Sixth of the World' [by Hewlett Johnson, who was Dean of Canterbury and a supporter of the USSR] *to school with me …*

Mrs. Mapother [with whom we stayed] *is very kind, but her house is very untidy and she talks nineteen to the dozen all the time about nothing in particular—Mommy and I just stood it— Daddy hardly could.*

After a tiring supper we went to another flick—a funny French film (very funny) with English translation written, called 'Ignace', and 'Dangerous Moonlight' [1941 British film about the war]*—another wonderful film—about Polish musician—composes during very well done blitz ...*

Back Mrs. M., miserable goodbye to Daddy, miserable bed going. Miserable more for what I'm leaving than for what I'm going to.

to Newquay

May

Friday 1st
May day, but no mass meetings etcetera. Not very happy. … I spent most of the time [on the train to Newquay] *gazing out of an open window, sometimes wanting to leap out and let the train go on without me. At Plymouth I went and got a cup of tea. Very shy making—a girl from Benenden came and sat opposite me. Despite pink face at first and silence for much time, I managed to politely help her flirt (pouring out her tea), tell her that it was Plymouth, and make two monosyllabic*

remarks. She was really quite pretty. Anyhow, my confusion showed how female-shy I am. … I wrote home, not all that miserable …

Sunday 3rd
… As Daddy and Mommy disapprove, I will not cut chapel anymore, but will read there …

Monday 4th
... Little news. I never put in that 2 Govt. candidates were recently beaten in by-elections. Dissatisfaction with war management—Labour in …

I cleaned the bathroom ceiling, removing lots of black mould (and some white paint) and I prepared the walls for distempering. When I removed peeling paint, the sand (capitalists' plaster) fell out …

Tuesday 5th
… In the afternoon I made a very valuable contribution to Britain's war effort. At 2.15 I left the house dressed in white flannels (How to Save Soap) but without boots (I had gym shoes), pads or bat of my own. At 2.30 (approx.) I walked out to a grassy field covered in 14 other similarly garbed blokes, and for 65 minutes I stood about, stopping some, missing many balls. … I then lay in the sun for 1½ hours … on one occasion I protected my legs, took a complicated structure of wood and rubber, and stood before three stakes in the ground while someone hurled a hand ball at me. I hit the ball once, and ran aimlessly to another trio of stumps, I then missed 2, the ball hit the stumps and I walked back to the sun.

I got back, just changed in time to learn … that I had a net at 6.5. I was extremely angry. … A half holiday! Not more than 10 mins. of free time, and the war effort in no way better off. Total war!

News:- we've occupied Madagascar, Russian local advances.

Friday 8th
Big naval battle in S.W. Pacific. Both sides claim enormous casualties for other, but I think the odds are in our favour so far. Several aircraft

carriers engaged etc. Gullible hon. housemaster tells terrific tales of whole fleets sunk for only three planes ...

This was the battle of the Coral Sea. In fact only one Japanese carrier was sunk but two others were damaged and this reduced their capability in the subsequent Midway battle. Naval power was crucial in the Pacific war and both Japan and the USA relied increasingly on carrier-borne aircraft to which conventional battleships were very vulnerable.

Letter from Mommy—one of our (gallant) night fighters brought down a Stirling [a British bomber], *the crew landed all round Glatting, but Mommy found none. All safe. Did not dare show flares believing to be over France ...*

In the evening I received one jaw from (very hon.) housemaster re: cricket. 2 alternatives:- I play cricket with a more co-operative spirit, or I go on no NHS expeditions (I chose the former). In a violent attack he showed how I ruined the game for the others (about 8 people in the game liked it), and how I have a mean and childish side to my nature. True, my attitude to cricket is not, to put it mildly, constructive, but it was partly as a (childish) protest and partly in the (vain) hope that I might get left out of games [I thought we could be doing more useful things].

He squashed war effort arguments by saying—free time—though why I should not do bird watching and works, and no cricket—O hell I dunno, but I must play cricket as I don't like it. It won't harm me anyhow.

Sunday 10th
... with RJC and Smith iii we went and rang the 3 young tawny owls—in fear and trepidation, having been told that one person per night was attacked. Luckily no parent appeared ...

I did lots of Chaucer [in chapel]. *Habershon preached, began by apparently damning capitalism but changed to* [talking about] *shepherds, so I reverted to 'Prologue' ...*

Very good, optimistic Churchillian speech 9–9.30, the best I've heard from him.

Monday 11th
... A p.card in the break from Daddy—poor old Mommy got acute appendicitis, rushed off to Hove (whence Daddy was writing), had successful operation and I wasn't to worry. I managed not to on the whole, sending her a letter after lunch. Poor Mommy.

News recently. Lull USSR. Big naval action in S.W. Pacific, so far very favourable to us, now only planes active. 2 aircraft carriers less for Japs. 15 down over Malta over weekend.

Malta was our air base for attacking German ships supplying their troops in N. Africa, and for protecting British supply ships on the way to the Eastern Mediterranean. It suffered incessant air attacks.

Tuesday 12th
... letter from Daddy ... Mommy is getting well nice and quickly and "is looking very pretty and well with her two plaits spread out on her pillow". Daddy also sent a very good book on electricity and photography—trap photography [setting off shutter remotely] *by means of an electric contact. Cheap and simple—I shall do it, and I ought to get some very good bird pictures if it is successful.*

It rained all day—good for the crops. (more crop-conscious nowadays).

News: German attack on Kerch peninsular—I hope Russia still has the initiative ...

Thursday 14th
Long letter from Mommy sympathising and advising re: Max and cricket.

Reference to Philistines—who are they? When I got the leave for this afternoon's expedition signed, he said the attitude was no better—I respectfully suggested I had not played since, but apparently some satellite had reported a heresy of mine to him. In the interval I will avoid the word 'cricket' and will be a model of application and almost enthusiasm. Then, if he tries to stop me going—well! I shall disobey Mommy's advice—to side step— and oppose it as she advised John and Martin …

Friday 15th
… In MT I had to greatly modify my plan of the electric shutter release, as it was too tiddly and complicated. It now consists of 10 pieces, with no joins …

Sunday 17th
… On the end of the headland we watched the sea and a seal for about an hour—the seal had white marks down its neck. We tried singing to it, but observed no effect—I think it needs a woman's voice or a wind or string instrument. I love watching the sea, but it's better to do so in utter solitude—time and life and death go, and nothing is left but water on rock and sand and spray.

Tuesday 19th
… Letter from Mommy … told me about a meeting of Daddy's—[with] *representatives from factories—Daddy spoke and was received enthusiastically* [I presume about a State medical service] …

Thursday 21st
… JTC Church Parade next Sunday Morning (Our Glorious Empire day). When it's a socialist union and we don't go to church I won't mind. The day is drawing near when it will be—and I'm glad I'm here to be able to help the new civilisation in.
… reading 'The Grapes of Wrath'.

Empire Day (Queen Victoria's birthday) had been an offical celebration in Britain since the First World War.

Saturday 23rd
There was to have been an expedition [Natural History Society], *but rain cancelled it. At breakfast Max said I was selfish to go so often—we pointed out that anyone who wanted to could go, and then he said he's*

only let me go 3 times a term. He said my attitude was typical of the socialist haves to the havenots—I got livid … and asked just what he thought he meant, and told him he was talking utter rot. He got a bit annoyed and soon left.

Thursday 28th
… We got up in uniforms and fell in at the Pentire at 15.15 hours … No. 5 [platoon] *marched to Crantocks, and then about 2½ miles towards the pylons. Here we split up, and with M and his section we rushed off across fields. We soon split up and I lost sight of all the rest of the section except M and R. We met no opposition for some time, and in response to my urgings we advanced quickly to Penpol, where we saw the first steel helmeted parachutists. These, however, disappeared, so we crossed over the marshy bit to the field beyond Penpol by the bridge.*

Advancing along here, I fired two shots at a sten gunner, who I believe was made a casualty, and then I suddenly found my self behind an enemy post of 3 men—Snelling, R and T. I bayoneted Snelling, but they were already dead so I ignored them. After that I wandered around nearly freelance, killing R and T again, and being killed by them. The battle faded out, but not before I had had sufficient exercise for weeks to come!

Sunday 31st
… we left for Kelsey Head [on an illegal outing]. *Another party was going, so we joined on … We arrived, and swam across 12 feet of flowing channel, many feet deep. The Chick* [rocks in the sea] *(where we'd swum to) was riddled with nests, and smelt strongly of guano. We found two dead shags and saw about 15 live ones. We then rushed back, the current having considerably increased in speed. M and L couldn't swim, and came across on a clothes line. Fun. We biked back … arriving at 5.10, rather tired …*

Biggest raid ever on Cologne, more than 1,000 bombers, all in 90 mins., one bomb each 6 seconds or more. Blimey.

June

Monday 1st

… I went to Frank in the first part of prep to have my maths paper corrected. He wants to get Daddy's opinion about his arthritis of the hip, which seems to be extremely painful. He liked Daddy's 'Fears May be Liars'—in fact he admires Daddy a lot.

Tuesday 2nd

… Max jaw. (a) I'm aloof. (b) I'm selfish. … By aloof he means I don't mix with the rest of the house well. Considering (a) their lack of interests and (b) their lack of morals (this applies to some 30% of the possibles for mixing with) and (c) their unattractive personalities, I'm not surprised or ashamed that I don't. I do occasionally go out with crowds, but am not usually well received or happy. Perhaps I suffer from (c) but actually I think its just that the effort of talking about uninteresting things is too great. … I remained comparatively polite and uncommunicative throughout. Silly worm …

1036 [planes] *went out to Essen, 1001 returned. Small loss* [35 planes], *horrid mess there.*

Initially described in terms such as 'attacks on marshalling yards', it was soon apparent that the targets were less clearly defined—as indeed was inevitable given the inaccuracy of bombing at that time—and that in reality mass attacks on civilian targets had become a deliberate policy.

Much is still made of British experiences of the blitz on London, Coventry, Plymouth, Liverpool, Belfast and other towns, but our civilian death rate during the war was one tenth of what we inflicted on Germany in raids such as those on Cologne and Essen, and later on Hamburg and Dresden, where the RAF had perfected the technique of creating firestorms by the combined use of explosive and incendiary bombs.

But the losses of RAF aircrews were also oppressively present for those who could count; aircrew flew for a tour of 20 operational flights and on average about 5% of bombers failed to return from most missions. RAF bomber command losses of over 50,000 aircrew over the whole war amounted to more than half of all those trained.

Thursday 4th
A visit to the Marine Biology station in Plymouth.

[on the train] *we passed through some lovely country—hills with tiny valleys criss-crossing, and all the slopes thick with either oak or larch or fir. When we got there, we bussed through the remains of the town to the Hoe, where we sat on grass and ate lunch. The damage was widespread and often severe, but I expect a fleabite compared to Cologne and Essen. We watched a Sunderland* [flying boat] *take off* [from] *the Sound.*

After lunch … we went to the laboratory, which despite blitz damage and the fact that the bloke showing us round tried to breathe in his upper lip while talking, it was pretty interesting. I was drooping with heat and thirst …

News. Rec. commando raid, Boulogne-Le Touquet area.

Sunday 7th
… After lunch I changed into the remains of my games clothes

and went to Kelsey head with B and T. T went down on the rope to a kestrel's nest, containing 3 1-week-olds; I didn't go, disliking vertical grass slopes and not wishing to strain the rope (I'm a hell of a funk climbing); and before B could, A [a prefect] *was sighted on the beach. Did he see us?? Anyhow, we quickly hid the rope (I twiddled 50ft. round my waist, T the other 50 ft. under his mac), and we visited an oyster catcher's nest on the end of headland ...*

Tuesday 9th
… Crawshaw [teacher and assistant chaplain] *wanted a few of the better birdwatchers to go with him to Ellenglaze in the afternoon where*

a ? grasshopper warbler had been seen. He asked Max—Hah! Course not. Much too much to do. B can go, no one else. They did hear the bird. The important alternative proved to be a one hour's fielding practice. The man has a blighted soul …

Thursday 11th
[Truro schools'] *festival is a show of talent by Cornwall's schools. … we went and looked at the Art exhibition. Benenden, of the Bristol hotel, a girls' public school from Kent (?) had some frightfully good portraits in, and so did another girls' school. Really professional charcoal and pencil portraits (of very nice subjects!). One was painted in just over the face, frightfully good … Then we went to the Theatre; 1st item, nice music by combined Greshams and Benenden. Then Greshams 'Glee'— Glorious Apollo—then the plays … us, scenes from Julius Ceasar. Good acting, but Shakespeare's semi-circular stage scenes never seem very real to me …*

I was much impressed by the girls' schools (not all the members, true) but then my standard isn't high, as I've none to compare them with …

Because of the war, events such as this, and the crowded school trains to and from London at the start and end of each term, were a window of opportunity to mix with girls. A more experienced friend (AWW) was quick to initiate and sustain contacts, and helped me overcome my timidity to some extent.

Friday 12th
… In JTC we had a lecture on gas by Capt. Shand, with smell tests—phosgene [chemical weapon used in the First World War] *don't smell very nice …*

Letter [from home, including] *Sov*[iet] *War News and report on Parliamentary debate—Mr. Macniel* [MP] *"… to quote Prof. Ryle, who can hardly be called a Tyneside red—".* [The quote was] *out of Daddy's State medicine* [paper].

Saturday 13th

[To Truro festival again] … *I went with Watkinson, who had a date with a member of Benenden, and in this manner I gained a new experience—how to talk about nothing to comparatively pretty girls. After much manoeuvring we got into the neighbouring compartment, whence we went into the corridor. About five girls appeared, the highlight being one Anne, or Andy, with nice long golden hair behind the ears, big brown eyes, a pretty face and a good figure. The conversation started when Watkinson gave them his lunch, which he did not want—they had just had lunch, but appeared to be starving. After a short sausage fight, we spent the whole journey talking utter rot—some of it, however, quite witty. I was amazed how easy it was to do this. … The journey back was occupied in equally ridiculous waffle …*

The thing which got me down was the giggling and shrieks. Their behaviour was not ladylike. They were quite intelligent, but didn't sound it. I enjoyed the novel experience a lot, but have no wish to continue the acquaintance with any of them, as they did not seem to share my interests—they were just rather amusing. Without Watkinson nothing would have happened, for it was due to his past experience and tenacity that we found them at all. ... Anne had lovely eyes.

Sunday 14th

… Watkinson has found a method of discovering Anne's surname, via a cousin of M's. He's going to write to her—what tenacity!

The sermon was extremely good—by the headmaster of Clifton [a public school from Bristol, currently in Bude]*—a young man. … The gist of the whole sermon was 'ought the church meddle in social affairs'. He praised Temple (Arch. Canterbury, new) and told how Shoran Singha had found out from a reliable source that a deputation of Lancashire cotton* [mill] *owners had sent a deputation begging that he* [i.e. Temple] *should not be elected. He then blasted the church, showing how Buddhism, Mohammedanism and Christianity all professed high ideals for living but none of them had carried them out. After quoting Rowntree on York's statistics* [of] *40 years ago (1 child in 5 underfed), he pointed out that there was no public conscience about social* *inequality, and suggested that we should find out about the injustices. Very good.*

William Temple had recently become Archbishop of Canterbury. He was a Labour party sympathiser, and former member, and supported the idea of a state welfare system. The statistics were from 'Poverty: a study of town life' by Seebohm Rowntree, sociologist and chocolate manufacturer, who was now assisting William Beveridge with his welfare proposals.

Wednesday 17th
… 5ft 11 ½ inches, 10 stone almost …

After tea I had works—mowing the Bay [Hotel] *lawns again. No shirt, great fun. I enjoy hard physical labour if it don't last too long and I need not wear a shirt. … No letter from Mommy yet this week.*

Friday 19th
V. good JTC parade—I was one of 20 paratroopers defending the Bay yard from the rest of the Senior Coy. and no. 5 [platoon]. *A short, very fierce battle, bangs all round and charges over tin roofs. We built barricades everywhere. I grenaded 2 people, and then came up a wall and saw a rifle sticking out of the gun store. I pulled this out, and killed two enemy by unspecified means at close range. I was given dead. Terrific muddle, few survivors. D on the other side, managed to kill two of his own side.*

News—We've swept back (or rather been swept back) to the Egyptian frontier, leaving a garrison at Tobruk.

Benghazi ← → Suez

Sevastopol still holds—just.

Sunday 21st
… News is bloody, I think Sevastopol may well fall, despite hellish fighting costing the Germans 3,000 men a day, and beside this they've pierced Tobruk's perimeter and have occupied much of the inside. I

suppose it may mean a sea evacuation, in which John's boat may well take part—and his relief hadn't arrived in his last letter …

Monday 22nd
… Sevastopol holds. Tobruk has fallen—25,000 of our troops with it—not exactly exhilarating. John may have to help in the evacuation, if there's time for one. 'After two weeks of constant dive bombing …' —extract from one of his medical reports. Poor John—and Mommy and Daddy. What a lousy life for him—and God knows how many others. Japs in one of the Aleutian isles. Cheerful, what!! …

John's report extract was probably included in a letter to my father. He subsequently wrote his DM thesis on fear, and noted the importance of keeping occupied.

Tuesday 23rd
… Tobruk quite gone, action as follows. We at first appeared to be doing well, but the Germans established a base through our minefield, so we had to withdraw, as the 150th Brigade and S. African division were about to be cut off (June 19th). We withdrew to the [Egyptian] *frontier, leaving a garrison at Tobruk which proved to be insufficient. A strategical error losing some 200 tanks, 29,000 men. Bad …*

Wednesday 24th
… After 3rd prep., Donald Soper answered questions—explained 5 points of the Malvern conference [of 1941, where Christians discussed the principles on which peace should be made when the war ended]*—a combined religious basis for post-war social system, it boils down to socialism, and when I asked him he agreed about it—he is one. I also asked him what he thought of Russia as compared to Christianity, and he said that Russia Christianised must be the basis of p. war reconstruction—good. They certainly could do with some I should say. All this was very interesting. (He's the bloke what answers questions each week on Tower Hill). I also asked about the soul and essentiality for future life—getting unsatisfactory answers—I'd like to go on.*

Thursday 25th
Field day … I was with three other blokes, all of whom were temporarily put out for ten minutes. Then we advanced along a stream, ran into a machine gun post, which I managed to grenade … we later did it again, and were ourselves killed for a short time. After that casualties were casualties …

Eventually I went up by a top stream where I had a hand to hand fight with B—I shoved his face under the mud, we both got filthy and gave it up … the whole thing was very enjoyable, except I got two blisters. Back … tea, bath (needed—we'd blacked our faces with burnt cork).

Friday 26th
Fine hazy day. A Henley [training aircraft] *crashlanded in the sea; the crew, I believe, were picked up very soon by an RAF launch which I saw. … Bren gun in JTC …*

Saturday 27th
Lovely day. Uniform parade for Guard of Honour at 8.20. … After tea I went down to the harbour and learnt to dive—I improved a lot with valuable criticism …

Watkinson has arranged a date next Sunday (tomorrow week) for M (who has a cousin at Benenden), H, who amused them, and one other—he asked me, and despite school cert. I did not say no!

Sunday 28th
… I spent the whole morning doing geography and chemistry, learning a fair amount. About 2 cwt. of crude rubber covered with crude oil was washed up on Fistral beach …

Not a very exciting sermon—'Captain of my soul, master of fate' or vice versa—I read physics 'Light'. Walked back with Watkinson, talked about next Sunday and other things. He's a bit of a cynic but has at the least some original ideas—some good ones—I quite like him on the whole.

Monday 29th
Letter from Mommy—Martin came [home] *for 1 day—tired but glad to be so useful …*
Battle of Mersah Matruh in Libya.

Tuesday 30th
Speech day. … Last night we had another very interesting Soper woffle, which altered many of my views slightly. … I wandered round the exhibitions—Physics, Biology, Chemi. At 12.0 I reported to S with other prize-winners in the tennis court. I was lent a book for the occasion as mine hadn't come …

After tea I biked down by the Gannel, along past the viaduct a short way, then I returned and watched waves past splash point—a very fine occupation.

News. Mersah Matruh fallen, [Germans] *claim 6,000* [prisoners], [General] *Ritchie sacked,* [we have] *retreated past Fuca. Alexandria when? Not very encouraging.*

July

Wednesday 1st
A very fine day. Message writing in JTC.
News, [Germans] *100 miles from Alexandria—bad. John has sent cable: 'Relieved—but not coming home'. Fleet mail office, Alexandria,* [is his] *address …*

Thursday 2nd
News. Battle in progress at bottle neck, 65 miles from Alexandria, so far we're holding our positions. Sebastapol fallen, but fighting continues nearby. That is war, and brave. A blow, however, as it'll enable a switch of troops up further North. The Hun lost a good many in the attempt, however …

I wrote off for two pamphlets issued by the Malvern conference of the churches—re: postwar and nicely Socialist, I believe.

Friday 3rd

Grey, damp day. Astounding news, Rommel has withdrawn some way westwards. I hope we keep him there.

School cert. timetable went up—not too bad …

School Certificate was the nationwide school examination taken at about 14. It had to be passed as a whole, reaching the required level in a combination of subjects.

Sunday 5th

… we … rushed off to the meeting place [with the Benenden girls]*—by Trenance. However, half way along the bottom of the Gannel they met us at a trot, having cut a singing recital and being pursued by monitors. … After hiding over a wall until all monitors had vanished, we walked up the Gannel, crossed the footbridge and up the longish track. The conversation was less facetious than in the train …*

They had to be back for a 4.25 callover, but weren't—all their watches were 10 mins. slow [was their excuse]*!—we hope they don't get in a row, their school play was cancelled through the noise made in the train due partly to us …*

Monday 6th

… Egypt now going well—we've captured important ridge S. of Alamein, and 600 Germans gave themselves up to us—they'd had enough. The battle is pretty vital, and seems to be swinging over to us …

Tuesday 7th

A long letter came for Watkinson, self, S and H [from 4 of the girls]. *… The watch trick worked for tea, but they all had to go and see various housemistresses, and they had to admit that they'd been out with us. They failed to see why not (good for them!).*

Anyhow they all went to the headmistress, who is pretty sensible. She agreed that they could not have left us in the lurch, but thought their conduct was 'housemaidish'. They are off Trenance, 3 day gating, and sundry other punishments. Most unfortunate. We had a conference and decided to all write letters, which we finished just before prep. … We suggested seeing their headmistress to explain, or failing that, writing to her and asking if she minds. Rather amusing developments, but I hope not too distressing for them.

Wednesday 8th

… News—Russia, poor, back on Don River, Germans claim [they have gone] *beyond. Egypt waiting for next phase, odds equal.*

Watkinson and I realised with trepidation what it would be like if we really had to see the Benenden headmistress. However, they are quite kind girls and would not let us in for it I don't think …

I decided last holidays that I'd be a doctor, but sometimes I wonder if I've the ability for politics, as I'm interested in world affairs fairly intensely. I don't know then if a doctor's training would be the best. I must discuss it with Mommy and Daddy.

Friday 10th

[School cert.] *10.26 French oral. He was impressed by my accent at reading, so that's presumably OK. 11.15–1.45 Chemi. Titration was very easy, but I got answer wrong through not READING THE QUESTION. I thought it was Na_2CO_4, it was $NaHCO_3$—I did not see the bi …*

The awaited reply came [from Benenden] *… of sympathy, they've not been forbidden to see us permanently, but either us or them will ask permission …*

Saturday 11th

… I had a very interesting discussion, chiefly with Alan Watkinson,but also with MF Wood and RJC, re: matters of religion, politics and sex repression. … My views on religion are changing, I am really a Christian, am open-minded but sceptical about future lives (though so much depends on all the definitions of these things). However, I see no connections with the churches nor does Watkinson. He is a good and deep thinker, and I like him.

As for politics, we're in agreement and sex repression makes us both livid. 2 bodies of youths living in separate compartments, doing the most ridiculous things to try and obey their instincts and meet each other, while narrow minded fools tell them that it's silly and wicked.

Sunday 12th
… I wrote a joint letter with Watkinson to the Spectator about educational reforms—chiefly co-education …

After lunch the same force as last time went out, having arranged to meet [the girls] *down Henver Rd. However, as we approached the Hotel Bristol we saw three friends pointing down a side road, and eventually we were guided into one of the 'Bristol' garages. … Anyhow, we talked a bit about future arrangements, and they said that Miss Sheldon* [headmistress] *had forbidden us meeting, and they'd fetched us just to save us waiting hours for them. Then one of their housemistresses entered: "This isn't a very satisfactory way is it, I think you'd better come up and see Miss Sheldon in her study".*

Our hearts increased their speed, but otherwise we remained firm and determined. We were led up to the study, followed by a crowd increasing in size. Then we followed the girls into the study, where we were greeted with an affable handshake from Miss Sheldon, the principal. Then she explained that she couldn't have the two schools seen out together, but she saw our point, and did not think that we were wicked. She had tried to get dances and tennis, and she promised to try again. She also said that she'd ask us out to tea sometime.

We agreed to be good and not meet on the sly, as she was reasonable, and her position was obviously difficult. We disagreed, however, about the theoretical side and we made it quite clear that the system should be changed. Then we trooped out under only J's escort, and left followed by waves from the window.

Watkinson got a note, largely confidential, saying who's keen on who. … We got back, and wrote a polite and appreciative letter to Miss Sheldon. … What would Mommy and Daddy think of this? Personally, I feel no shame, and see nothing wrong …

Monday 13th

... a letter for me from J, in reply to my letter telling of my beliefs etc. It was a very nice letter, and she is a socialist, which is good. However, she holds some strange reincarnation theory about future life—I will argue about this when next I see her ...

After 3rd prep I went to see Max. "Hah! Lamentable behaviour in the Truro train". It was all about Benenden etc., Watkinson had been before and told the whole story—Max had only been told about the train.

Then the garage business came in—we agreed that that seemed silly, and I made it clear that I felt no shame. He seemed to think that Miss Sheldon was livid with us—not the impression she gave us anyway. He was rude to me, and I did not mince words ...

Wednesday 15th

3 exams. ... Latin—nice ... Tempest, which was easy but I didn't do very well. ... Chemistry, which I dreaded but eventually liked. Then we spent ½ an hour clearing the tables away for a dance band ...

War news—Russia bad, Libya OK. Don well crossed, Rostov threatened now. Litvinov forecasts that 4th round will soon begin, knock out for Jerry ...

Saturday 18th

... House match in the afternoon, and our Benenden friends had said they'd come if they could. ... Anyhow, they turned up, and in view but away from most people we spent about ¾ of an hour talking. ... Unfortunately, we broke the promise made to Shelley [Miss Sheldon] *and my conscience was very active ...*

War news—Libya tank battle odds even at Alamein. Russia resistance stiffening in battle for Don, Voroshilovgrad fallen. Counter offensive soon. What a damn waste.

I read some of Blundens 'Undertones of War' and got pretty depressed.

This was the first battle of El Alamein; it was a stalemate but halted the German advance on Alexandria. Edmund Blunden's book is a memoir of the First World War.

Tuesday 21st
... English essay; I wrote—I believe fairly successfully—on 'Keeping a diary', which I ought to know something of ...

Thursday 23rd
... Geography B—Synch. ... Latin 2—Synch. Swimming sports in the afternoon. ... Biology II not too bad. FINIS !!!!!! THE END ! Clouds of relief, walking on air ...

Friday 24th
Free day ... I went towards Trenance not very far, biking leisurely along cliff paths—enjoying the solitude. On the way back, as I passed Mr. Crawshaw's house, I saw him cleaning his windows. I offered to help, and he accepted, so reinforced with a cup of coffee, I cleaned 10 windows with him (he's leaving this term).

Over the coffee he discussed monastic segregation of Benenden and Gresham's re: last Saturday's effort. He was awfully reasonable—regarding a friendship between opposite sexes perfectly normal for a change. If he'd known, he'd have asked both parties to tea—a thing he's done before. Pity he's leaving, for that and other reasons ...

Sunday 26th
Grey day. I spent nearly all the morning packing etc. [it was end of term].

After lunch the usual lot of us + RJC went to Newquay beach to meet our fair ones. Six were forthcoming ... They couldn't stay as the tide cut them off—they had to paddle. 15 mins. only. They'd re-seen Shelly who'd been v. nice, but had forbidden writing. She'd appreciated our letter—we'd feared otherwise! Still shy in the flesh with them ...

News. Libya, we've advanced a bit (5 days ago) and we're consolidated. Lower Don situation poor, Rostov threatened.

Am reading my French prize—'Mission to Moscow'; some good criticisms—very good book I think for stimulating mental processes [it was by Joseph Davies, former US ambassador to Moscow: a broadly favourable view].

Tuesday 28th
Up at 5. Down to the station with AWW to see the girls off. We did, being observed by many of their mistresses and by Max …

After breakfast went to station again to meet Margaret [my sister, who was going to cycle with me back to Glatting].

Log of trip

Left [Bay] *hotel at 10.30. Very good weather all day, with only a slight wind … Journey all very hilly. … to Wadebridge, which was further than expected, and then a distant and fairly hilly ride to the Camelford stn.*

From here we were directed to Tintagel by a kind van driver, and there was a glorious down hill [ride] *into the setting sun. We … were welcomed by Mrs. Coxeter and her sister* [relatives] *and some grand vegetable stew. … After supper the sister took us for a stroll and we saw Arthur's castle and Merlin's cave …*

Wednesday 29th
We left, after despatching from our packs a heavy parcel of superfluities, at 9.30. It was raining a thin very wet drizzle, and we were soon soaked. We made quite good time to Launceston, however, where we had some dinner in a pub which did not seem to approve of us.

… we stopped for tea after a quick 500ft. climb past Tavistock on the edge of Dartmoor. The country was hilly but almost too bare, with rocks lying everywhere on the surface. 12 miles past tea, after seeing the ugliness of Princeton gaol, we reached Bellever hostel after a cross country push …

Thursday 30th
… At first uphill, but then long glorious down ride off Dartmoor to the small town of Moreton Hampstead, built round a church on a hill. From here was a long climb through a different sort of country—smallish fields, all cultivated. We reached Exeter soon after 1 o'clock, and did there a little shopping. Tempers were getting short from hunger and

exhaustion, so we stopped by a main road and ate lunch under an elm to the roar of lorries and a nearby 'drome.

… after Axminster began the quest for somewhere to spend the night. This proved fruitless, so at 7.30 we ate supper in the gutter of a main country road (the only flat place for the meths stove)—we had sardines, bread and stewed plums. Also coffee without milk or sugar.

Feeling fresh, and as the evening was lovely (also feeling rather mad), we biked on to what we hoped was Beaminster. Actually it was Charmouth.

Past here, in twilight, we made a halt and lay down under a hut's side propped against a haystack, and after being relieved of our identity cards by the owner, we 'slept' here, getting colder and colder as the time went on …

Friday 31st

… we left at 6 o'clock, and had a cool but fairly lively ride to Beaminster, where we had to wait for ½ an hour for the shops to open. Today was the hottest yet …

After a rest for lunch, we went on, reaching chalk hills at 3.30. Having been very misdirected, we eventually found Cerne Abbas, complete with old carving of giant. The hostel was just foul. No cooking facilities, all dirt and smell and overfat women.

We fled, and ate supper in the field (liver) with a lab. boy from the Cambridge Engineering lab., who was on holiday and felt like us about the hostel. Luckily the dormitories weren't too bad …

August

Saturday 1st

Crept away from awful hostel early, after breakfast in the field. A very stiff climb at first, and then all flat country. … The journey was along two rivers, eventually reaching Wimborne and then along straight ribbon-developed road to Ringwood. Both sides of these towns was grand rolling wooded country.

We went along a slightly hillier road from here towards Romsey, and already all accommodation was advertised by queues of cyclists. We had a large supper of tough steak, and biked on losing all hopes of bed.

... we decided to spend the night out, so after losing our way leaving Winchester, we climbed onto the Downs towards Petersfield, and at 11 o'clock settled down in a hollow by the road wearing all the scanty apparel we could muster.

Sunday 2nd

Half past midnight. Cold enough, so we decided to continue. We followed the road, lit by many green glow worms and a Solent lightship. The moon, after several feeble attempts, at last emerged to help. We had no lights. We soon left the Downs and descended into the valley, where the mists were icy. Nearly collided with a couple standing on the road, but apart from these and one cyclist we saw no-one ...

At last, exasperated by cold, we stopped; and choosing a dense tree, we lit a fire underneath in a rabbit hole, the draught entering by the other holes, through one of which could be seen a ghostly glimmer. We wandered miserably round holding a candle collecting firewood, but remained cold. At last we damned the blackout, increased the fire, made some coffee, and finally slept ...

We left at dawn, with orange clouds and ominous thunder on our left. We were soon soaked by heavy rain. We reached Petersfield at 7.10—having decided to train from here. We ate a soggy breakfast in a waiting room which smelt nastier than most things, and caught the 8.20, wet and tired. Rain[y] *ride home.*

Nora and Martin and Daddy and Mommy and Margaret and me all there—only John missing, the biggest gathering for nearly two years. We spent the morning asleep ...

Lovely to be home, after a lovely holiday. Martin suffering from insomnia after 2 years of overwork, Daddy also rather tired, Mommy rather thin after her operation ...

at Glatting

Monday 3rd
... Margaret and I went and helped Martin clean his car in the morning, getting soaked on the way there and on the way back.

The news recently has been very bad; the Germans have crossed the Don at Rostov, and are overrunning the Caucasus, but are held further N. on the Don and in the loop a certain amount. Lull in Egypt.

Tuesday 4th
I started work for Major Shiner [at Coldharbour Farm, next to Glatting]. *Hoeing from 9–12 with old (deaf) Mr. Bone, and from 1–3.40 with him and a land girl (Mrs. Hare's daughter). I stood up to the exercise OK.*

Friends of Margaret's arrived—Margaret Clifton who'd been to Bedales, who is rather nice and fits in well with the family, and Pauline ? who brought her brother Colin (aged 13), who is rather shy. Both communists (all 3), the latter working class—she's at Oxford.

Thursday 6th
Stooked (shocking up) from 9–12, 1–4. In the afternoon we caught up the binder, as the one broke (canvas torn). Pauline came too, and two more friends—called Vera and Mickey. I had to try and teach Vera how to stook, not quite without success. I hope there are no gales.

A tractor-drawn reaper-binder delivered bound sheaves, which had to be propped up in groups (stooks or shocks) of 6 or 8 to keep the grain-bearing ears off the ground.

Several of these girls are reading at Oxford Politics, Philosophy and Economics (PPE) and I was wondering if I might not do this. Now is the time to decide. Daddy has written to Ramage [Biology master] *about my career, assuming that I will be a doctor. I must change now if I'm going to.*

Friday 7th
Drizzle after 12 o'clock, with quite a lot of wind. Many stooks down. I stooked and re-stooked from 9–11.50, and then had lunch.

Everyone except Mommy and George was out for a walk miles away, and arrived late, having stopped to cook some soldiers' dinner. Talking of soldiers, a Canadian artillery private spent the night here … having got hopelessly lost …

Margaret's friends are a jolly lot, Margaret Clifton fits awfully well into the family and is very helpful and cheerful. … All are atheists and communists, I think.

The war news is awful, Germans doing well on 3 fronts in the Caucasus.

Saturday 8th
Shocking up 23-acre 'Crooked Six' today, but I only worked for the morning. I was paid 13/6—6d per hour—so was George (11/6), but Major Shiner discovered later that this was the wrong rate.

Lunch was at 1.30, by when one Herbert, Daddy, Dr. Tom Garland and his two sons had arrived. 16 at table was quite a squash! … Learned discussions on metaphysical selves and other weird subjects.

Sunday 9th
… Have just finished reading 'Darkness at Noon' (Koestler) about the Moscow trials (novel). I don't know how true it is, it is certainly very clever and good …

Monday 10th
Back to work [on the farm]. *Daddy is now having his yearly holiday. … I spent the time shocking. I did it with Mickey in the afternoon, but after spending 10 mins. under a stook and a macintosh (Mrs. Willams'—a land girl, who saw us getting wet—kind of her), we gave up at 5.20. Talked on politics and education—she's sensible as most of the people here at the moment seem to be …*

Tuesday 11th
News—Riots in India, 100 members of Congress arrested, crowds fired on. Chaos. I suppose that the govt. had no alternative when the mass civil disobedience campaign was started, except to quit India which is hardly practical ...

Tuesday 11th [sic—in parts similar to above entry, with variations]
Shocking up—with one Hugh Davis as company—he is a boy staying at Coldharbour, just taken school cert., 14½, doing medicine, and seemed quite nice. We discussed respective schools ... and I comparatively convinced him on socialism.

More in the afternoon, but I stopped at 3 o'clock due to rain. The job gets boring.

News as depressing as ever, India is quietening down but for 'hooliganism by irresponsible students'.

Friday 14th
... Last night we stayed up arguing until midnight. ... Mommy and Tom got furious with one another so Tom left. We were all arguing in various shades against Mommy, the point being that Mommy thinks that the Revolution should be moderate, and bloodless at any cost. We think it is urgent, and that it must be successful at any cost. Mommy very depressed and very depressing; I think the idea of John, who is almost reactionary, probably makes her fear intra family strife. It's a pity that we have to disagree. Anyhow, there is a good chance of the Revolution being both quick and bloodless—but we must be prepared to suppress the reaction. Miserable having to disagree with Mommy.

70 years later I cannot recall having ever really believed in the possibility of revolution, bloodless or not. But the threat of elected left wing governments being overthrown was not imaginary as, for example, some years later, the fate of Allende in Chile demonstrated. I suppose the mythology informing the discussion served some function for me and the other participants, perhaps signifying that things would be much better after the war, while life continued to be scary in the real world.

Saturday 15th
… Tom Garland and family left at 9.30—taken in the car to the station by Mommy—we get 4 gallons a month now. At 9.40 Mrs. Shiner called to fetch me, and she dropped me and Hugh at the bottom of Duncton hill. We walked on for 40 minutes until the bus caught up. We arrived in Chichester at 11 o'clock.

After meeting his mother and sister and having an ice cream with him and his sister, he and I went and successfully bought a tweed jacket for me—quite a nice bluish-green one for 39/6. Then we wandered around a bit and bussed to his house, about a mile from the centre of the town. Here we had lunch—his mother is a comfortable nice sort of woman, his father looks like a business man but is actually director of education.

After lunch we drove down in the car, Hugh and I being dropped at the cinema. … Met the others [Margaret and friends, who had also by chance been to the cinema] *in the bus. We got off at Dog Kennel cottages and trudged back in the rain singing. Supper, woffle, bed (happy woffler).*

News bad in Russia. Malta convoy fights through, 'Eagle' (old a-c. carrier) sunk.

Monday 17th
News—Maikop oilfield very scorched and left by Russians. More threat to Stalingrad. America consolidating with very heavy losses in the Solomons. I shocked up in the morning 9–12, repairing fallen ones—a miserable job …

Tuesday 18th
More shocking up. … It was a scorcher of a day, and we were doing horribly floppy and tickly barley—I was miserable and we were all bad tempered and worked badly, getting little done …

News. Churchill has been having important talks with Joe [Stalin] *and* [Ambassador] *Harriman (USA). (This yesterday published). Daddy said*

Said Churchill to Stalin
"I think you're a darlin'."
Said Joseph "You've said it,
But a 2nd front would be more to you're credit."

Wednesday 19th

Cooler day. I was woken at 7.30 by Margaret shouting excitedly "Mommy! Mommy! We've started a Second Front!". I leapt out of bed saying "Good God!" and went to hear the details. Francis had heard in the village, we'd landed in France. What excitement! We turned on the news—a raid by a force, largely of Canadians, was in progress in the Dieppe area. This is not an invasion. DAMN RUMOUR. My goodness what a flop. Awful anticlimax.

We worked six hours on the barley field, hard, and we just finished by 4.15 with help from Mrs. Shiner …

The Dieppe raid was a disaster—as a result of poor security, the Germans were ready, and the Canadians suffered heavy casualties.

Thursday 20th

… We went off to Petworth by car at 9.30, to shop and to have Margaret and me vaccinated for smallpox, of which there is an outbreak. He cleaned the skin, poured on serum, and then jabbed slightly painfully with a needle six or seven times. Margaret he scratched and rubbed …

Letter from J [of Benenden]*—thank god I met the postwoman today. She too is sobered. It's a silly business, because none of them share my interests really, though I suppose few at school do either. Quite a nice letter, though …*

Friday 21st

Shocking up barley in the morning. David came to stay, as his mother's gone to have two growths on her back operated on (due to X-ray burn 12 years ago). In the afternoon we first tied up loose bundles, then we thinned swedes until it started to rain, when we went into the piggery and entertained the pigs …

Wednesday 26th
… we went to two really bad films—but not bad enough to be funny—'The Man who came to Dinner' and 'The Stork Club'—both Hollywood at its worst. The news had some quite good Malta convoy pictures …

Thursday 27th
… 2 exhausted soldiers (Canada) came in for a wash, eventually stayed for supper and night. One was feeling (and looking) rotten—he had eaten too many apples (whose??)—we gave him bicarbonate of soda, which worked.

News—flare up expected in Egypt; fierce sea and air battle in Far East; Stalingrad threat held at the moment, serious. Big Russian attack N.W. of Moscow—35 miles advance.

Sunday 30th
John's birthday. Not very good weather. During the morning and after lunch I painted a beehive and then helped in a glorious honey separation and bee utensil wash, which only ended just before tea.

After tea I went for a 'nice quiet' walk on the downs with Daddy. Up the green slope, and then we found ourselves in the middle of an enormous camp of soldiers, with all the lorries etc. hidden under blackthorn, and a nice white table cloth for supper (officers). Our quiet walk caused some amusement. We went on to Bignor Hill and down through the woods, back past Salter's.

2 soldiers arrived, to whom we gave tea and sandwiches—one had fallen down the hill, hurting his knee and back. The food was George's, taken away in punishment for being 20 mins. late yet again for a meal. Eventually Mommy took them off in the car to the Bury-Arundel road, as they were making for Goring (Worthing).

As she left, a cyclist (soldier) came in, who was similarly fed. All three were very nice. Then as we started supper, 4 'whacked' 'deserters' from the HQ platoon came in—we gave them a wash and then they came and had supper—minus the first course. All were very nice—[Canadians] *from the country. Amused at scale of* [English] *farming. From Angmering, which one failed utterly to pronounce.*

After supper we all (except Nora who doesn't like alcohol and is having a fit of depression) drank John's health. Nice having all these people in.

Monday 31st
... Margaret and I spent the whole morning cleaning and greasing Martin's car—quite fun, and we worked together, better than usual. (There are apt to be rows when we do this). ... we poured out the honey from the centrifugal machine, getting over 20 lbs—2 x the expected. Good ...

David came back. ... He'd spent the morning [at Shiner's farm] *gossiping—the men are discontented with the foreman, JB, because his interest has (noticeably) switched from the farm to the nice (both are) landgirl Joan (who is Mrs. Williams), and he's neglecting the farm ...*

Margaret leaves tomorrow for 4 weeks in a shell filling factory as a guinea pig to study the effects of TNT poisoning (blood etc. tests before and after).

September

Wednesday 2nd
... we flattened some pennies under the train (David's pennies). What's the penalty for 'defacing a coin of the Realm'?

News—a stand before Stalingrad, 1,000,000 axis troops there. Flare up in Egypt, no major engagements yet.

Thursday 3rd
The post brought the following card, much earlier than I'd expected: from the HM Gresham's School, Newquay. School Certificate, July 1942. You have obtained a certificate with Matric. Exn. in the list of subjects which follows. ... [signed] *Excellent (PSN). Gee! Far better than I'd dared expect ... 6 VGs* [very goods], *3 Cs* [credits]. *I felt quite happy ...*

At 11 o'clock we had been at war for three years. How many more? This must be the last war ...

Sunday 6th

… [Daddy, Nora and I] *went up Farm Hill where we basked and collected blackberries, seeing two interesting birds—a redstart and my first nightjar. On the way back we collected rubber salvage (half a tire used as pheasants' drinking trough, pre-war), which I had to carry and roll; and I arrived back hot, dirty and cross, after having to make a detour due to its refusal to roll straight. Also Nora annoyed me, as she refused to carry anything …*

Stalingrad drive held, Germans claim Novorossisk.

Monday 7th

Daddy left by the 9.5, after a happy weekend. There were nice letters awaiting him too, 2 from John, happier with nice rooms, sailing, swimming and more medicine; 1 from Martin who had flown from London to Malvern in a 'Defiant' in 20 mins. They'd gone up in a Blenheim, but no planes large enough for 3 were available for the return, so they went in 3 Defiants flying 20 ft apart.

Margaret is filling landmines, and has a lovely hostel to live in. Her hair may go orange if exposed (TNT) …

Tuesday 8th

… *Stalingrad still holds, we … won victory in Egypt when Africa Corps* [German] *tried to advance last week; Churchill reviews war situation in house …*

Wednesday 9th

Lots and lots of Dieppe leaflets [dropped] *in the night. … after lunch David and I collected some 70 each from Shiner's big field, and we left the ones chewed by sheep …*

These were German propaganda showing pictures of dead and captured Canadian soldiers from the Dieppe raid.

Friday 11th

I spent the morning doing various jobs and reading 'I Believe—the personal philosophies of 23 eminent men and women of today' (George Allen and Unwin 15/-)—it is extremely interesting.

... went and bathed with David ... but it was rather spoilt by the fact that they were building corn ricks (or threshing) nearby, and I felt awfully guilty doing nothing. To make it worse, one of the men walked past and said "Nice to be some people" ...

Saturday 12th

News to date: Novorossisk evacuated, Russian slight withdrawals W. and S.W. of Stalingrad, Mozdok fighting held. Grim, it is Sept 12th. Churchill severely and well criticised for India speech. Lull in India ...

Letter from AWW. I told him my attitude about Benenden—I have lost interest—because I don't think real friendship there was possible, and as it was seemed silly, especially to my holiday self, whom I respect more than the term one ...

After supper Daddy read from Bernard Pare's 'Russia'. Daddy also brought down the 'Daily worker'—very respectable but good.

'12th Sept' may refer to 1941. On that day the first snowfall in Russia began to impede the German advance, and the first ships arrived with supplies for besieged Leningrad.

Tuesday 15th

... During the morning there was lots of cooking going on in the kitchen, and the old lady paid her weekly call with the belladonna leaves. At 11.30 Henry Bassadone arrived for the week—he had now a good job on some hospital staff ...

I read the Webbs' 'The truth about Soviet Russia'—an abridgement of the 2 volume super-exhaustive 'Soviet Communism, a New Civilisation'. Very good. Then we went for a walk ... picking up queer bomb fins of unknown origin.

Wednesday 16th
… Henry and I left for Petworth quite early, leaving the accumulator [battery] *to be charged at Rapley's. In Petworth I changed his Ration card for Emergency coupons, and also bought some canker lotion for Tinker's ears. We then had some nice cakes and coffee at 'The Hobby Horse' (6d) (he paid). After he had bought some handkerchiefs (and after we'd seen the Black Market Indian) we biked back by Duncton …*

We can't hear the news as both accumulators are down. Stalingrad fights on, with occasional withdrawals. Bloodiest battle ever. We've done some raid on Tobruk and have lost there 2 Tribal Class destroyers. So far it seems to have been rather a flop, though we've not heard much about it.

Thursday 17th
Mommy and Nora left for London at about 10.15, Nora is to be interviewed for a job there …

I painted a beehive, and then we went for a walk. … Grey day, with yellow sun on the Solent and Chichester harbour. Two mushrooms of black smoke in Worthing and the sound of a raid warning suggested bombs. Back for tea.

Mommy and Nora arrived back at 2 o'clock … She's [Nora] *got an LCC evacuated children job in Kent, starting on Tuesday. Poor Mommy will be all alone.*

Friday 18th
… I went with Mommy in the car to the station to meet Daddy, who was carrying a petrol tin containing a present (illegal) from Melody for us.

After supper we went down to Francis' to hear the news, our batteries being down, Daddy having seen headlines of sensational counter attacks. Unfortunately this proved to be an exaggeration, and there is fighting in the suburbs [of Stalingrad].

Melody was brother John's fiancée, who lived in London.

Saturday 19th
…An ailing rabbit gave Henry a chance to dissect one, so we dislocated its neck and cut it open. The intestines—to our delight—contracted still, and if pinched went tight: Then when he opened the thorax, we found the heart, distended, still beating. Soon only the right auricle was working and eventually this too stopped. Death was due to many small flat white nematodes …

Mr. and Mrs. Hill and their daughter … came to tea … [the latter] *has a messy foot from 3-month old graft for X-ray burn, which Daddy and Henry examined …*

Sunday 20th
…biked to Francis' with Henry for the news. Streets in Stalingrad recaptured, bloody fighting and still no second front. We are a damned awful country, and the Russians are beginning to say so. We woffle about our allies, the Americans; we boast what we are going to do, but we do nothing to help the 3,000+ casualties per day which Russia is suffering.

to Newquay

Tuesday 22nd
Up, breakfast, goodbye Glatting and everyone in it, and off to Pulborough. Uneventful, melancholy journey to London, where we bussed to Paddington, had coffee in an ABC [cafeteria], *and went on the platform. Same faces, same goodbyes, same coma in the train. Mommy and Nora walked away just before the train left.*

AWW there, he went after Benenden after a time. I declined. Spent the day (mostly in the corridor) looking out of the windows. Talked to Treweeks, who had infantile paralysis—headache—oblivion, no fear.

Arrived late, in the dark, supper, miserable; and wrote a miserable letter, bed, asleep. Am sharing in a big room with AWW only, RJC has a single and anyway won't return for a few days as he has impetigo.

Wednesday 23rd
... I'm in the Upper 5th form. ... I read A.S. Neill 'That awful school' (Summerhill). Interesting, but I'm not entirely in agreement with it. I started to read André Maurois 'The Art of Living'. 3.30–4.45 potato digging—quite fun really.

Thursday 24th
Work began, but much nicer work ...

News better, strong Russian attacks from N. of Stalingrad, no more streets yielded.

Preps, in which I read 'Gulliver's Travels' and Bernal 'Social Functions of Science' (Physics prep) recommended to form from school library by Mr. Candler (whose last term this is) ...

Friday 25th
... Nice periods, am really enjoying school now. ... 'The social functions of Science' is very interesting, and it makes it clear that Soviet science is far better financed and organised than ours or the USA's.

The news remains better, with successes north of the city [Stalingrad] *and no more withdrawals elsewhere. Also (significantly?) there have been no recent reports of German reserves thrown in. Either they're being collected for final fling, or there are none.*

Saturday 26th
... Periods: Biology (evolution), English, study, study, PE.

Height 6ft, weight 10.2 ...

After tea we talked A.S. Neill with Snelling (who is left, if anything), and then AWW and I went for a walk to see the sea. He got a letter via Croydon from Benenden—they are all forbidden to write ... As a matter of principle I'm quite with them, though I have no particular inclination to write. After supper we wrote a letter with Snelling to Picture Post about it—quite fun, I don't care if it's printed or not (anonymous—for school reasons and personal).

Sunday 27th
... biked off to the Dome (Mr. Candler) for lunch ... walked back. I saw paddling A and J [from Benenden], *and grinned half-heartedly at them. On the way back to school we ate our last wartime ice-cream ...*
Music Club. They played Beethoven's Violin Concerto. I read at first, but then listened—it ought to be played outside on a still, clear, cool night. Sometimes happy, sometimes beautiful.

The manufacture and sale of ice-cream was banned from the end of September.

Monday 28th
... I'm not too unhappy—only slight homesickness—it's nice here, but so much much nicer there; and I don't like to think of Mommy all alone at Glatting, and Daddy all alone travelling so much. I hope he gets the social medicine chair at Oxford which has been created (everyone assumes that he will, but he's heard nothing). He was offered a seat in Parliament—cert. but declined, probably correctly as he'd be rather ineffective and overworked now, and his State medicine is useful.

October

Tuesday 6th
... In JTC we did silly battle drill four times.

Wednesday 7th
... Have just read a book—'Back from the USSR'—Gide (French). Short, with many well-deserved criticisms. Danger of orthodoxy—not enough criticism—may be excusable but very regrettable.
About the world future I'm in a ferment. I've several beams of light, and I'm certain that some things must come for moral reasons. The way in which it will come, just how it will come, I don't know. There are problems in my mind still unsolved—a mass of conflicting ideas pierced with occasional certainties. May it straighten out in time to be of use. How badly ideas are expressed by my words!

Thursday 8th
... I read 'The Road to Wigan Pier' [by George Orwell].

We were supposed if pos. to make toys—I don't know what to make, and I don't fit in with the atmosphere of the house storeroom (carpentry place). Max would say 'aloof'—I don't know—I think it's a form of shyness really, and also I know I'm not liked much by most people ...

2 letters ... Nora is settling down well, is in charge of junior nurses who like her. I do hope she does her job successfully—it would make such a difference to her if she found that she was capable.

It strikes me that when I read this in years to come I'll want to know what I think now of my physical appearance—I'm 6 ft., not very broad now, 10 stone, my nose is wide, snub and original, I have a very large mouth of which I'm sometimes shy, with thick almost negroid lips. None the less, I've been told that people think I'm good looking, though I'm very inclined to doubt it! ...

Friday 9th
I want to get into the habit of writing down my dreams—testing the theory of dreaming in the past and future. I'm now sceptical. One dream was that I went and sat down at the 3rd table and Max told me I would listen to the wireless at ? o'clock. I knew that this was when Mommy would broadcast from S. Africa (personal message) as she'd told me in the letter before. She had been sunk off that coast. I saw a photo in the paper of airmen in the sea ... who were also going to talk, as it said underneath.

The second dream was in the chemi. lab. I created an elephant, about 1 ft high. In the lab were about six boys and two girls, one looking like B (who was also there). Outside the window was another form, which came in when it rained. Mr. Dodd was taking us.

Theories as to origin—(1) Mommy's letter, photos in paper—why sunk?
(2) Doing chemistry, 'Co-education' (a book I'm reading—very convincing)—why the elephant—the school pigs also came in the dream in connection with Mr. Dodd ...

I read two books today—'The Road to Wigan Pier' and 'The Lion and the Unicorn'—both George Orwell. He's very prejudiced against Russia and English Communists, the latter partly excusable, but he does not see the good and potential good in Russia. Socialist however, and thinks we'll not win the war until we are (Lion … written in 1940).

In *The Road to Wigan Pier* Orwell described working class life in the 1930s, and then discussed why many are hostile to socialism. *The Lion and the Unicorn* presents a vision of socialism with a particularly English character.

Saturday 10th
… I went along the rocks past splash point with Snelling and H—both of whom are really very nice people. … Then the music recital.

… after supper I read and wrote criticisms of the Conservative sub-committee's report on Education. Re: Religion, they were incredibly fair to Russia.

The report consisted of recommendations to the party on policy towards youth and education, advocating the development of a sense of civic obligation, and proposing a national federation of youth organisations, one of which every 14 to 18 year old would be expected to join.

Monday 12th
… Excitement at 12.40—verey lights [flares] *by Baker's Folly. … Rush out when the bell went, to see rubber dinghy and 5 men there. A Whitley* [bomber] *had apparently landed* [in the sea] *at 12.23, and sunk later. At 1.15 approx. the Newquay lifeboat arrived—quick work! Pretty disgraceful …*

Soc. Soc.—[lecture by] *a Norwegian who had recently arrived* [by boat] *at the Shetlands—and had had difficulty in contacting the police! Interesting, and I should say a nice man.*

Tuesday 13th

… News—Stalingrad lull over (one day only), counter attacks in Caucasus. We sit. The British paper in Moscow publishes a photo of pigeons being fed in Trafalgar Square (typical, but hardly propaganda!).

Wednesday 14th

3 studies [private study periods]—having no Chemi books and having read the Physics book I finished off a novel—'Night in Bombay' [Louis Bromfield, 1940]; the steamy heat and continual alcohol consumption depressed me—presumably it was well written, but I did not really enjoy it.

A very brief note from Margaret and some scalpel blades.

Analysis in chemi … Barium Carbonate would not dissolve in HCl so Mr. Hughes and I decided that an evil spirit had broken it …

News—little from Russia; naval success for Americans, but I'm sometimes sceptical because they usually announce heavy losses months later—The Yorktown [aircraft carrier] and 3 cruisers or something.

Thursday 15th

… Potato digging … in the afternoon; to get on quickly with the field, we worked from 2.20–4; I was with M and we did more than anyone except R and H—the rest stayed together and talked too much. We didn't work frightfully hard but just all the time, which is much more satisfactory. There's an enormous pile of potatoes now.

A postcard from Daddy—he's read parts of Bernal's 'social functions of science'—which I read a summary of in Physics today; the period ended with a discussion of patents and libel law—two iniquities.

Saturday 17th

[Rugger match in Truro] We arrived, changed and went to the pitch, where we had an altercation with a local farmer for "climin' in his bliddy 'edges". The pitch was small and on a hilltop, the ball was small and they were big; the game at first was very fast and good. … 4 nosebleeds (one me slight), many shirts and trousers [torn]. … R … bust a collar bone, T's forehead was cut open. Then showers and a little *tea. Wandered about Truro eating chips. … Saw a bad case of rickets—horrid.*

… debate 'Little boys should be seen and not heard'. 1st K—poor; 2nd B—good; 3rd Mullins—good speech, reactionary and irrelevant; 4th F, then G, H, me. My first speech. Probably inaudible. I said that Mullin's conservative 'good old days' policy was OK—if you're the gentry. I also said that you did not learn self-mastery by being mastered …

Sunday 18th

… Misty damp morning, with blue sky forever showing through the mist, but never coming right out. We saw the first waders arriving—redshank, ringed and grey plovers.

… three M of I [Ministry of Information, or MoI] *films—'Silage' (good), 'Stretcher Parties' and 'SDS'. Then RJC and I went up to the Biology lab. and dissected rats.*

Rather a good sermon by a German pastor, who, however, was convinced that a new world could be built only by Christians on Christian foundations. On Christian principles, yes, by the present usual type of Christian, no …

Max said to Roger that my only common ground with AWW was Benenden—I wonder. Actually I often find him very aggravating now—he's so damned superficial in everything he says or does, that one never knows whether to believe him or not. However, he'd thought a little about some things.

Monday 19th

… Began reading Aldous Huxley's 'Ends and Means'—he takes a very gloomy view of the USSR today (written during Moscow trials). The terrible developments he mentions are (1) Vested interests in rulers and (2) Militarism in schools. I think the first is probably rather exaggerated, and the second, though partly necessary, worries me. He sees it as wide self rule under Lenin, and iron discipline under CP and Stalin.

Things to avoid here—where, with our tradition of the principle (if not practice) of freedom, it should be easier. The conservative plan's [for education] *as bad re: militarism. (Another point) It's painfully obvious that complete disarmament at the end of the war is essential.*

Thursday 22nd
… we discussed with Mr. Candler the Yugo Slav who spoke in Soc. Soc. last night. … [Mr. C] *spoke to him afterwards, and brought out two points: (1) The Mihailovič* [royalist] *regulars still fighting don't work with the partisans. The latter are revolutionary and disapproved of by the government here. (2) The 'free' governments will have no say in Europe* [after the war ends], *because leaders will have arisen. However, if there is not soon a second front, they'll all be killed …*

It was some time before Britain accepted that Tito's partisans were the effective anti-axis force.

Friday 23rd
… read 'Middletown in transition' [an interesting sociological study from the USA, by Robert Lynd].

Wednesday 28th
… I am in the house play—'The Blue Comet'—as paternal colonel at head of the Bedale family, when a blue comet very nearly hits the earth. Really rather a good play—we skimmed through it after tea.
News. We advance in Egypt, Stalingrad still see-saws, Wendell Willkie repeats Second Front call.

Willkie was an American Republican politician.

Friday 30th
… I am doing the house cuttings book each week (things from newspapers)—must get some from the 'Daily Worker'! A good chance of getting the right (or rather left!) point of view across.

Saturday 31st
… Saw a nice [religious] *tract in the morning—the motor car is a sign from God—chariots of steel and fire = internal combustion engine. Also Russia, Germany, Turkey and Persia are going to attack Jerusalem, but*

God'll save it at the last moment; and the wicked Russians will perish by their own mustard gas, the exact symptoms of which are described in the old Testament. Pathetic and silly.

November

Tuesday 3rd
... I read a very good book by a journalist—'North China Frontier'—about the Chinese Red Army. ... I had not realised that a Soviet state had existed in N. China for ten years, despite Chang Kai Shek, under the leadership of Mao Tse Tung—the Chinese Lenin this man calls him. Very interesting anyhow—now there is guerrilla warfare there—written actually in '38.

Watkinson, Snelling and A wrote a damn silly letter to Picture Post protesting about the interception of letters—so silly a venture really that I did not sign it—and Picture Post's published it, heading 'Three love-sick swains give their view on progressive education', and signing it with their initials, and Newquay—this being the only boys' school here! Quite funny ...

Wednesday 4th
... In Soc. Soc. there was a talk by Dr. Willoughby (φ) on—billets or hostels for evacuees. She chose the latter, and argued it out very well ...

Thursday 5th
Fireworks in Libya and Russia! In Libya, Rommel's in flight, we've captured 9,000, two generals (one killed—the commander of the Afrika Corps). Lots of planes (500-600), 260 tanks, 270 guns etc. We are following up, and are harrying from the air. Good ...

Friday 6th
... News, advance and destruction continues, papers as usual terribly over-optimistic, I expect we'll be rolled back again soon (pessimist!). Actually it seems not too bad.

We were not. This was the decisive (second) battle of El Alamein, fought by Australian, New Zealand, Indian and British troops.

Saturday 7th

... Colts [under 16s] *match here, v. Truro, at 3.15, with the Dome* [Mr. Candler] *as referee. He had strange ideas of the rules, but they were at least the same for both sides ...*

Today is the anniversary of the October [Russian] *Revolution. Twenty-five years, I think. There are many true criticisms to be made, but the system has proved to be the most economically sound, it has done more to promote health and happiness than any other. ... Anyhow, I think the communist ideal is the hope for the future.*

Sunday 8th

News. American forces, to be followed by British, have landed in French Morocco and Algiers from the Atlantic and Mediterranean. Gen. Giraud, who recently escaped from Germany, has called on his troops from Algeria to assist us.

Some Vichy forces resisted the landings, but other French troops and resistance units cooperated with the British and US.

There is a hope, and a possibility, that the German and Italian armies in North Africa, outnumbered and surrounded, will be liquidated. Then, or before then, France will be invaded also. The outlook is brighter than for some time.

... we had a rehearsal—or rather a say through [of 'The Blue Comet']. *I quite know my part, so I can now concentrate on the acting and expression more. I think this play will be fun, even though it means missing three days at home—and I think this is now definite ...*

Monday 9th

... Letter from Margaret: ... USSR meeting—Red Dean spoke, very good. She ends up "Do you know exactly what's wrong with Daddy—I can't make out except that it's due to overwork. Anyhow, as he gave me no cause to worry, I'm not worrying". I, however, having heard nothing else about it, am. Not frightfully, but Daddy's father died of cancer ...

News. Americans doing OK, but coastal batteries and naval forces of Vichy France are opposing us. Rommel still flees, with awful bombing of Halfaya pass. Scare headlines in Telegraph 'Only 28 tanks and 20,000 men left'. If it is true, or only exaggerated x2, it looks pretty hopeful. A lull at Stalingrad, which is dwarfed out of all proportion to its size in the news—many more Germans there than in Libya.

Tuesday 10th
Normal day. A letter from Mommy in the morning—Daddy is in Guy's, having broken down after long months of hard work, but she doesn't think it's anything worse than fatigue. He's going to have some weeks holiday at Glatting. Poor old Daddy—he always works himself too hard, and Guy's were awful to him …

In fact this was the first episode of coronary artery disease. After it, any exertion was liable to provoke anginal pain and he had a number of heart attacks (coronary thromboses) and finally died in 1950. Despite this, his last few years were active and productive and during them he set up the Institute of Social Medicine at Oxford and visited India, South Africa and the USA.

Wednesday 11th
Germany entering rest of France, Corsica, and troops landed in Tunisia—Rommel's retreat continues. Things are certainly happening …

Letter from Daddy at Guy's, dictated (he apologised for laziness). I do hope there's nothing more than fatigue.

Soc. Soc. was a talk by Rev. Coleman [an American] *on America. Besides telling some very funny stories (blue silk pyjamas) he was very good and fair on the colour problem. Negroes have the vote, but the poll tax is too high for them to pay; in the South, tradition and prejudice are very strong. I enjoyed it anyhow.*

Friday 13th
… We had a grand Chemi period, sitting round the fire while Oscar [the teacher] *told stories about one Hughes* [himself] *who in his youth had*

been very wise, good, industrious and immoral. He told good stories marvellously well—he must have been quite a lad, besides working hard before he got the nervous disease ...

He suffered from Disseminated Sclerosis (as Multiple Sclerosis was then called), and had to have someone assisting him with all physical manipulations and writing on the board.

News—assault again on Stalingrad where the Volga freezes. Halfaya pass captured ... Bardia and Tobruk reached ...

Sunday 15th

... we [AWW] *discussed the shortcomings of school life. I can't believe that a system which by its nature makes 50% of the boys in the school sleep in each other's beds for the physical pleasure obtained therein, there being no other outlet for sexual feelings, is a good one. The blokes who do it aren't particularly wrecked psychologically, but it don't seem natural. God knows at times I feel in need of an outlet for my sexual feelings, if I didn't practice self control I'd probably do what they do—but on the whole I don't expect I'd be happier. Still, it's wrong—the system I mean.*

Monday 16th

Another week. Feeling rather annoyed all day—though considering what some people are going through I suppose I've no right to complain—though that's no argument for the system I'm annoyed with. 'The End of Economic Man' is a good book—he maintains that capitalism and Marxism both fail because they are built on the basis of man as an economic animal, and both have failed to secure equality. I wonder about that—I think Marxism pure and simple is useless, but if even Russia—which is admittedly very imperfect—has advanced so enormously in culture and the standard of living, surely this shows that they do not believe that the only important aspect of man is the economic one. Anyhow I can't write it down, it's too involved, and I've no time to spare ...

Peter Drucker, who wrote *The End of Economic Man,* was a theorist of how business corporations should be run.

Tuesday 17th

… JTC—I have now a battle dress, minus spats and forage cap. First we had a talk by Major Low, who turned out to be none other than Prof. A.M. Low [physicist and radio engineer]. *It was a lecture on how to avoid boredom by observing nature—very good, with frequent humorous interludes. Then he showed us some scientific conjuring tricks with military significance.*

We then inspected a reccy armoured car (Humber!) [which carried a 25 pounder gun], *carrier pigeons and, very interesting, a field dressing station. The description of the uses of the various instruments was given by the sergeant, a cheery individual* [who] *caused faintness on F's part. He was rather cheerful about the importance of sharpness in an amputating saw.*

Saturday 21st

News for last three days—we have passed Benghazi, fighting starts in Tunis, Russian victory in Caucasus, Stalingrad unchanged, Jap. defeat in New Guinea …

Monday 23rd

… Works in the afternoon—to Mrs. Hamnet at Trevone. There was next to nothing to be did, but we did it as long as we could …

The Russians seem to have made a successful offensive on the Don, cutting railway lines important for Stalingrad …

Thursday 26th

Nice long letter from a recuperating Daddy, growing fatter at Glatting. He said "I think as a family we have combined the job of remaining individuals and a loyal group pretty well"—he hoped that it had been partly due to Mommy and he not being too coercive and dictatorial—and in having married young. Which is very true and lovely, and also is what we are aiming for in the world. Poor old Johns had dysentery—but was cured 48 hours after diagnosis by one of the new drugs [sulphonamides] *...*

Got the Webb's 'Soviet Communism, a New Civilisation' from the school library. ... I want to look up points on: individual freedom, the part of workers in Industry etc.—partly to see how right it is, and partly to learn how to argue for it, if it is right.

Sydney and Beatrice Webb were respected social researchers and reformers—Fabians—who wrote this totally uncritical account of the Soviet system.

Saturday 28th
... Russian attack in S. and Moscow front, both big and successful. However dull this life may seem, I've no right to complain and I've always one job to do—to behave in a way which will show what communism in its true sense expects, and to be an example, atheist or not! I could do that job very much better.

This is the nearest I got to seeing Communism as a quasi-religious belief system with implications for how I conducted my life. The error, as I now see it, was in linking my beliefs to a deeply flawed state, not in investing political belief with moral significance.

Sunday 29th
Speech by Churchill—he said very little very well.

This comment in many ways summarises my evaluation of Churchill's contribution. He was wrong on nearly every social and military issue, but his unifying and at times inspirational rhetoric sustained the unrealistic hope and commitment of the British through the long and dark days of 1940-1945. His distress at the Labour victory in the 1945 election, and the major contribution to that of the Forces vote, demonstrated the limits of his understanding of the people he led.

Monday 30th
... I read another play by Auden and Isherwood—'On the Frontier'. Not nearly as good as 'F6'. I also read many of the poems in Auden's

'Another time'—some are a bit deep, some are very nice, some are funny. Anyhow I enjoyed a lot of them—I thought before it was rather drivel.

When I re-read the diary for the end of last term, I feel tempted to tear it up—but the fault is not mine. The first experience of the opposite sex may have knocked me rather silly … I think I see things in a saner light now.

December

Thursday 3rd
… Economics lesson in the afternoon—I tried to ask if he agreed with the principle of private ownership of land and resources, but he wasn't having any—said it was ethics.

In prep I digressed and said that the only justification for a science was in its application to human needs, and these should be studied with the mere facts and laws.

Thursday 10th
Slight fracas in Physics with ACC … I said I could not write out the proofs of the formulae for Newton Rings, 2 slits and Doppler effect. The Dome had worked through them once on the board, with masses of greek letters which I never remember the meaning or name of; he leaves out the intermediate arithmetical steps, and he proves the formulae without explaining the groundwork. We're supposed to learn the latter from the book, which I find impossible to inwardly digest except in very small doses, and even then I don't often see why …

In the evening was the house play, 1st performance. … The play went absolutely wizardly, no hitches, no pauses, and we and the audience both enjoyed it immensely. We all acted more and better, and several new jokes were unearthed. Afterwards several people classed it as the best, or certainly 1st Class. Lovely satisfaction feeling.

Sunday 13th

… prep, reading more of 'The Art of Living', André Maurois—I like his section on growing old, and his one on leadership is good.

There is so much in life to do—books to read, music to hear. … And then there's the general task of trying to put an object in life for all, however many there are members of the Human race.

The A's in the 'Ascent of F6' impressed me. Life—I've got it all to come before, to make what I can of it. Profound thoughts! When I read through them in future years I'll probably make some cynical remark! (like this!)

Mr. and Mrs. A, a white-collar working couple, in Auden and Isherwod's *The ascent of F6* are a sort of disenchanted chorus to this political play about a mountaineering expedition.

Tuesday 15th

The end of term approaches. Habershon asked me if I'd like to come and discuss things with him—I said yes, he's rather a woolly but quite a good old chap …

7-a-side rugger in the afternoon, but as we arrived there was a terrific downpour and the games were cancelled …

Double theoretical physics without incident. The Dome gave me a copy of the Week to read—good.

The Week was a left wing magazine produced in a hand-to-mouth way by Claud Cockburn, which specialised in revealing corrupt goings-on amongst the European ruling elites, especially the British. It was banned by the government in 1941, but reappeared in October 1942.

In 3rd prep I made toys. Some Dartford [a women's physical training college] *carol singers serenaded us from the hall—in aid of the Red Cross—we watched from the banisters. It's possible that some of Woodlands will go out carol singing (Smith suggests with mistletoe on our hats)—it would be quite amusing. This time next week ---*

Wednesday 16th
… In Chemistry we had a happy little sing-song with Oscar [Hughes], *starting with carols, and gradually descending …*

[We were given] *essays to comment on—I liked Oscar Wilde's 'The Soul of Man Under Socialism'—however bad an advertisement Oscar Wilde may have been!*

Thursday 17th
… we went out carol singing. Our party was very lucky, we did all Dartford … [We] *sang two long carols with a circular stair crowded with Dartford above us. … Our total, for bombed and distressed areas, was 27/3¼, the other party got 24/-; not a bad total earned very enjoyably …*

Friday 18th
… I spent the morning doing various jobs on stage and auditorium [preparing for 'The Blue Comet']*—surrounded by nicotine inhaling and generally decadent youths.*

After lunch we changed and made up. The audience at 2.30 consisted of about 100 wounded soldiers—quite attentive and appreciative but not very quick on the jokes. However they enjoyed it.
… 2nd performance—general visitors from Newquay—quite our best audience so far—and quite our best performance …

Saturday 19th
… Usual routine performance in the afternoon (!) to an elderly, quiet, but appreciative audience. It went pretty well. Then off with moustache—no regrets! and into civilian clothes again. Tea, and then a general tidy up in preparation for the do [a dance as a reward for the cast of the play].

At eight o'clock the first girl arrived—I was introduced, and was astonished to find that she knew me (as a small boy) … by name (S)Cylla … now at Dartford, living with her mother in Newquay.

Her brother John had contracted polio while their father was in India, and he had stayed with us when out of hospital, and in some school holidays. He was now a medical student.

… we played silly but amusing games and danced in between. (S)Cylla taught me very patiently (and probably on her part painfully) [the dances], *and everyone else I danced with was very kind and patient, and I was doing a good deal better at the finish. Taylor played us some things and Hales did a little act. Then the end came and they went.*

A lot of people were seeing people home, so I offered to see Cylla home. … [Her mother] *brought us some cocoa, and we chatted awhile about our respective families. John is entirely recovered* [from his polio] *… except for occasional mental blackouts …*

Sunday 20th

[To London in a very crowded night train] *D, RJC and myself got into a 1st Class carriage. … we left our luggage and went out to recon (how the hell do you spell it?) make a reconnaissance for 3rd Class seats, and to stretch our legs. We went the length of the train, unlocking about ten doors with penknives, but found nothing. We then … opened one, and came into the mail coach—we shut it quickly, but the guard saw us and gave chase. He took our identity cards, took us to his office and spoke of Newton Abbot jail. D's HG* [Home Guard: he was a senior boy already with military documents] *and naval identity cards, and our tact and assurance that we were not mail bag robbers, eventually freed us. We returned, and I took a seat in the corridor and dozed …*

to Glatting

Monday 21st

I was woken by a very drunken sailor, who confided some most unpleasant facts about his recent doings. … The train arrived at Paddington on time … by tube to Victoria. There I had a cup of coffee, and after a short wait in which I bought the 'Daily Worker' and the 'Labour Monthly', I boarded the 9.13 … got to Glatting at 12.15. Daddy looks much better and fatter and is also much jollier …

Tuesday 22nd
… Listened to the Brains Trust in the evening—I'd never done so before—Joad sounded like you'd expect. Good news, Russians on Don still advance—almost a rout. Rommel nearing Tripoli.

'The Brains Trust' was an immensely popular radio discussion programme with questions sent in by listeners. C.E.M. Joad, a philosopher and lecturer with some very unconventional opinions, was a panellist.

Thursday 24th
Another lovely clear morning. Daddy, Margaret, David Wolfe and myself went out in the morning and obtained a very squat Christmas (yew) tree. … after lunch … Margaret and I went out for another walk, getting holly and hawthorn and sloes for decoration. Also one primrose …

After tea we knitted, and Daddy read chapter II of War and Peace.

Margaret and I went to the MoI film show at the WI—a very good lot—cartoons on digging for victory, on vitamins for health, films on dockers and shipbuilders, and the siege of Tobruk.

News good—Middle Don offensive continues. Daddy read us a 'Christmas story, 1942' from Punch—extremely funny about a would-be operational dynamo.

Bed, after Daddy's yearly Christmas eve poem:

One Xmas eve when Santa Claus
Came to a certain house ---

Friday 25th
We exchanged what presents we'd got in Mommy and Daddy's bed, à la pre-war birthday. … I got two books—'Monkey'—the most widely read Chinese novel (in China) and 'The Amateur Poacher'. … good news—Darlan [former head of the Vichy government, who had made a deal with the Allies in north Africa] *assassinated. There will be repercussions. The nationality of the hero is 'not known'* [he was a French royalist].

… the two soldiers we'd invited from Duncton searchlight post arrived for Christmas dinner … they soon thawed and started a conversation which lasted for nearly ten hours (!) with breaks for meals. Dinner was magnificent with tomato soup, two pheasants and very fine pudding. Also parsnip wine.

… tea, to which David and a bloke staying with him came, then more conversation, then supper, with an excited harangue by Margaret on Socialism, supported by rest of family. … at last they left—they'd enjoyed it all immensely, and we'd enjoyed most of it. The strain of following George's [one of the soldiers] *talk was terrific—he told hundreds of (some very funny) anecdotes with a Cockney accent through closed teeth. He was a builder. Ted was a woodworker from Dagenham—quiet and sensible and kind, and he agreed with socialism. … an exhausting but happy Christmas day.*

Saturday 26th
… I helped Margaret pin out rabbit skins [to make gloves] *until 11 o'clock … We did the animals after tea and then were cosy and lazy … in the drawing room—we sewed or knitted while Daddy read 'War and Peace'* [aloud].

Tuesday 29th
… I took my mattress out to my house after lunch, and spent part of the afternoon there, reading my old diary. I withstood the temptation to burn it …

Thursday 31st
Much milder, and it had rained in the night. … Daddy and I went for a short stroll—along the stream and down through the fields to the white bridge, where we played Pooh-sticks. After lunch Francis came in; he has been told to find other agricultural work on a nearby farm within ten days. A blow.

We are going to try to prevent it, for without him we'd have to sell most of the livestock and let the garden go; Mommy would have to stay here or we'd have to let Glatting go; Francis has never worked on a farm, and anyway is producing much food here. Everyone was plunged into gloom …

So ends the old year. This time last year I wrote: what does next year hold for us? Invasion? Victory? This year I can repeat it, but thanks to Russia, the invasion should be of Europe.

Over the year I seem to have taken some interest in the patchy military training we received and I had become less fascinated by the collection of bits and pieces and more concerned with the overall situation. I clearly identified as 'us' not only British but also (especially) the Russian and, in a more distant way, the American forces. The military situation was still precarious in every theatre of war, and only the RAF represented something positive.

Chapter 5: 1943–1944

World events: January 1943–February 1944

The German army at Stalingrad surrendered. Rostov was soon taken and over the year the Red Army, with high morale, the T34 tank and a more effective air force moved westwards, winning the world's largest tank battle at Kursk and liberating Smolensk. In the first months of 1944 the German siege of Leningrad was ended but German, Estonian, Finnish and volunteer SS troops from other European countries held up further Russian advances on this front.

Africa: the Afrika Korps finally surrendered and 250,000 prisoners were taken.

Far East: some gains were made by American forces in the Far East. In particular, in their first major offensive action, US forces captured the Pacific island of Guadalcanal, safeguarding the supply route to Australia and providing a base for the future campaign. In Burma, British jungle troops—the Chindits—were active but had no decisive victories, and Japan continued to threaten India.

Europe: the Allied invasion of Sicily and southern Italy led to the Italian surrender in September, but German troops took control of Northern Italy. The allied bridgehead at Anzio was fiercely attacked, and the first assaults on Monte Cassino involving American troops were repulsed. The RAF continued the systematic bombing of German cities and developed the technique of creating firestorms; in one Hamburg raid 44,600 civilians died. The first ghetto rising in Warsaw was crushed.

The Atlantic: improved techniques for detecting submarines (sonar and radar), more escort vessels, and extended air cover led to the sinking of many German submarines, and eventually to their withdrawal in May 1943.

In the year before, Allied ships were being sunk faster than new ships could be built. The German battleship Tirpitz was damaged and the Scharnhorst was sunk, reducing the threats to convoys of supplies being sent to Russia and to the transatlantic flow of US troops and materials.

The economic balance of the Allies and the Axis powers was crucial. The Russian re-creation of an industry beyond the Urals, which now out-produced Germany in tanks and planes, and the mobilisation of America's vast industrial base, were providing the material means which Germany and Japan lacked.

Diary for 1943

at Glatting

January

Saturday 2nd
Martin was expected all afternoon … he rang up from Pulborough at 7.0, and was fetched. Very tired and non-receptive. I always used to feel awed by him, and imagined that he was contemptuous of me—probably quite unwarranted, but I've never really been at ease with him—or John.

Sunday 3rd
… I went for a longish walk with Margaret and Martin (who wore a lovely furry [lined] *leather flying jacket)—the walk was not hilarious, for Martin is still pretty exhausted, and has rather a headache I believe …*

Good news—while the capture of Veliki Luki was being described, news of the capture of Mozdok came in. Three big towns on three fronts in about one week. It's wonderful.

Wednesday 6th
… Daddy examined Martin and discovered that he had a dilated heart. Usually this means rheumatic fever, but Martin has never had that. He suddenly felt ill about two weeks ago—presumably it's due to constant strain and working at high pressure. What makes it worse is that he's

working on a very important piece of apparatus which will make safer bombers, and it can't go on without him. That's two war casualties in the family …

The village brains trust took place at 7 o'clock—Daddy on it, we went (O wicked ones!) by car—it was very wet and Daddy's not too well, as a sop to my conscience. The questions were very good, and so were the answers, which managed to be both informative and witty—altogether a great success, followed by refreshments, then back, supper, the slow movement of Beethoven's Concerto no. 3 in C minor in Martin's room—lovely, and bed.

Thursday 7th

Mommy and Daddy went up to London for Daddy to see his doctor Lord Horder. … Daddy is to give up everything until the Oxford job [professorship] *starts so as to be quite fit for that—and he's to be up only from 11 to 9 each day.*

… while we were having supper—who should ring up but Harry [Martin's friend]. *Hooray (boo). I fetched the car (where it is now, one goes round by road and there's time to change gear) and went with Mommy to meet him. He's thinner but as cheery as ever. He'll do Martin lots of good. Martin wants to go back* [to work], *whether it kills him or no, because others will be killed if he does not. Apart from family considerations, if he did go back now he'd only get crocked and never be able to save any more lives afterwards …*

Later in his life he would say bitterly that all his work did was to save a few hundred RAF crews so that thousands of German civilians could be killed.

Saturday 9th

Harry had to go off to Birmingham … I went to the station with Mommy to take him … Back to find house cleaning in process by both Margarets and Melody …

I went and read in Martin's room—but he was so damn gloomy that I went out to expend energy in a solitary walk, which restored my spirits.

… Martin was allowed to get up for supper, and was much more cheerful under the influence of young female company …

[With my parents] *had a long heart to heart talk on sex—at school and personally …*

Saturday 16th

… Roger [who had come to stay] *and I set off in quest of goat husbands, the telephone finding all known ones already sold. We biked to Bury Gate, where the owner—a woman dressed like a Chinese—very sensibly told us that unfortunately their Billy was too young, but she told us of Mrs. P. at Graffam.*

The pedal broke off Daddy's bike which I was riding, so we called at two garages, at the second of which we obtained a new core and balls [bearings], *which with the help of a nice hand, we affixed—they had lots of bits …*

At 3.15 we left in the car with the goat Bumpbox—who soon settled down all right with some hay. She was suitably dealt with by a very odorous billy—whose mistress smelt as bad …

Sunday 17th

Roger and I went for a walk—up Farm Hill, where we re-directed some lost map-reading and somewhat profane RAMC privates …

New Russian offensive south of Voronez (spelling?) [Voronezh]. ... *One can't think about what an offensive like this means in lives.*

to Newquay

Tuesday 19th

... All the same bloody faces in the station, but we at least got good seats with comparatively unobjectionable companions …

Then some of our old Benenden gang walked past (I'd seen them and said hullo when returning from getting some 'coffee'). ... After some hesitation Snelling and I went and talked to them ... We talked for most of the journey—trivial but quite amusing conversation, which I enjoyed. ... I don't think I'll try and carry on in the term time ...

On the train I heard that M [a fellow pupil] *had killed himself with explosives* [making fireworks] *in the holiday—I was not really surprised, but rather shocked. One can only be sorry for the parents. It will act as a deterrent to other similar experiments …*

I'm in the same room, with AWW, and I'm captain of the Juniors.

Saturday 23rd

Today school life continued with all its monotony and pettiness, and I felt more homesick than before this term.

The news was good, Salsk and Tripoli both taken—Rommel, however, has been very successful in extricating his forces …

Tried Stravinsky, but one side was enough. Weighing and measuring—6′ ¾″, 10.8. 10 weeks before I live properly again.

Sunday 24th

It dawned with promise, light blue sky with a few pink trailers and dark blue on the horizon …

Another mealtime argument with Mullins, I being assisted by Wood—Wood's philosophy has changed somewhat—from a once orthodox Christian he has become an agnostic. There may be more in him than meets the eye …

Tuesday 26th

… I had my first music lesson [flute with Mr. Taylor]*—learning (a) how to make the noise and (b) how to read music. The flute is OK but one stop needed a pad, and later in the day the handle* [lever] *broke, which is a nuisance. Taylor does not know the fingering, but a book is on the way. I hope it can be repaired. Apparently there's lots of good music for flute and piano.*

JTC was a uniform check etc, then drill—I've been put in No.1 platoon, which means Cert. A. [a national assessment of basic military training] *in March. Then a hard working 80 mins. of Physics—pretty concentrated but also illuminating. After tea I played the last part of Scheherazade—which I like a lot. Hard work in prep—also Physics—I got on well with it.*

Wednesday 27th
... News—Stalingrad army [German] *is now practically annihilated, Churchill and Roosevelt meet in Casablanca—Stalin unable to come due to being C-in-C etc. Max suggested at lunch that this was because "Dictators never like to leave their controls"—which started a long and heated argument.*

Friday 29th
… Martin went back on Monday. Poor Mommy, to have to see him go back still seriously ill, to go on working at terrific strain, like the others, under the short sighted policy of working flat out till death (practically) stops you. May officialdom be moved by this plea of expediency if not by humanity—which of course with their vital work would plead the other way, only Martin is my brother and Mommy's son …

Sunday 31st
A Rainy dawn. After discoursing on the comfort of beds before getting up, we were just in time for breakfast. Then I messed around, did some daily flute practice, and looked out on the grey view. Feeling disgruntled I walked out quickly alone along the headland, where a magnificent gale and big splashy waves quite restored my spirits, and I came back and wrote about it …

The usual drag to and from chapel, Habby preached—he's not an orator, and I read more of Lin Yutang's happy philosophy. It's all very well, but it wants to be distributed …

Lin Yutang was a Chinese writer who wrote in English about Chinese philosophy and culture, and commented on Chinese and world politics.

February

Monday 1st
59 days till freedom. Of 320,000 men round Stalingrad, 48,000 (I think) are prisoners, the rest are corpses. What a world …

Standards [physical training], *unchanged, in the gym, lasting ten minutes. I did six press-ups—distinction, and only two rollups—pass.*

Then Roger and I went to the Gannel—a very high tide, so we rock-clambered along and returned, due to the rain, to quote Shakespeare, wet (Tempest, Act 1, Scene1, enter Mariners, wet). Dogfish in Biology, not a very successful dissection on my part.

A letter from Daddy—quite happy I think, with large fan mail coming in …

Friday 5th

I finished reading 'Penguin Island' [by Anatole France]*—a cleverly and amusingly cynical book with a morbid ending. I'm now reading Aleck Bourne's 'Health for the Future'—*[about] *social medicine, and as I write he is taking part in a wireless discussion on Social Medicine—which Daddy was to have done but for his ill-health …*

Saturday 6th

… Games after supper—I quite like the atmosphere of many people doing silly things to the sound of modern 'music'—unmusical but with a strange rhythm, so that I can imagine people liking it; but not the stuff where the noises are ugly and there is no rhythm. Hot and sticky to bed.

Tuesday 9th

Periods as ever, with an explosion of various chemicals in Chemi affecting my neck, and of molten lead in Physics, which covered H's clothes, face, Stony-Smith's coat, and me on face and clothes a bit. Indoor JTC—maps and Sten [gun] *...*

Music was not very encouraging, due to bad blowing and bad stops. I must get over the initial period of noise making so that it becomes music. In the evening there was a lecture by Capt. Knight on eagles which—despite an unpleasant affected accent— was very good …

Russians have captured important town of Kursk plus garrison and supplies.

Saturday 13th

Another Saturday. Usual sort of bad hockey game 2nd, PSN ref, me wing, and I was very glad when it was over …

Music Recital: Taylor, after a dissertation on the power of the Modern Trinity—Press, Radio, Cinema—played Bach, quite nice.

A very poor and silly Debate 'This House believes in the survival of the fittest'. I made a poor but not silly speech.

Monday 15th

… we did the headless frog experiment. A 2-volt current down the spine, however, made it cease work.

Works were digging on the [school potato] *plot; I enjoyed it—I always like digging—we went on despite two very wet and windy hail storms.*

Wednesday 17th

Kharkov has fallen, so hopes of German recoveries they may have had are somewhat blasted. Our gallant American allies in Tunis have lost three airfields and several thousand men as Rommel advances.

Soc. Soc. was on elevating London children's characters with clubs and camps—some quite good ideas but a very stupid old fellow [who gave the lecture]. *I asked if he "did not think it more important to change the schools which produce the bad characters than to change the bad characters which the schools have produced", which I thought was neat. His suggestion was a twelve hour day for teachers and the abolition of the Teachers' Union.*

Thursday 18th

... I saw [PSN's] *letter being sent to parents re: Penzance potatoes* [proposing that a school workforce should help lift a farm crop], *slimy—the idea being to give a good impression of public schools. A bad one* [i.e. bad reason]. *Profits and money saved on food to Newquay scholarship, perhaps 7/- to us. I would ask if my earnings could not go to something better ... it being unlikely that public schools would continue.*

Beveridge report debate [in Parliament] *has gone two days. ... the House is very eager about getting on with it—it looks like a crisis, and govt. defeat if they don't give ...*

Sir William Beveridge had been a civil servant with a particular interest in employment before going on to be Director of the London School of Economics in 1919. In the 1930s he played a part in helping German-Jewish academics to come to the UK.

His report, published in 1942, provided an outline for the reform of employment and social security. His proposals were not popular with the Conservatives, and the publication and debate on the proposals was delayed. It became an important focus of political concern. He argued that the serious poverty endured by so many in the 1930s could be abolished by a universal system of insurance, and public support for the proposals was a main reason for the success of the Labour Party in the 1945 election. It provided the basic structure of the Welfare State which the Labour Government put into operation in the immediate post-war years.

Friday 19th

... The House of Commons rejected the Labour amendment [not to postpone proposed improvements in social security] *by 230–119 (approx.) The biggest govt. opposition yet. One can see the govt. point of view, just, though I don't agree, but one feels that the reasons given for the delay aren't the only ones.*

We had a lecture on the Indian Army by a real one; no gs in 'ings', and what a lot we've done for India, and how the trouble is only caused by a few agitators etc. etc. ...

Monday 22nd

... welcome letter from Mommy at Oxford. No houses [to be found there] *at all for two years—rather depressing. Martin came down* [home] *for a day awfully tired again.*

Daddy replied to the slimy circular on Penzance potatoes like this "Potatoes, I think lifting them is a social necessity". Good! They had tea with Sir William Beveridge who is not too unsatisfied with reception [of his report].

My father was visiting Oxford following his appointment as the first Prof. of Social Medicine. Beveridge, now the Master of University College, was welcoming, and lent us his house while he was away.

Wednesday 24th
Soc. Soc. was the Bishop of Truro on 'Vocation in life with special reference to the clergyman'. ... He spoke at length, grinning broadly, emphasised the leisure and cultural attractions of the C. of E., almost forgetting to mention service at all but remembering income—I was rather disgusted and eventually rather bored ...

Thursday 25th
... Discussion of theology at lunch. Wood has changed a lot since I was his friend—what a long time ago that seems now! He is now an atheist, a disciple of Dunne's [J.W. Dunne produced an influential theory about time and reality]. *Mullins is just as foolish as ever, and says of course you won't find God until you put him first—i.e. until you believe in him. He's a maniac.*

Saturday 27th
Mr. Stony-Smith has infinite capabilities for talking the whole period on Physics excluding anything related to humour or humanity, and I feel bored and annoyed in his periods. ... Mr. Taylor did a copy of the 'Daily Worker' with his English set ...

Sunday 28th
Roger and I had made plans for an expedition to Porth, so of course Max chose him for rolling the by-our-lady [bloody] [cricket] *pitch. ... In a bit of a temper I went off for a bike ride along the cliffs past Porth, and solitude and silence improved me. Gulls and jackdaws are already congregating, and I saw a raven several times. Also two women marooned on a rocky island, the tide still coming in. It would not have been nearly covered, and they seemed quite happy.*

... played the gramophone and read part of 'Cripps, Advocate and Rebel' by Patricia Strauss ...

Cripps, a lawyer, was a left-wing (initially pro-Communist) Labour MP, and a friend of leaders of the Indian Congress Party. It was as a result of his views and contacts that he was made ambassador to Moscow 1940-1942, and then was involved in the mission to India described before.

March

Tuesday 2nd
Sixteen years have passed since first I saw this earth. Today was not an inspiring anniversary—a dull grey day with dull, grey periods and JTC. A letter from Margaret ... promising a gramophone record, and letters from Mommy and Daddy, cheered it up a lot, so did the parkin which came by parcel post.

Wednesday 3rd
... News [received of a] *schools conference ... at Cheltenham; I think I might go despite missing a week of home ...*

Wattie met Jane C by arrangement—L is not keen on me despite rumours to the effect, she's busy with four already! Ah me.

Soc. Soc. was a sickening major (rumour says of the Salvation Army!) on the Good done by the British. He gave quite impressive facts, but also asserted that good colonisation was a British monopoly; we've a divine mission and colonised for humanitarian not economic motives. He evaded skilfully, if untruthfully, the barrage of hostile questions.

Thursday 4th
I fired 2 rounds Sten [gun] *in the afternoon ...*

Wrote to Cheltenham ... and also am writing thing on train journey back after the play [the journey to Glatting at the end of last term]—*Kelly has set four preps to produce literature for next Truro festival. Wrote amusing (to me) speech against Free Trade—making my sympathies obvious.*

Friday 5th
News—Jap convoy of 8 transports and 10 warships completely destroyed off New Guinea, also some 60 aircraft. For the loss of three planes, so the story goes ...

Nasty accident in London during alert—people entering tube when woman in front tripped, all fell on her, people behind pushed, and 167 people or so were crushed or suffocated with 70 injured. Horrible. No panic, anyhow before tripping.

... Map reading and compass work was interesting in JTC ...

Saturday 6th
... There was a debate, with outside speakers—two RAF men proposing and two Army men opposing—that 'In the opinion of this house, Parliamentary government is unsuited to post-war needs'. Both RAF men were exceedingly good and convincing—the usual points about the whip system, the electoral system, the out-of-dateness of the organisation, and the terrible failures of the last few years. The opposition brought forward British compromise and little else. A very good debate—I did not speak as little was left to say. The motion was carried 31–26, there being some 9 RAF visitors—the most deplorable apathy of the school is apparent [from the numbers] ...

Monday 8th
... another team jaw and another house match—in which after a hard fought battle we were defeated ... and I did not over-disgrace myself.

Letters from Mommy—Beveridge has offered us his house while he is in America—very nice of him.

Max announced that anyone in the A block might attend a meeting on Russia in the town at 8 o'clock ... I went. Also came 4 dayboys (just for the smoke). ... He [the lecturer] *was speaking primarily from the religious point of view, and was I think very fair.*

Back and food—while eating this we learnt from the 'skiv' Daisy that her wages for working 6.30 [am]*—10.30* [pm] *are £1 1sh 8d per week. The maids get the lordly sum of 19/2 ...*

Tuesday 9th
Am reading 'Between the lines'—a book on the newspaper propaganda, by D-T (Mr. Denys Thompson, late master here)—very good ...

Thompson became a prominent critic and educationalist.

Saturday 13th
I went down to town, bought a book 'Red Star over China' by Edgar Snow, about Chinese communists and the Red Army there.

... to the dentist; the hole I went for wasn't but she found two others ...

Then up to the Pentire to help Cook work the projector for a school film 'The Lady vanishes'. A good film, if melodramatic in parts, and the only hitch was a bust last reel. Then putting things away ...

Sunday 14th
... I read Somerset Maugham's 'Cakes and Ale'—a good but not great novel—during chapel ...

Not good news—Russians pushed back from Kharkov. Oh God—if there was one.

I am wondering about Communism. I agree with most of its ethical concepts, I think I agree that ends justify means, and I think men can judge that; but I am not so sure about, for instance, their attitude to family life. I do believe a form of it holds the future. But I don't entirely identify the British Communist party with Communism. Life is somewhat complex but worth living.

Thursday 18th
... Heard from Cheltenham. ... I'm in commission [group] *on 'Planning in the USSR'. Am looking forward to this a lot.*

Argument with Mullins—he favoured Franco because he might restore the monarchy—anger overcame my reason somewhat.

Friday 19th
... House game, junior team and others, quite good but very hot and too long.

Books from lecture other day arrived—'Christian approach to Communism' [by Tiran Nersoyan, an Armenian Christian priest in America]*—which seems very interesting.*

Gramophone after tea—2nd Movement 'Clock' Haydn is very lovely. I wish I could write down everything I think.

Saturday 20th

… I read 'Christian --- Communism' in English—very concentrated and deep, which defies first reading—but all the more satisfying when read.

… After tea I went out by myself on bike to the Gannel—a lovely hazy blue evening with a yellow sunset on the water, the tide being right in. Solitude is enjoyable too for itself. Otherwise I listened to the gramophone …

Quite good games after supper. Have finished Edgar Snow book on Red China—I'd like recent news.

Sunday 21st

Roger and I went far up Penpoll, finding nice fields and thickets, hearing the chiff chaff, and seeing a common snipe, brown owl and the pair of buzzards. A good morning. Back late for JTC (not sorry to miss it) with king cups and catkins to supplement the blackthorn decoration in our room.

... at nine o'clock the Prime Minister speaking. At 9.20, just as he got interesting, we were sent to bed, to my intense annoyance; and with the result of profanity and bitter reflections on the democratic nature of this x school, country and world.

Our basin gave up the ghost and parted in twain, the front falling on the floor and, being full of water, drenching the study below ...

Monday 22nd

... a school lecture on the war by Capt. Gammon MP. Quite good, in fact very good on the war, but outrageous on the freedom under the Union Jack (it must also be symbolic of power), and untruthful or uninformed about conditions of labour in the USSR—bayonets, told where and how

to work etc.—I've a good mind to write to him asking why, as he left immediately after that statement. 14,000 extra deaths per day of war.

Tuesday 23rd

… My last music lesson this term with my friend Mr. Taylor—a nice man. The school play should soon be casted—I wonder what he'll put me as. Ambitiously I hope for Malcolm or Banquo—if I'm capable, that is.

… Farfield house play in the evening—'It pays to advertise'—a very amusing very well acted farce; enjoyable …

Thursday 25th

The fateful day of Cert. A., which consisted of drill, drilling, map reading, weapon training, lunch, long pause, tactics. Anyhow, the result ... was a pass in parts I and II for me and most others.

After prep was the Howson's House play (who should come with Dartford but Scylla Cavell—she smiled and so did I, somewhat half-heartedly). The play was quite magnificent, with superb acting. ... Very hair raising, with much good comic relief …

Friday 26th

I had to show an old boy (35 years old) round the grounds—including a typical Pentire study and the Pentire roof, which appalled him. Little news …

I began to read again Remarque's 'Flotsam'—a book which impresses me more for its sadness and its beauty each time I read it.

Sunday 28th

… up to Pentire to set up the projector. … thread the first film. The films shown were 'Tawny Owl'—good; 'The Crawl'—good under-water photography and interesting; 'This was England' … and 'OHMS'—long sob stuff, amusing if taken the right way. Machine got very hot and refused to work three times …

to Glatting

Tuesday 30th
Up at 4.45, pack, breakfast, feeling happy, and then a long wait in the hall. At 5.40 we rang the bus station to find that no bus had materialised, and as the train was six-five, most started to walk ... only 39 there [in time]. *Hence a very comfortable journey.*

We contacted and chatted two Benenden acquaintances ... which was quite a welcome distraction ... luckily PSN missed the train and we had only S …

I went Underground to Victoria, bought my ticket, sweet ration and a paper, eat half the sweet ration, had a panic about having lost the ticket but found it with the chocolate (--ate half the ticket--), read the paper and boarded the 4.18.

On the way from the station my mother softened the news that my dog Tinker had been shot—it was impossible to get meat for him—with the news that John was home.

... Poor old Tinker has been done in, as his ears got worse and worse, but, joy of joys and dream of dreams, John arrived this morning!! He spent six weeks on the way, and his delayed cable and letters never arrived. He was there, very brown and different to what I remember, probably because I've changed a lot …

Daddy can manage mental work quite well, but has not improved much physically, but he is happy and on the whole OK. God it's grand to be home!

Wednesday 31st
Nora left today for a course in nursing in Tooting—she has improved tremendously from her last job …

After chatting by the fire, John and I left Daddy and went out for a brisk walk in the rain—the weather John dreamt of in Egypt. We talked a lot and I now know him better than ever before—because I'm no longer a much younger brother with quite different interests.

Mommy got back [from Tooting] *about eight o'clock; we talked happily round the fire. I'm sure family life is one of the best things in life.*

April

Thursday 1st
... Mommy, John and I went down to the village to shop, John and I going to see Mrs. Francis—who was very thrilled to see him. Then we went to the shop where hungry Canadians passing by had finished all unrationed food, and walked back ...

We're doing quite well in Tunisia, lull on Russian front, Americans are competing with Goebbels in claims. Three Canadians came in at about 9 o'clock, having come on foot from Eastbourne with very few meals in three days. We gave them 2 eggs and most of our bread, for which they were very grateful—they were to leave for Lewes at 1 o'clock.

John is not enthusiastic about the Russians—I think he saw released Poles. I don't doubt we think too much of them, but that will counteract the usual line—and there are the seeds of very great good there.

Polish troops captured by the Russians at the time of the invasion and partition of their country were being sent by way of the Middle East to join the army in North Africa.

John's philosophy is one hand for yourself and one for the ship, that being more for the ship than is given by most. He also believes ... that things always come right in the end, so don't be discouraged. He's a nice brother anyhow.

Friday 2nd
John went up to London, to see the Admiralty, Margaret and Melody. Apart from the Admiralty they are all coming here tomorrow ...

I spent some time in my house fluting and reading up the Webb's book [on Russia] *for the Conference. Before lunch I went with Daddy to see the Bones, whose son Colin is dying of a cerebral tumour (inoperable)—I went in with Daddy—the first person I've seen desperately ill. He was shrunk and semi-paralysed, with a terrible squint and unable to talk; his big toe curved up when the sole of the foot was tickled. Also he had bedsores. My first patient—unpleasant, but much worse for the parents than for him—their only child.*

After tea we went up the Gully at the bottom of the green slope and picked primroses and violets—lovely ones …

Saturday 3rd

A lovely still sunny day. I did a little reading and fluting, then Daddy and I went to the signpost and waited peacefully until John and Margaret eventually appeared, when we walked back with them …

After lunch we lay in the sun, and Melody came by the 3.47. After tea I went for a walk with Margaret—she didn't enjoy yesterday with John, I think she refused to because they spent so much—I told her she took herself too seriously. She's miserable because John likes that sort of thing …

Sunday 4th

A lovely clear sunny day, made much happier for all by the announcement of John's engagement to Melody. I thoroughly approve of my new sister-in-law elect (right word?). They are to be married in London next Saturday … with a short party in Melody's flat, and a honeymoon at her house at Wittering. Daddy and Mommy are so happy too. Unfortunately I probably won't get up for the wedding from Cheltenham.

We spent a very happy day, having taken a picnic lunch and tea up to the chalk pit with Daddy in the car (no hills allowed)—the excuse being to fetch chicken food from Shiner …

to Cheltenham

Tuesday 6th

Went up to London with John. … we walked along the Embankment, John instructing me in the geography of London. We had lunch in Leicester Square, and then I took a tube to Paddington, wishing John a happy wedding—he's an awfully nice brother. ... My diary is now going to separate into (1) account of lectures etc. and (2) what I did the rest of the time.

The Inter-Schools Conference was organised by the Council for Education in World Citizenship. It had been founded just before the war to promote international understanding and co-operation, but most of its conferences focused on social reform, as exemplified by the speakers at this one.

John Boyd Orr was a research nutritionist, advocate of international planning of the use of food resources, and adviser to the Minister of Food.

Cecil Powell was a nuclear physicist and internationalist.

Ralph Wedgwood, who had been a railway manager, was an advocate of a world development plan, on the model of wartime Lease-Lend, run by an international economic council.

The following entries were written after the conference ended.

CHELTENHAM CONFERENCE

Tuesday 6th
Opened by Mr. D.L. Lipson MP Cheltenham—who said nothing worth recording.

Sir John Boyd Orr: 'Fighting for what?'
Civilisation has gone into a metamorphosis—the beginning of a new era. Inevitability of (i) World govt.—far distance had been annihilated by science—no boundaries. Finance has already become largely international.

Note FDR's food commission towards a world food policy. Trade expansion is not an end. A master plan for a new world is needed into which the others fit. ... Freedom from want for all men in all lands beginning with the elementary needs of (a) Food (statistics of inefficiency of present diets) (b) shelter (similar statistics relating to environment generally).

There is no <u>*need*</u> *for unemployment. Is the plan materialistic? Idealism essential—rich countries must make sacrifices. People who are now comfortable do not like change—youth's drive and courage is needed.*

Wednesday 7th
Science and Society, Dr. Cecil Powell.
A decisive epoch has come in man's history as a result of the control over nature by science. The burden of labour can be lifted from mankind. The problem is the establishment of a society where science can be utilised to benefit all the people—but we must not forget present danger in our contemplation of the future. Deal in two themes:

(1) Application of scientific method to every phase of human life. Science must be applied to the ordering of science. The scientific method is the objective study of the thing itself. The emphasis has been too much on the technical, not social side. Science's benefits are not more fully enjoyed only because of conservatism.

Will international govt. come? By generalising from the past and deducing laws and drawing conclusions, which enable us to understand the direction of human society, we can see a definite tendency towards internationalism—parts of world more interdependent. 'Ask not for whom the bell tolls, it tolls for thee'.

(2) Relationship of scientist to society. If we are going to apply science to every aspect of our affairs, we must increase time spent on it in schools and universities, especially on learning the scientific method. When industries develop as a result of scientific discovery, more scientists are drawn into industry.

Today research is no longer individual, the apparatus cannot be made without industry; people of science, as was the case with industry, are becoming collectivised. Only if the state acts as the patron of scientists can science advance—but scientists must learn to work in teams. Science must be subject to social control.

Economic problems, Sir Ralph Wedgewood …
Industry will be different. … Workers still have very little interest or influence in the management of industry. There is a monopoly

tendency—combination not competition. Monopolies are interested in the producers—the consumers must be represented in the management of industry. Production must be subject to public criticism, workers must influence control. … Shareholders not to be dispensed with—state control increasingly, but not ownership …

Brief Diary of Life at Cheltenham.
When I arrived at the college I was directed to the hall by two girls who later were prominent adversaries in the commission. In the hall I was taken in tow by a fellow called John ... from Glasgow Academy—a lovely accent … [and met] *two Hertford Grammar School blokes. ... People generally were secondary school, and very friendly and quite as well educated as me—I don't know why Mommy and Daddy spend £130 a year on me.*

In our free time we went about together, and with four girls from a Dorset secondary school. I took one of them to the flicks—'Thunder Rock'—a very fine film; she was very quiet and kind and quite good looking—but it took me four days to find that these still waters did not run deep as I had hoped; but she was quite a pleasant puddle, though I'd have liked to get to know more interesting people really—there were plenty.

The conference was predominantly socialist, a sprinkling of Christian preachers, one anarchist, one ardent federal unionist, very many atheists of various types. ... We had a good discussion in the dormitory on atheism—in which I was honoured by being the first convincing atheist a bloke had ever met.

[On the train to Oxford, where my parents were staying] *I got into a coach with two Oxford conference girls—both Socialists, one an Austrian refugee—rather nice. We talked politics and agreed on them—and were joined by a progressive woman who knew of the conferences. The other occupants were the latter's daughter, doing medicine, and a woman reading a book on the USSR—a very progressive compartment!*

at Oxford

Monday 12th
Mommy was waiting on the platform—had been for a long time. We caught a bus (crowded as everything is) and had lunch in a British Restaurant …

The widely available British Restaurants sold simple, reasonable food at basic prices and did not take coupons from one's ration book.

We then bussed to Daddy's department and took him to a flick—quite funny—Arthur Askey, 'King Arthur was a gentleman'; and an excellent newsreel of the fighting at Mareth [Tunisia]*—rather ghastly.*

We boarded a taxi in the Broad and collected luggage from Daddy's depart. and the hotel where they had been staying. Then to 49 High Street—our digs [they had been staying in a rather expensive hotel]. *The first impression (fully confirmed) was unfavourable—the hall smelled of dog and socks, and we were on the top floor—bad for Daddy* [with his angina]. *The rooms were little attics, we get only breakfast, and the charge is 9/6 per night.*

We had supper out and returned early to bed—Mommy is not feeling too well and her depression is aggravated by these digs …

Tuesday 13th
… I spent the morning exploring Oxford—not awfully successfully, as I walked out along the Banbury Rd getting nowhere—still it was pleasantly sunny …

We went out (perforce) to lunch … then returned to the digs meeting Margaret C [sister Margaret's friend]. *… Margaret and I having failed to get a boat, we went through Magdalen—Addison's walk—and sat peacefully by the river in the sun, watching jackdaws and a magpie quarrel …*

We had a goodish supper of rice and curried lentils and papar at the Indian Restaurant …

Wednesday 14th

I spent the morning shopping and seeing an exhibition of Paul Nash 'Applied Design' at the Ashmolean; his ordinary designs were nice, but dirty old bits of map and snakeskin and bark are just silly—we were very openly irreverent—I liked one painting, the forest of Dean.

Then we waited for Daddy at Municipal Restaurant No. 9 [another British Restaurant], *opposite Somerville , and after queueing got a quite good but chilly lunch. Mommy went back home, still gloomy and unfit, I basked with Daddy in the park for a short time and then went with him to his department ... meeting an old friend ... in the RAMC.*

I went home and tried to cheer Mommy up. ... The hag (our landlady) delivered a message: Mrs. Summers [an old friend] *wanted Daddy to ring up, she was worried about her son. She* [the landlady] *would not let Daddy use the phone—it would disturb her dogs! so Daddy had to cross to the Eastgate. This incident aggravated the situation, Mommy and Daddy were both rather depressed and not too well.*

Thursday 15th

... Daddy went up to London; Mommy and I did a little shopping, and walked through the Christ Church meadows by the Cher[well]*—a lovely part. We returned for lunch at Restaurant no. 8 (St. Aldates), then I went off to the War Memorial* [to go sailing with Margaret C], *leaving Mommy to go lonesomely to the Park.*

I ... arrived back at the digs at 6 o'clock—Daddy's train was at 6.15 so I decided to wait there for them. I read for some time, and then went to the Virgin Mary's church, to find that it was seven fifteen. This somewhat distressed me, but I presumed that Daddy had missed his train. I waited for the buses watching all those from the station, then tried unsuccessfully to ring up the station about train times, and then anxiously took a bus to the station, leaving a note to the effect in the digs. There I found no Mommy, and 7.50 train had come and gone sometime before. Back running to the flat—no one. I was by now in an almighty flap, for I was sure that Mommy would have come and told me had Daddy missed both trains, and if he had come, then why hadn't they returned to take me out to supper?

Desperate, I tried to ring up Margaret [Clifton], *being the only person I knew in Oxford—but they were not in the book. Now hopelessly distrait, I ran to the police station who were unsympathetically unhelpful ...*

A lady in the digs was very helpful and comforting when I somewhat tearfully (I know it all sounds damn silly now, but there I was in a strange town with my parents apparently quite vanished) confessed my trouble. Unhopefully, I left the digs to walk to the station—and there they were walking towards me! I felt sick and cried from relief. The explanation was quite simple—the only one of many dramatic, lurid and painful possibilities that I had not considered. They had thought that I was staying out to supper, and so when Daddy arrived they had caught a bus out to Abingdon and had had supper there—very enjoyable. My two hours of anguish and my exposure to the contempt of others less affectionate or less sensitive than our family had been—as is usually the case—unnecessary.

Friday 16th

... Mommy and I went to Folly Bridge and got a punt. We went up the Cherwell—a lovely little river and good for punting—which I gradually improved at. We decided to go up and fetch Daddy and food to the punt, contrary to our previous decision. We got to 'Parson's Pleasure' [male-only bathing in this section of river], *where I rested until Mommy reappeared with Daddy and lunch. Kingfisher flew past as we ate our food, moored to the bank in dappled sunlight and great contentment ...*

We ... went three doors along [from our digs] *to 'The Golden Kettle' for tea ... the manageress was the sympathetic lodger of last night—shyness of my state then prevented me from being duly grateful ...*

The last entries demonstrate a number of traits which I still recognise as aspects of my nature. My attachment to my parents was linked with a rather morbid concern. Most of my references to my mother concerned her vulnerability, her mood or her health; and since my father had developed angina I was naturally anxious that he might have another heart attack, and was concerned about how stressful situations might affect him. My own dependent needs were usually met indirectly by being a helpful person, but on this occasion my vulnerability found a childish expression.

to Glatting

Monday 19th
[via London] … *we went to see* [Nora]*—a long tram and bus ride to Tooting Broadway. She was in bed with fear—of people and new things and her lack of book knowledge—her only escape, and the only way she becomes important, is by illness, and she probably convinces herself that she is ill.*

She wanted to give hospital nursing up, but Mommy, after talking to the Matron who was very understanding and sympathetic, told her she must at least try it first—Mommy was very kind but very firm. Poor old Nora—life can't be easy thanks to that damn midwife doctor [she was born after a long difficult labour and suffered minor brain damage] …

at Glatting

Wednesday 21st
Margaret and I went for a long walk—all day with lunch. We went first past Bishop's clump along the North edge of the downs. ... Eventually where a N–S line of trees was, we stopped and ate lunch—near a big crater.

Then we turned south, and followed a long path down the valley and up the other side—containing tileless stone farm buildings and many mortar bombs etc. Also large white boards like this about 30ft high. At the top we rested in the sun for a while ... and we learnt that we had been through a military range from a notice on the other side: 'W D DANGER. Artillery range. Dangerous when the red flag is flying. Any objects you touch may explode killing you and others.' The way we had come in had no notices or obstructions.

We pressed on through a little village with a nice church on the Singleton road, and up through beechwoods. ... Here we found ourselves

surrounded by well camouflaged Canadians, one of whom jokingly said "Do you know you're liable to get shot walking in front of us like that". We risked it as they were only using blanks.

... cauliflower cheese for supper, and outburst from Mommy on our lack of hilarity, which we mollified eventually.

Infantry are attacking, Enfidaville [Tunisia] *taken, 3 mountain ranges ahead—God what a prospect!*

Thursday 22nd

A grey day, with rain a lot of the time. I spent the morning here in the hut, and reading 'Macbeth'. Martin's colleague's sister ... Mrs. someone—anyhow a doctor—came to lunch and tea, to talk about a job with Duddy ...

... Daddy experienced one of life's greatest joys—listening to a nightingale while lying in a hot bath. I heard three I think later on—lovely them being so near this year.

Friday 23rd

... a lazy afternoon by Daddy's fire reading Lilliput and 'World Education in Science and Ethics'—a grand book. Good statistics too; about juvenile delinquency—the number per 1000 in Liverpool for state schools was 21, C. of E. schools 35, and Roman Catholic schools 45.

... Mommy fetched sister Melody from the station. She said she'd heard I'd had a nice conference—I replied "I hear you had quite a nice wedding"—"Yes, we quite enjoyed it" ...

Sunday 25th

... I fluted, and Mommy and Daddy came out to my house, and we walked to the deserted orchard—where there were fewer orchids than we expected, most being very early this year. After this we talked about Jews, and then I did the rabbits. Supper was earlyish, and then John and Melody went off in the car to Petworth ...

I wonder if John is so entirely un-idealistic as he sounds—he thinks it [a better future] *will come without working for it. After all, most of the happiness today is owed to people who thought the future was their business, and we jolly well ought to pay back our debt by spending some time on the next generations.*

Monday 26th

... I went down to the village in the afternoon and fetched the paper from Mrs. Francis—who told the latest gossip, such as the editor of Picture Post walking down the road holding a bottle in his hand wandering from side to side—ought to write to Picture Post about it! Though Mrs. Francis' gossip is not entirely reliable ...

On the 30 secs. allowed us by the [radio] *battery we heard that USSR had broken off diplomatic relations with the Polish Govt.* [in exile] *in this country—which has been consistently and violently anti-Soviet.*

Old and complex enmities had been exacerbated by German reports, later clearly validated, of the Katyn massacre of Polish officers by the Russians in 1939-1940.

Wednesday 28th

Last day at Glatting ... Margaret helped me carry the canoe to the lake, to see if it was worth taking to Oxford—it did float high enough for a quiet river like the Cher or Isis. Then we went for a goat walk.

... off on cycles to the Holdings for tea. I spoke very little—don't feel sociable today at all, rather cross. Silly how moods come and go. Maybe because the 30th is in two days.

to Oxford

Thursday 29th

A hectic departure from Glatting, but an uneventful and fairly comfortable train journey to London. Then by Taxi to Paddington, while Margaret biked perilously through a Canadian army convoy. ... During the journey I read with great interest 'The RAF in Russia' [H. Griffith, 1943].

We ... taxied to the Master's [William Beveridge] *Lodgings, Univ. ... All beautifully prepared for us; Margot Klein* [his housekeeper] *very helpful and cheerful, and Mommy was very relieved and pleased. Tea was brought (!) to us, and then we collected parcels and things to the house.*

I read rapidly Saki's 'The unbearable Bassington'—witty and clever. Sad last-night feeling …

to Newquay

Friday 30th

... goodbye to Mommy. ... Not too happy, but it is better to have them both less ill and better housed.

I got on the school train, all the same damned faces of which only Roger's was really welcome. Soon all the damned dirty jokes. What an anti-climax after meeting all the thinking people at the conference. I read most of the journey D.H. Lawrence's 'The Virgin and the Gypsy', which did not strike me as being sufficiently immoral to warrant banning in the school—better than many other novels in that respect—but not very inspiring …

I share now with Wallop [CMGS—youngest Smith. The Smith brothers were nicknamed Crash, Bang and Wallop, but only the latter stuck] *and Wood which might be nice …*

My parting from home was softer than usual, but I think I am fonder of Mommy—and even more of Daddy, whom before I scarcely knew—than I have ever been. Indeed I am fortunate in my parents—they are well chosen!

May

Saturday 1st

… Roger and I set off Gannelwards and spent a sunny hour talking. He is deciding not to join up [the call-up of a medical student could be deferred]*—for he would probably not qualify till 30 yrs old—which is awful late for marriage and for medicine. I begin to think I will not join probably, because it would rather wreck the career, and I think I am as much use to the society as a future doctor as I would be a sailor …*

Monday 3rd
… I fetched a JTC wireless set from Pentire, for my practice and familiarisation [I was now in the signalling section and involved in maintaining a radio link with the Pentire hotel]. *Then mowing, and then a Biology extra, 6–8, cockroaches, including the setting of the mouthparts thereof …*

Tuesday 4th
… established radio contact with PENtire (link sign Peter Easy Nan). … I get on pretty well with my study mates, I think—quite OK.
After tea a short rehearsal [Macbeth]. *I learnt after Prep my parts for I ii and I iv—about 20 lines in all.*

Wednesday 5th
... JTC—10 mins. W/T [wireless telegraphy], *then lectures to beginners and Cadre pl.* [platoon] *on procedure and organisation; I think I will be a permanent signaller—far more fun than drill.*
Afternoon periods—very interesting electronic structure in Chemistry, too complex Physics …
After tea helped B lay telephone line, fluted and listened to gramophone.
Soviet forces near Novorissisk, French, American, 1st Army near Tunis and Bizerta.

Thursday 6th
... A mine was sighted ... which was eventually detonated by a coastguard at 9.25 off Splash Point, to the detriment of seven Pentire and two Bay windows—the former blew in, the latter out, no casualties …

Saturday 8th
First class gale blowing, grey, wind and surf a mile out. Struggle walking, and very heavy showers …
Rehearsal after prayers which went pretty well, and I like my part [Malcolm]. *The lone scene with Macduff has been suitably shortened.*

This is definitely Roger's last term, as he's going to a Scottish University to read medicine and can't take 1st MB from school. Next year will be lonely—but busy if I'm to get my schol[arship to Oxford].

Sunday 9th
The gale remained, diminishing, but there was brilliant sunshine … [Roger and I] *did a rock climb, and watched glorious waves on W. Pentire. One cove was thick with cream, breaking into froth like lace, into which waves roared breaking over a 30 ft islet—grand …*

A boring service, but as in divinity prep, I got on quite well with 'Macbeth'.

> *Tomorrow and tomorrow and tomorrow*
> *Creeps in its petty pace …*

Monday 10th
Tunis and Bizerta fell on Saturday—great news. Russo–Polish squabble continues. ... After tea up for a successful rehearsal. I brought the house down successfully by, when Macduff says "Your royal father's murdered", saying "Oh! by whom?" in a bored matter-of-fact way. These brighten already brightish rehearsals.

... a jaw from Max on reading in chapel. I said I never asked to go to chapel, he said I wasn't asked to come to the school; I said it did not distract people, he said it did; I said it didn't and anyway most of them wanted to be. He said "well anyway, I want it to stop", to which I made no reply. Nor will it.

Tuesday 11th
… There is a literary competition at the Truro Festival this year—I'm sending in three things, an account (not true in detail) of the night train journey back for last Christmas; one 'They have their reward'—short, humorous article; and 'Stephen dies', three sides—can't explain plot except by reproducing it. Taylor had seen the train one which was done in form last term, and thought it was quite good. Fun writing, when there's time.

Thursday 13th

Africa cleared!! Hurray for that anyway. Europe—when?

The day cleared up to warm afternoon and clear lovely evening. In Leagues [non-serious cricket] *I excelled myself, bowling* [Mr.] *Dodd (satisfaction!) and two others, and making 41! ... I almost enjoy leagues, but I don't think cricket matters, and it's inclined to be a bore, so I couldn't do it seriously (speak above in excited whisper for correct effect).*

Friday 14th

Two big bomber raids last two nights. 1,000 tons type. 35 [planes lost] *each time about. What a hellish but necessary business …*

JTC was lamp signalling on the headland—good fun, practice and interesting …

Saturday 15th

... 'Wings for victory week' parade [part of a national fund-raising campaign]. *March down to games ground, where long wait, then the procession through the town. Grand sunny day, rather sweaty and a bruised left collar bone, but not too bad.*

Remarks from the crowd and other soldiers varied from "Coo! The Norfolks!" (two tones of voice—pleased surprise and contempt) [coming from Norfolk, the school Training Corps wore their regimental cap badge] *to "Garn, they're only kids", and mostly "'Ome Guard", with an occasional "Greshams" …*

After tea to Baker's Folly, where we got talking to two soldiers who'd been in the parade—brencarriers—Northants Regiment. One was keen on and knew a lot about birds—he was collecting eggs (leaving one per nest) for eating purposes at the time. We talked for some time and gave him an address so that he could write for an NHS report.

... a fairly OK rehearsal—Macbeth, recovered from measles, arrives next week.

Monday 17th

... Divers jaws to house by Max. I think the school system is wrong because, public opinion [i.e. the pupils] *having no say, nobody troubles about the organisation of their community. An autocratic rule is useless to train democrats—I think school councils in each form and for the whole school are the answer; no executive power except in its own concern would be necessary even—but to have opinions which pass unnoticed or, worse, to develop no opinions, is wrong, I'm sure.*

Have just read 'Children of the Soviet Union' ['Children in the Soviet Union', pamphlet by Beatrice King 1941] *which impressed me a lot.*

Tuesday 18th

More sun, with East wind. An unsuccessful Music period—why I don't know—feeling off. ... I went to read C. Day Lewis by Splash Point in the sun. 'Overtures to Death', 'The Nabara' and 'Newsreel' impressed me most—I like his poetry.

To continue last night's outburst on school government—I think 'socialist competition' between forms would be excellent (... but the general environment here has already worked it's way into people, and it probably would not be a success). The open criticism in form would be most healthy, I feel—and the relation between staff and pupils in the Soviet Union seemed much healthier than here ...

And now to bed—and autocratic rule from above decrees it, but I don't mind this one as it's based on medical reasons!

Wednesday 19th

Letter from Nora (yesterday) and Mommy—she's had to give up nursing. Poor girl, she is so terrified of other people—no self-confidence. Still, I hope she's happy with children. Daddy is going to enter me for a medical student at Christ Church, and I am going to work harder and harder, and I hope I'll get a ruddy scholarship in the end. Mommy has already found an exhausting job, so any hope of her getting fat and rested are blasted—she's visiting homes of service men for some society and the Citizen's Advice Bureau.

... being free after tea I went out and read 'Poems of this War' by Baker's Folly wall. Some I liked. Feel uncomfortable and unsettled today ...

Saturday 22nd

News—Announced from Moscow that the 3rd International has disbanded itself on the proposal of the executive, due to the impossibility of meeting in war time. [It] *calls on its followers to exert 'utmost effort' towards end of fascist tyranny. This may be regarded by some as an admission of failure, or as the removal of domination of the world CP by one country—supposed to be using it for its own ends. I don't know quite how to look at it, being ill-informed.*

... biked down town ... and shopped—chocolate, pencils and brake cable for Wood. Then my job—standing by a model Spitfire, the propeller of which could be turned, and in front of a 1d in the slot machine for the War Effort [part of 'Wings for Victory Week']. *I had at first a small boy to turn the prop, but I let him go with a piece of chocolate as his hands were blistering. About 12 orphans passed and all had a turn on the wheel. Quite amusing.*

... Then back seeing a query query young skua—strange bird ... very aft legs, used wings in diving. If it is a young skua it really has no business to be here, but strong winds may have blown it.

... Got permission to take lunch out tomorrow. Myra Hess is playing in the town, but seats are 5/- reserved or 3/6 and I haven't really the cash—if it's raining I'll try to get in.

Myra Hess was an internationally famous pianist who gave popular 1/- lunch-time recitals at the National Gallery in London throughout the war.

Sunday 23rd

A holiday. Roger and I, as arranged, took lunch out ... with food and water and 'costumes de baigner' (wrong) artfully concealed. ... Down to the valley beyond Porth—onto the beach, where we bathed briefly ... Then up along the road to near Mawgan, where we cut down to the cliffs through hay and cornfields, all this in half sun—warm.

Here we discovered Beacon Cove, where I went years ago with Mr. Candler—a grand steep sided, real, romantic Cornish cove, caves galore, a stream coming from inside the cliff and stalacmites. The towering cliffs were awe-inspiring, and imparted a sense of foreboding.

We sat on a flat sheltered rock for lunch during which Roger, causing a shower of crumbs, shouted "choughs!" Sure enough, a pair flew over and we saw them collecting grass. ... Also during lunch three buzzards and a peregrine flew over—grand place.

After lunch we explored, bathed, and trotted around fairly naked among rocks, nests etc. Then rather sleepily back, along Watergate beach where Americans were playing baseball …

Monday 24th

Up in uniform [it was a JTC field day] ... *talk from Major Took (?) ... then some sort of* [signals] *demonstration. I concentrated on the wirelesses and pigeons. They had no.22s, a no.11, a no.18 (what a contrast to our hefty 8s) and (even more contrast) 38* [wireless models]. ... *We were acting as intercommunications with umpires—but it was raining and altogether unsuitable for V/S* [visual signalling, i.e. with flags or lamps]—*my only message I shouted.*

However, I quite enjoyed the battles with the elements while curling up the wires etc.—the day was cancelled before the conclusion due to excess of water from heaven …

I fluted and played some Petrushka—Stravinsky ballet music—rather fun …

Wednesday 26th

... Letters from Mommy and Daddy—Nora going (now gone) to nursery near Guildford—Mommy on to Glatting for a few days. I'd mentioned the possibilities of war service in my letter—they told me not to worry—I don't really, I think the final decision then [when I'm due for call-up] *will be made easier—if the war continues hard I will feel prickings of conscience …*

Friday 28th
... Argument in Divin[ity] *on jingoism of pamphlet read by PSN in chapel ...*

Kuban [in southern Russia] *fighting on again—strong Soviet attack. Lots of raids on Sicily and S. Italy.*

Monday 31st
... It is amazing how we have come to accept the air war—in one normal large raid we dropped 1,500 tons on a little place I'd not heard of, while 600 tons on London was a hell. It must be pretty damnable dropping them, but quite hellish under.

This is the beginning of my disquiet at the RAF's mass bombing campaign. A few public figures voiced concerns about it as the military effect remained uncertain, and the morality of targeting civilians as a main strategy was disputed, but the policy remained unchanged.

June

Tuesday 1st
Another wet day. More raid news, coal strike on in USA demanding $2 per day more—rather a big bill—both sides are, I expect, too fond of 'filthy lucre'.

... good and enjoyable music period—quite successful. After lunch, a run in the rain ... I played 'Eine kleine nachtmusik' twice. ... Music is a very great and lovely blessing here.

After consideration these are the opinions I have formed on the Comintern dissolution.
(1) Make America far more amenable to post-war co-operation.
(2) Have a very good effect on national C-Ps. They will consider far more sanely the background and suitable methods of (for) their own countries. ... I think there is far more chance of the CP here gaining influence now, after all suspicion of foreign control and money from Moscow is removed. It will become much more truly our CP to build on our own system ... the Russian Revolution wasn't Communism. ... I'm

wondering seriously about the YCL [Young Communist League] *for me.*

As for the question of CP–Labour Party affiliation ... the CP is essentially different to Labour, the latter is purely an electoral body with general agreement (woolly idea'd too) on policy in the terrible (they [the Labour Party] *regard it almost like that) eventuality of a Labour govt. coming to power. The CP, on the contrary, is a definite education—body of leaders with their prime interest the working class.*

Sunday 6th

By bike from Newquay to a farmer at Newbridge (near Penzance) for whom we lifted potatoes (others went by bus).

... hectic off with Roger, M and S. They went a good speed, the latter two having 3 speeds, with pauses for smokes (not me). ... then Roger's axle bust off. After much searching, and seeing the bus with others in whizz past, we found a garage with an extremely helpful man who fitted a new cone—there had only been 5 ball bearings in the wheel.

On, sunny, cheerful, to Hoyle. Then when the others were right ahead, Roger's tyre burst. ... found a man and bought an inner tube and pump, put it in, blew the pump connection, and failed to find any Cornishman willing to sell us half a loaf. Rather depressed we rode out. Roger on a flat tyre ... to Penzance, St. Michael's Mt. looking lovely, and up out of the town …

Monday 7th

... We arrived at eight, up the field, and dug and lifted potatoes behind a horse and plough with an energetic farmer. Hard work. 10 min. break at 10 with lovely creamy milk. ... Occasional rain ... Hard long day. But good supper.

Tuesday 8th

A similar day. Just about as wet. As hard work, welcome change in the morning weighing sacks for a GWR [Great Western Railway] *lorry. ... Then off with Roger, M and S to the woods, returning in song. Life here hard, hungry (we're adequately fed though) and on the whole enjoyable. Would like some sun.*

Wednesday 9th
Ditto. Better weather. Harder work. OK. More tired …

Thursday 10th
... Biking across the misty moor as usual before eight, but after a little rain it cleared to quite a decent day. ... after tea, usual walk and sing.

Friday 11th
Another good warm day. Work since Wednesday has really been pleasant and untiring. Mr. Prowse our farmer is a very nice man, in every way. He has treated us very well, and we have been given tea often (we provided the tealeaves) …

Saturday 12th
Our last working day, only half one. ... Then goodbye (really regretfully, with the prospect of back to prison soon) to Mr. Prowse and family.

We were free from 12.30, so (Mr. Prowse having given the party 10/- 'to buy a drink') off to Trengwainton [home of the Bolitho family]. *... at 7.45, off to Morfa (?) in Col. Bolitho's car (he is the Lord Lieutenant) where was a kittiwakerie. Quite unjustified but pleasant use of petrol. Grand place, where besides masses of nesting kittiwakes we saw a fulmar petrel, razorbill, shags etc. ... When we got back we asked the 'Bird'* [teacher in charge] *if we could go out to see the badgers, and to our amazement he said we could …*

Sunday 13th
The end of the happy interlude—happy despite 8½–¾ hours work each day and rain and little sanitation. ... We got paid—the pooled wages came to 9/6 each—which is OK. ... Rather tired we reached the dear old place ...

Walked [to chapel] *and back with Taylor, who very unfortunately is leaving after this term for the BBC. Life next year will not be jolly. ... I am an expectant uncle, good show—January …*

Tuesday 15th

... an enjoyable music period—with the prospect of terrible few more with Taylor ...

I haven't put down much news recently—nothing big in Russia; it was announced that all four of the Italian islands in the Sicilian narrows have now fallen. ... The only army casualty in the last was one man bitten by a donkey!

Saturday 19th

... up to the Pentire to try on play clothes and wigs [for Macbeth]. *I have a lovely deerskin jacket. Our wigs make us very glamorous, if not masculine by modern standards ...*

Tuesday 22nd

Two years ago, on a Sunday, the German attack on Russia began. Casualties given as German killed or prisoners six million, Russian four.

... after tea listened to Tchaikovsky's 5th symphony—glorious; he appeals more strongly than any other composer to the emotions—sometimes perhaps too sentimental (6th) but I like it ...

Wednesday 23rd

Der Tag (that is German for 'the day' isn't it?). After morning periods and a very slack signallers' parade—the senior hall being at the theatre—and lunch, we bussed down with our clothes and swords to the theatre, there to rehearse Macbeth. It was largely a sound and lighting rehearsal; acting had to be left to its own devices. Anyhow we started on time; apart from wobbly knees in the first scene I enjoyed it a lot, and it went off very well. B [as Macbeth] *was very good indeed, nobody was bad (not even me) and the audience was very appreciative. Then the ordeal of the curtain call (chief six on alone to bow) and back. Taylor very pleased ...*

Thursday 24th
Speech day. ... I was demonstrating the short-sighted and long-sighted eye, and the curing by spectacles—a simple and very effective demonstration—much enjoyed by all I think. I enjoyed doing the talking too, especially to the bevies of fair damsels who came from the Bristol [Benenden]. *I also contributed a dissected frog, which was not appreciated on the whole, though nobody was actually sick.*

After lunch there was a very good Art exhibition too (a lovely Gannel by K), the guard of honour, and silly speeches ...

Down to the theatre, dress, make up, and starting at 8.15. All OK, if very hot. Two ITW [RAF Initial Training Wing] *blokes came to firewatch, and we sent them in to see the play after the first interval—they liked it a lot; as we left they were helping the stage hands.*

The audience clapped more, Macbeth and Lady M had two curtain calls, Mr. Taylor [director] *was made to appear, and it was one of the best plays ever; and we enjoyed it as well a lot, and were very sorry indeed that he is leaving us ...*

Sunday 27th
... we had a lovely afternoon sunning and swimming. Back, stopping on Crantock beach for more sun. Many fair damsels around, and I do not approve of segregation. I wonder if something might not arise out of the play—anyhow I hope some female contact occurs—especially for next year when I'll be pretty friendless here.

I slept through part of an incredibly poor and boring service. Dejected this evening ...

Monday 28th
Very hot and lovely. I did work fairly hard. Bathe in Gannel ...

News—S. Greece railway to Europe thoroughly cut by guerrillas—good for them.

Wednesday 30th
Cloudy. Life was very normal, we did heliograph and M/L lamps in corps. There is a horrible plan for an all Sunday do.

Free after tea, up Penpol with RJC and back—oppressive, disturbing evening …

July

Thursday 1st
Better weather again—good enough to do Fraunhoffer lines outside with the wavelength spectrometer, anyhow. I have managed to keep my resolution of working hard this week. Another year of working to a crescendo before I can stop. I am taking school exams fairly seriously too ...

English prep was to write a description of a building. After reading Hardy's magnificent descriptions in 'The Mayor of Casterbridge', I wrote one of Glatting, which made me feel quite homesick. Must improve writing.

Fraunhofer lines are dark lines which can be seen in the spectrum created by refracting the light from sunshine.

Friday 2nd
More perfect weather. Hard work. Discussion of [Oxford scholarship] *syllabi in Biology; not too encouraging and possibility of having to take it in MARCH! I hereby make a solemn resolution to work to the utmost of my ability, and if, through lack of application or refusal or failure to utilise my natural talents I fail to obtain my scholarship, may I simmer in hell for eternity; may the word 'scholarship' become engraved on my corneas that I may never forget to work hard. Etc. …*

Sunday 4th
... I dived, swam 60 yds. breast in 50 secs., did 50 yds. on my back with my arms folded, did 175 yds. in under 4 mins. and so became —with six out of about 18 others—a 2nd Class swimmer.

After lunch discontent fell upon me; I walked and biked aimlessly, and then tried to drug myself with sad and angry music—but didn't feel a lot better.

Divinity prep was to suggest improvements for the services here—a violently sarcastic half hour helped to relieve my feelings.

But still this damned restless unsatisfied feeling; I don't know the reason and know the cure still less. I think triviality, pettiness, monotony, aimlessness, not full friendship and hence loneliness, and lack of sexual contact make up the reason. I do not think the answer can be found while I'm at school.

Just after writing this, Mr. Taylor came up and talked to me. My depression went with him, because he—well I don't know, he restored my sense of perspective in myself for one thing, and also talked a good deal more intimately than previously. His philosophy is, he says, on the lines of Daddy's 'Fears may be Liars', also Hardy's novels—I must read some more ...

He promised to lend me a book by Bertrand Russell. Why must the man leave now? … [he] *said "I suppose you've got a certain amount of confidence in yourself already". I've more than I had two years ago, and then it was too much for Max, who called it arrogance …*

Max, incidentally, seems to have abandoned me more or less—I've not spoken to him now for nearly 1½ years. I'm none the worse for it either. I wonder if I'll be a prefect—there are advantages and experiences in it, even if it is a rotten system.

My housemaster (Max) was doubtless correct to see my self-righteous challenges to the school system as arrogant. But looking back, I can understand why his alternations between authoritarian stamping of the feet and phases of friendly informality had irked me, and do not regret my rejection of the banality and hypocrisy involved in compulsory religion. I do regret my provoking teachers who did not deserve it. Mr. Hales, for example—the music teacher who was now required to teach French—was a poor disciplinarian, and I recall earning cheap popularity by provoking him. I owe my reasonable French accent to him. And I had been no trouble to teachers who earned, and granted, respect, of whom Mr. Taylor was one.

Monday 5th

... Mr. Ramage was disgustingly gloomy about scholarship prospects—a seven-term course he said, and gave lists of people who tried earlier and failed. ... I'll have a shot I think. Work ahead! ...

Sikorski [head of Polish Government in exile] *killed in air crash—personally I think a small loss—perhaps that is too biased and callous, because he did what was right by his standards, I suppose.*

Wednesday 7th

... HRH Duchess of Gloucester visited St. Runions [military hospital] *after lunch—I did not go and gape—several did, cutting first period ...*

A Doctor Dicks (or Dick) was in for lunch—I think a prospective parent, he had a diminutive son with him. He is a very ardent Social Medicine fan, who was examined (kindly) by Daddy at Cambridge. A nice man from the few minutes I spoke to him ...

News. Big German offensive on three Russian fronts, heavy losses, small headway.

Friday 9th

In Biology I showed the exam data to Mr. Ramage, who has just about convinced me that I would hardly have a forlorn hope in March. I wrote to Mommy and Daddy, and also sent off an application for a place at the Queenswood Conference [another inter-schools conference at Hatfield].

If I don't take a scholarship, it'll mean a comfortable 1st MB, and then I could start off hard on the medical course. If I then did well enough ... might be granted an exhibition—I don't know.

I was anxious to avoid another year at school.

Saturday 10th

Grey wetness all day. News good—at 3 o'clock today British, Canadian and American troops landed on Sicily. A good Russian commentary after the 9 o'clock news (Alex Werth)—the Kursk battles are the biggest mechanised battles ever yet. So far little ground, great cost. A good quotation from an old Russian peasant woman: "More sweat in the fields, less blood at the front". Let it be remembered when I harvest [Alexander Werth was the BBC's correspondent in Russia].

The Sicily invasion was costly, with many troops killed by friendly fire, and many airborne troops landing in the wrong places, including the sea. There were problems in co-ordinating the different armies, and in due course a large proportion of German and Italian troops were successfully evacuated across the straits of Messina.

Sunday 11th
... Read one of Taylor's books—Bertrand Russell's 'A Free Man's Worship'—that essay only. The idea seems to be that man has got to accept that he is quite powerless in the face of Fate and Death, and until he accepts these inevitabilities he cannot be free. When he has realised that, he can choose for himself Power or Goodness to worship, and his mind can still expand in the face of this rather awful inevitability. Which, especially in his more adequate prose, seems fairly sound.

Tuesday 13th
... I was accorded the unutterable honour of representing my house in the 1st cricket XI. ... H and I had a happy period together getting 20 (him) and 27. ... I did not think I would ever sink so low as to be congratulated on my cricket in house prayers!

Friday 16th
... Dodd was wise again in French re: international affairs. Trying to put 1940 events from the French point of view, he was banned as a pro-Nazi by the majority of the class.

... down to the theatre for a combined schools concert. ... Benenden suitably singing Humpty Dumpty, wretched girls! Finally the Clock Symphony in D by Haydn, with combined orchestras including us conducted by Taylor ...

Saturday 17th
... Am reading through Browning's 'Men and Women'—I like Fra Lippo Lippi particularly.

… Thunder began at 9.30 [pm], *we did not sleep. 2 carrier pigeons arrived from over the sea; having failed to entice them with cake, Wallop climbed up the wet roof and saw that there was no message. Almost sleep, then watched* [the storm] *again—grand—so grand that Wallop and I decided it was too good to miss. We donned gym shoes and bathing shorts, and in an extremely heavy downpour, we slipped down the porch pillar outside our window and nipped up the cads' walk* [so-named because used particularly by prefects].

Thence we ran down past the range to the Gannel; the track was a torrent, and everything was brightly lit by frequent vivid flashes, with occasional forked lightening. On the Gannel was a flock of curlew making disturbed noises. Back by the road (passing someone—we must have looked queer).

We first entered through Kenyon, but finding the lights in our corridor on, we retreated to the front, went in through the dining room window, then up the pillar into our room. Dried there and watched the storm die away. Sleep (1.50).

Wednesday 21st

… out to Mr. Taylor with M and S and Roger, where we drank tea, ate sandwiches and indulged in civilised conversation—as I have said before, a very nice man. Back by eleven to tell fairy stories and then ghosts—amazing how one can frighten oneself by discussing that sort of thing.

Saturday 24th

… After a light tea, up for prize giving, speeching etc—I got a 5/- voucher for economics …

House supper at eight—sitting next to Mr. Taylor—lots of speeches, the unfortunate singing of 'For he's a jolly good fellow' three times, then charades.

And then, oh joy, an 11.30 bathe on Fistral beach. Grand, and when you moved your hands through the water, little sparkles of phosphorescence streamed from the finger tips. Glorious. … At 1.10, out of the window -- oh but

Sunday 25th
and along the headland with Wood and Wallop, looking for Watkinson and H who were trying out a tent by a quarry. We made a double round tour of the quarries but missed them. A fine starry warmish night—very lovely. Back up the porch, welcome sleep …

Monday 26th
… I went to say goodbye to Taylor in the afternoon—we talked for a bit, and he told me to look him up if ever I passed through London. I am very sorry to see the last of him.

There was startling news this morning; Mussolini has resigned [in fact deposed]. *Badoglio has succeeded, with blaa about the king, more fighting and martial law. Fascist militia incorporated in army. Signs of cracking I wonder? …*

to Glatting

Tuesday 27th
Diary brief for a few days.
… caught 4.18 from Victoria after a short time spent in the flick. … Margaret home, Nora for two days … and Daddy's secretary Gwynneth (how spelt?) …

Wednesday 28th
… After tea Margaret and I went and bathed with David Wolfe, returning to find Roger installed here, after a goodish hop including a lorry loaded (by him) with 9 tons of Brylcreem which later had a blow out. Off tomorrow walking.

Thursday 29th
… we went off—Margaret, Roger and I, loaded with heavyish haversacks. We stopped for lunch past Bishop's Ring, then after a little doze, on through hot sun, skirting part of the artillery range; and so at last down into Cocking. Beyond we found a fine camping site, and settled down to hot food and drink and early bed. No sleep came, so up and bed again towards dark. Fine searchlight.

Friday 30th
… A good breakfast, then off through already hot sun; we lunched in a lovely cool wood, and rested for about an hour. Then on over bare, scorching hill, in (me) a bad temper. We turned south opposite Harting, and called in for water at a place where a very nice gardener gave us—for the price of 2 lbs, 2½ [lbs] *of tomatoes and, free, some raspberries.*

On feeling better … at last reached a fine spot, where we ate a great deal of vegetable stew. Had to move after supper due to flying ants. Bed with dark, nightjars. Saw today a hedgehog also. Trains passing.

Saturday 31st
Up and off down the valley to the next crossing; then through the woods of Up Park by an erratic, long short cut to Compton, where we bought food, and had half a pint of watery beer.

Above Compton we had a fine shady lunch, then on through pleasantly shaded walks for some way, aiming for the river Lavant at West Dean and a wash. The river was, of course, bone dry, but our souls and tempers were saved by some kindly people who called us into their garden, where we were waited on by daughters with tea and food, and then let loose in the bathroom. Heaven and thank god for such people.

Up the downs by a walled-in estate, and then as the first drops fell, a rush into the private woods to a ? waterproof pine. A real thunderstorm; we donned bathing things, put everything into a waterproof sleeping bag, and in this manner I washed (for no-one saw us); we ate rawish stoup from the billy can, by a fire we made from an army petrol can.

The storm passed and we dressed and passed the Trundle [ancient fort] *in search of a barn. RAF men's only suggestion was Chichester, which was out of the question, so we decided to make for home.*

… by failing light, and with a pause for food, to Up Waltham. Nerves were ragged, and the woods were too dark to go torchless, so we went on towards Chichester and up by the Willow Herb patch

August

Sunday 1st

using the candle in woods. Cheerful now, down the greenslope, and let in as the first drops of the second storm were falling. Sleep came easily.

The day was lazy and bad tempered. Daddy had a bad day. It is decided, practically, that I stay an extra year at school.

Tuesday 3rd

[On the way to the inter-schools conference at Hatfield] ... *by train to Potters Bar with a very nice schoolteacher who knows the Bignor area—leader of the education commission.*

Usual female preponderance. ... Before tea and during tea, got talking to a very nice (I think) girl from Queenswood who showed us round—medical and nearly communist, very small, pretty ...

A reactionary opening address from Sir Francis Freemantle [doctor and Conservative MP], *well questioned after—clever evasion and good use of a deaf ear.*

... a very excellent, realistic, useful talk from one of the wardens—a headmaster ... I think it will be a good conference.

Wednesday 4th

... a lecture on education by a local secondary-school teacher, headmistress—Dent of the Times educational supplement could not come—she was adequate ...

Then commission meeting—we've a good leader. I'm one of the two secretaries, and tomorrow I give a short talk on health in USSR. We got going but made no decision today. ... I spent the rest of the afternoon with various people talking—have made a large number of acquaintances.

At 4.30 the future housing talk by Mr. Carter of the RIBA—extremely good and interesting. After tea I bought some pamphlets for tomorrow's lecture, then I talked to Ursula F. until the social—she accidentally missed the lecture, and spent it talking communism with a policeman. Games in the social quite amusing …

Thursday 5th

Spent the early morning preparing my talk on the Soviet Health services. The first lecture was on the Beveridge plan by a woman liberal candidate for Devizes; she spoke loudly, well, and there was really nothing to disagree with—but much to learn. Good.

Then commissions; we had the four talks, mine was very successful and I spoke better than I ever have before; we passed a few summing up resolutions—almost unanimously favourable, especially regarding the health services. A good meeting.

During the afternoon I did a little stooking on the local estate farm, having bathed, and then I wrote up the commission meeting …

After tea I went for a short walk with the Queenswood girl—she is, I think, very intelligent, and her political interest is fairly well developed. Her friend, Lucy someone, is YCL and extremely sensible.

Then Prof. Levy on the Jewish question, which was really excellent; I have taken notes and must keep them for reference when discussing anti-Semitism …

Grand news today—Orel fallen [to Russians] *and Catania* [to the 8th Army].

The last speaker was probably Hyman Levy, mathematician, socialist and broadcaster.

Friday 6th

… I wrote up a little stuff and then off for the first lecture, on China. It was interesting, and entirely able, but not exciting. Then a commission meeting discussing education.

After lunch I met my fellow secretary and together we compiled the report up to date. At 4.30 an extra commission meeting on Planning. Then tea, and after an informal discussion on emotion and reason, the highlight of the week. Our very Rev. Comrade the Red Dean of Canterbury, Hewlett Johnson, who was just magnificent …

Saturday 7th

First lecture was very good—Mrs. Mead, a virile American on America—a strange approach but conciliated me; reasonable. The commission meetings, morning and afternoon, became heated on subject of political democracy, but eventually we did attain a reasonable and agreed decision.

ISC [Inter-Schools Committee] *election today—my school being apathetic and not in reach of London, I could not stand, though I do believe (from indications) I'd have stood a goodish chance. And I'm going to try to get a thing going at school—'Society for Discussion of World Problems'—SDOWP (s'dope) …*

Sunday 8th

Summing up day. I spent the morning with Noah (a fellow commissioner), who was typing out our report. After lunch the reports of commissions, ours third; I read a little badly at first, but then ok—I think it was a good report …

New girl friend—dark girl not really very pretty but damn nice. … She's attached somehow to the ISC—a friend of our commission leader, YCLer Barbara P.

Monday 9th

… busy before breakfast carry mattresses etc. about. New friend Eliz. came to my table—deeply honoured! After breakfast, many goodbyes, especially to Ursula (awful name, nice girl) and Elizabeth, neither of whose addresses do I know, or am I known, and I don't know the latter's name.

I'd like to get up to the ISC dance on Sept 11 to meet all the many nice friends I've made here, but I can't dance, have no party clothes, and would need other excuses also to go up—we'll see. The friends I made here are the people I'll probably like best in this country, and the more I see of them the better. … Decided not to go to lunch hour National Gallery concert, where many I knew were going, so caught 11.56.

Now I will sum up the results of the Conference, because it is a place remembered from home, and the journey constitutes the re-adjustment period. I have liked all the people immensely. I have enjoyed the many arguments and also the frivolities. I have learnt a lot in the Commission, a lot from some of the lectures, a lot from being secretary, and a lot from experiencing a week of live contemporary company. And I have returned re-armed and re-determined. I think I have got an important task ahead, and I believe that the conference has helped to emphasise this and to prepare me for it. Blessed be the Council for Education in World Citizenship!

The train journey was long and largely standing, also hot. I walked from Petworth with my rucksack—hot but pleasant.

All well at home, and Martin here—fairly well and just becoming less depressed …

Thought for the year:

	N. of Himalayas	*S. of ditto*
Amount spent on health	*£5.10*	*1d*
Amount spent on education	*£39*	*1/6d*

at Glatting

Wednesday 11th

Started work today, after having done some cow-rounding before breakfast. The work was loading carts—with pauses while the cart is taken and a new one fetched—quite pleasant. David there. Hot …

Mrs. Wolfe to tea—after she'd left there was a family disagreement upon her world utility, with Mommy defending—my how it's left me depressed. When I'm depressed I think of all the other things that depress me, and 2 years at school is quite sufficient—if I ever want to stop feeling happy, I just think of that. It will be so entirely isolated for me. I will concentrate on getting politically—and to some extent culturally—educated in my spare time, but it will be bloody. Conferences will help. Oh! hell and damn.

Friday 13th
Roger arrived at 1 o'clock (a.m.). I left for work before he woke—carting—loading for me …

After tea we heard that a rear gunner had bailed out in the morning, and was believed to be 7 or 8 miles due south of Petworth, his plane having collided; we rang up the police, and then Mommy, Martin, Roger and I combed the woods from the pylon … along to Duncton hill—we could not do it thoroughly. The only other sign of searchers was one Lysander for 5 mins.—no police on the downs. … Absolutely exhausted, to bed.

Wednesday 18th
Binder again largely. New land girl, 17, no chin and hunts and makes up. Work OK. Bathe in the evening—nice; then damn silly row with owners, because we took away a commando hand paddle which we found 5 ft. from the shore under water …

News—Sicily clear for 25 thousand casualties. Russians advancing—tough—1 mile from Kharkov.

Saturday 21st
Here my diary must return to proper length and legibility. The morning was grey, with downs at cloud level and frequent rain; … left work for good with 24/- in pocket …

Roger and I cycled in to a flick—a quite amusing Joe E. Brown film—anyhow I'm uncritical as I see so few …

Sunday 22nd
A happy day. Margaret, Roger and I went out for a walk—over beyond Bignor hill—sunny and windy. We picked greengages, and I started on the 'Fall of Paris', Ehrenberg [Ilya Ehrenburg, Soviet writer, 1943] …

Wednesday 25th
… Roger and I went up and dug for pottery. About 1.6 down, I found a marl paving stone—flat and horizontal; much pottery. In this hole I found four or five [pieces] *of the same rim …*

Thursday 26th
Roger left today, and I went up too to get the records which cannot be sent by post ... went to the HMV show rooms, where we played through and got Beethovens 7th, 8th and Violin concerto. ... We had tea then parted. Roger to Norwich and home. His was a highly successful visit, enjoyed by guest and hosts.

Friday 27th
... Mommy heard that her Father has died—not too sad as he has not really lived for some years.

Sunday 29th
Went for a walk with Margaret after rabbits etc.—we collected marjoram for the WI show for Mommy to dry. Examined the combine harvester—a nice machine ...

The Danes are being very tough—there is martial law, and street fighting and sabotage is going on to a very great extent—so [German] *troops can't easily get to Norway, now the Swedes have stopped them through their country. Poor, brave Danes.*

Denmark had not resisted the German invasion, having no adequate means, and had retained initially some autonomy. Fewer than 500 Danish Jews out of over 7,000 died at the hands of the Nazis, by far the best record in occupied Europe. Two days before deportation was due to begin, the news was leaked and the Jews disappeared, hidden by all kinds of people and betrayed by no organisation, in contrast to France where the police actively cooperated with the round-up of Jews. Large numbers escaped in small boats to Sweden over the ensuing months.

Monday 30th
... After lunch I biked in to Petworth station to see about sending off carpets to Oxford. A rather grim evening with two overtired parents ...

September

Wednesday 1st
4 years since the attack on Poland—I never thought it would last as long. No real second front yet, but the Russians are nearing Smolensk, and threatening the N. Ukraine.

In the morning I lined a small case with velvet, having fitted it up to take my flute—satisfactory. Women's Institute produce show … Mommy did very excellently, with three prizes—dried vegetables, salad vegetables and most entries.

Thursday 2nd
Re-covered an old tattered ironing board in the morning; two Canadians called for water in a carrier—whom I had given pears to yesterday. We gave them pears and tea again.

Later we discovered that they'd left in the pump room a box of tinned food—months of points—very nice of them!

Rationing included under the 'points' category a range of food, particularly tinned food.

Rather a moody day for me—bad.

Sumi [in Ukraine] *captured. No big Allied European landing. Churchill's Tuesday speech—which was complementary to Russia—has produced little response there, but a demand for action not words.*

Friday 3rd
4 years at 11 o'clock. We marked it by landing near Reggio in the toe of Italy—no reports of what happened yet. Widespread Russian gains ...

I read and wrote during the afternoon and evening, and read 'Deirdre' in the evening. I'm very fond of James Stephens [Irish poet and novelist] …

Saturday 4th
… I wrote and fluted in my hut until John and Melody arrived, when we sat in a lovely warm, breezy garden …

John and I went for a walk up the Downs, returning via Coldharbour, where we collected two ewe lambs and drove them to Glatting. After tea I made a hurdle pen in the orchard—the sheep were a bit bewildered ...

Wednesday 8th
... I read 'The Brook Kerith' [by George Moore, elaborating on the life of Christ] *after lunch in the garden, and then walked with John to the Holdings' for tea, the others joining by car. We had a good tea and saw a lot of Holding's lovely paintings.*

I went back by car; on the pub was chalked below a Union Jack the words ITALY SURRENDERS. She has, unconditionally. Very interesting. We drank to it for supper. I wish John was not so blasted disillusioned, or to use a description he frequently uses himself, bloody minded. One has to feel apologetic if you're enthusiastic when he's around—especially about Russia.

Stalino and the whole Donetz Basin is taken. Things are happening.

Thursday 9th
I received a letter today (a rare occurrence) from Hilary Rubinstein—he is going to print [my] *article on the objective attitude in the next Phoenix. Good. I have written another about internal school democracy—'Training for Democracy?'—I'll send it off as it's written, but I doubt if he'll print both.*

Phoenix was a magazine published by the Inter-Schools Committee containing articles reflecting the subjects of the interschool conferences.

We have made a landing near Naples, the Russians have captured an important but unpronounceable railway junction.

Went for a very pleasant walk with John, and thoroughly disgraced myself tree-climbing ...

Friday 10th

The removers came [to get furniture to take to Oxford] *and spent the day packing their large container, leaving to return tomorrow, having made no appreciable effect on Glatting's internal chaos …*

Tomorrow the ISC dance occurs—I would have liked to go, but am entirely resigned.

Saturday 11th

A lovely warm summer day. Picked pears early on. Melody's sister Pauline arrived 11'ish and we had tea in the garden—she is also nice I think—her husband is a Jap prisoner, and she hasn't heard from him.

I spent the rest of the morning making four bed legs for a spring mattress …

N. Italy now German occupied against riots and army, including Rome. Naples landing …

Monday 13th

An empty house. I spent a terribly lazy morning, and finished reading 'The Brook Kerith'—a very lovely book I think. … We packed my trunk after lunch, then into Petworth for tea, haircuts and petrol. Back via the Holdings'—a lovely clear quiet evening.

Tuesday 14th

A hectic morning, me pear picking and carrying things in from Margaret's [shed] *and my house …*

Daddy and I all alone until we go up [to Oxford] *on Thursday. Next week today I go into my segregated community of uninterested bourgeois contemporaries.*

During the afternoon I finished off jobs and read Anatole France—a rather naughtily funny man. One lovely prayer of an Italian girl to the Virgin Mary: "O thou who conceived without sin, have the grace to grant that I may sin without conceiving".

We listened to a rather woolly Brains Trust, answering rather good questions, preponderantly political.

Salerno bridgehead fiercely attacked, some ground lost.

to Oxford

Thursday 16th
… Journey to London was comfortable; I spent that and (after we'd had 'coffee' at Paddington) most of the journey to Oxford reading 'The Jungle' [by U. Sinclair about Chicago meat industry]*—a morbid but very fine book. Daddy took the journey fairly well. Arrived at Kybald Street house—no furniture yet, carpets and blackout just ready …*

We had tea at the Turins'—they are awfully kind and have made Mother's stay possible—they're Russian—not anti-present system [the Turins were attached in some way to University College] …

Friday 17th
… No furniture. Daddy went to the Institute at 9.45, Mommy and me went and shopped, had coffee, and then called at the Hobsons' and brought away a camp bed …

After lunch I went to the food office. … I slept in the flat on the floor, Daddy on the Hobsons' camp bed … News and coffee at the Turins'.

Saturday 18th
… ex-Polish pilot Stefan Gawel called and chatted. Mommy and I went to a flick …

A funny picnic living in an unfurnished flat—with 2½ knives, 2 forks, a teapot and little else! However we were given three chairs by the Turins—whose generosity is embarrassing.

Sunday 19th
… I asked Stefan to tea instead of vice-versa and then we went for a walk—Christ Church Meadows and Addison's walk. Back, and Stefan and the Turins (with cups) came in for tea—very nice party. After supper we went round to the Turins—good interesting company—West African girl and an English woman doctor who'd practised there.

Monday 20th
… I went to see Daddy off to London for a committee on 'Higher Education in the Colonies'! The luggage is in Oxford, but will not

arrive today, so at 4 o'clock we went and saw 'Mission to Moscow'—the film of Davies' book [read the previous year]. *Very good—criticisms are: too much emphasis on social life similarities with America—which is probably anyhow good propaganda. We returned and then had a nice supper at the Chinese Rest*[aurant]. … *Tomorrow, school—I can now face this awful inevitability with greater calmness and less emotionalism. I hope Mother and Father get settled soon.*

to Newquay

Tuesday 21st
… A coldish wait at Reading, then into the school train in a carriage ½ us, ½ Benenden. There I soon fell talking with old acquaintance Elizabeth Chitty—nicer now than before, older mentally and better looking—hair permed and fuller. She's taking up acting next term. … Spent the last part of the journey in pleasant conversation with a carriage full of them, including E. I asked F if she knew an Elizabeth at St. Pauls—she did, and the name was Zeaman, but how spelt I don't know …

Wednesday 22nd
… Mr. Hales thinks I'll have to go for my music lessons to Benenden, on Thursday—I'm willing! With two years I think I may become reasonable. Hales wants to teach me about the orchestra too. We're doing this term the 1st movement of the unfinished—the 1st flute is apparently terribly high.

I did not feel too homesick today. I'm getting so used to parting that the adjustment comes easier—and I'm happier about the health and comforts of my very dear parents …

Thursday 23rd
Into gear—bit of a grate at first with treble physics; re: that and chemi, I'm bloody minded, dejected, miserable, and utterly hopeless. Hell.

A 1st game run in the afternoon which I stood very badly getting an acute stitch—but we were not forced …

Saturday 25th
… interesting Classics with Maxi on balanced outlook on life. I think that extinction of me and universe is inevitable, life has as much meaning as we care to give it—Bertrand Russell's view …

The game (1st 1st one) wasn't at all bad for the 1st 1st one. Pretty stiff all day. Back for bath, music, and to read my prize book which has come, with 5/- extra required—called 'Leninism' by Stalin. Good …

Monday 27th
… Long good letter from Roger [now studying Medicine at Glasgow]*—with description of a slaughter house visit very reminiscent of 'The Jungle'—the floor drains to the bowl for black pudding.*

Thursday 30th
… At 4.45 I mounted my bike, and off with flute and music, for my period with Miss Stewart at The Hotel Bristol, home of Benenden. Miss Stewart met me at the door and escorted me to room 167 … funny woman, but I think rather nice. She rushed off at 5.45, leaving me with two other flute playing damsels, one of whom showed me to the door …

October

Tuesday 5th
… Went by request to see Hales after tea—he'd received a letter from flautist Miss Stewart saying (a) that I had ability (even talent!) (b) I would be held up by fingering (c) [she] *would let me have Bohm fingering flute for £12, and would allow me £5 on mine …*

Wednesday 6th
Normal day—I have no free time for boredom or misery nowadays, and am almost (whisper it not in Gath) enjoying school life—anyhow the out-of-school side ...

Orchestra practice—great fun, I did better …

Thursday 7th
There appears to be a lull in Russia—after what a storm! …

Blasted [athletics] *standards in the afternoon—I failed the 100 yds. (took 14 secs.) and the mile (took 7 mins.—1 minute more than allowed!). Have to repeat sometime I fear.*

Music lesson; after chat with fellow flautists, before Miss Stewart arrived—one quite nice—also plays violin and piano. Miss Stewart fairly normal despite hints of madness in letter—she did tell me to put the flute under a wardrobe when the sirens went (air raid, not flautist damsels she meant!). I came away with the new flute …

Monday 11th
… Midget submarines have damaged the Tirpitz.

Thursday 14th
… Italy declares war on Germany; what a farce, and that blighter Emanual and that b. Badoglio are on top—the dirty tricksters—and we, the silly fools, leaving (or putting them [there]*). I mistrust our govt …*

Italy under Badoglio had surrendered in early September, on terms which involved participating in the war against German occupation.

Friday 15th
… Was told of Sat. night illegal signallers do—no prefects coming—4 38's (with throat mikes etc.) arrived today. Ought to be fun—a night op …

Sunday 17th
At 4 o'clock I was woken, and having donned parts of JTC uniform, left with wireless set no. 38 by way of window. Was with H above Bay Garden, the group was OK but only satisfactory communication was with control. … We went on for some time, and then rendyvoused at top of Ispell Charlie Able Dog Sugar William Able Lone King.

Back at about 5.30, to see at 10 yds. range a figure wearing grey flannels and windjacket à la Max waiting on the roof—Wallop marched on as if to his doom, we scattered. I crept in about 10 mins. later, and slept dreaming of the wrath to come … went up to Wallop at 8.30 to find that it had been Wood all the time, so all was well …

Tuesday 19th
… an interesting lantern lecture which I enjoyed on 'The Old Masters of Florence'—the lantern was worked hitchlessly by self and M who [were] *congratulated to our infinite pride … ! …*

Wednesday 20th
… I have resolved into a clear issue a political conflict in my mind; I am sure that socialism is right, and I am sure that democracy is desirable (and only fully attainable under former). How to get it.

Will our democratic socialist votes ever outweigh the money backed power of our opposition; once we have our majority, how ruthless can we be? Can we be utterly, as the Communists—even if elected on that basis—or must we give reaction a chance, which it will doubtless do its best to use. … What I must decide is, will the end be attained without the ruthlessness? That is so hard to say, Marxist analysis of history says no; I must examine Marxist analysis to decide whether it, or the British socialist parties (not the moribund Labour, but, say, Common Wealth) are correct. A problem. More heads would be welcome, but I'll find few enough here!

[Added] *Mon 15 / xi / 43. Conflict largely resolved, for time at least, by Strachey's 'What are we to do'. CP for me eventually by that.*

Common Wealth was a new left of centre party formed in 1942, with J.B. Priestley amongst its members, to campaign for a non-authoritarian form of socialism. It was sympathetic to co-operativism and syndicalism (a kind of workers' control).

Saturday 23rd
… Soc. soc. on India by OG [Old Greshamian] *ex-commissioner of reforms (gave up, not enough to do!!). … I asked if he believed the British economic exploitation of India, the British support to the autocratic princes, the absence of general education, and the general poverty of the agricultural population, were a good basis for Indian democracy, and was he satisfied with the British govt.'s attitude to these questions, and if so, why? A long, non-committal and incomplete answer …*

Sunday 24th
… I'm in the position of being in the mood for writing poetry or music while possessing the ability to do neither; all I can do is sit and curse and play Siegfried or Cosi Fan Tutte, both of which express part of what I feel, but neither of which satisfy.

The feeling of utter hopelessness can only be relieved by expressing it in art, which I can't do, or sharing it with an intimate friend, which I have not got. I am feeling now the need for one, of my own stage of development, with whom I could share emotions, because we both felt the same things. … I'm a lonely soul in moments of emotional intensity like this, and when I'm feeling lonely I'm sad or angry and anyhow unhappy.

A bell has rung requiring my attendance at divine service—Christ! If I do not take care or develop one of the above outlets I shall become cynical or introspective or both. Meanwhile I don black clothes and swear, or weep …

Wednesday 27th
… A good Soc. Soc.; Mr. Norman on Probationary Officers—sounded dull, but a very nice oldish fellow who told many anecdotes, illustrative and naughty enough to make me regret the HM's absence—for it would have been amusing to study his reactions. I asked if he'd come across my late grandfather, as he'd been 15 years at Jo'burg—he had only heard of him but admired him …

Thursday 28th
Fairly contented today. I am writing a lot nowadays—probably useless in itself, but it may lead to something …

November

Tuesday 2nd
… Moscow three-power talks, conclusions thereof, published. V. unanimous; include trial and punishment of guilty ones,

democratisation of Italy, and military agreements for now, plus setting up of international peace-preserving body—good.

This meeting was the most cordial and constructive of any of the 3-power wartime conferences.

I … began to prepare a speech for next Saturday's debate. … Morse practice in the afternoon, I received 8 words per minute.

Nice Biology extra, then taking prep—N a damned nuisance, and punishment will be the only course if he refuses to be reasonable—but I think punishment is on the whole useless, and certainly very silly. Problems. But good practice for authority …

Friday 5th

No fireworks, but the usual Fistral mines which blew in the Art Room window …

Soc. Soc. was Sir Ronald Storrs [a former colonial governor] *on a recent ME* [Middle East] *tour—very interesting—a nice old gaffer who knew enough, but regarded the changing of Bulgaria's frontiers as the probable outcome of the war …*

Saturday 6th

Usual Saturday morning with the very cheering news of the fall of Kiev.

… the Debate: 'This house blames the whole German people for the war.' 1st and 2nd [speakers were RAF] *ITW cadets—1st able, competent; 2nd not awfully inspired; then a nice American staff sergeant … then a very amusing and useful American corporal—very good; then K—able; then Wallop—very good indeed, both for points and for speech. I spoke first from the house …*

A good debate, the motion defeated with my aid by 66 votes to 64. A controversial and difficult issue.

Sunday 7th

I fluted after breakfast, and then spent a rather boring time writing up cricket and rugger stuff for 'The Gresham'—a paper waste …

During the day I read parts of Hillary's 'The Last Enemy', a book which is interesting psychologically, but so far leaves me rather depressed—of course the subject is not one calculated to produce hilarity, God knows.

Richard Hillary had become famous for his account of his experiences as a fighter pilot, before being severely wounded.

I also read more of 'Leninism', on Dialectical Materialism—I am as yet not fully decided—can't be for a long time, and I must avoid agreement as a result of emotional sympathy. The emphasis on a fixed course of social development unchangeable by man seems unpleasing—it is important in this connection to make clear the point … that this explains only the origin of social ideas, and does not entail an underestimation of their significance. The ideas must, however, have the correct basis.

Monday 8th
… Letters from Mommy and Daddy. Mommy has just heard that her mother, too, has died—poor Mommy—because though grandfather's death was expected and was a release, this was not. I expect with Grandfather dead she had no particular aim in life.

Tuesday 9th
… A little notice went up saying 'A. Ryle has been awarded his 1st XV colours', which came as a very great surprise to me.
… a dogfish Biology extra in which uncle Bill gave vent to some eminently reasonable views on sex-education (not only sex instruction)—quite a wise old stick, but he does rather lack drive.
… The Russians are 30–40 miles past Kiev in all directions, with a bit of a rout in progress—Hitler made a not very inspiring speech.
Cesar Franck's symphony in D minor is grand.

Wednesday 10th
… heard from CEWC. There's a 4 day non-resident course in London—Westminster; I'd like to go, there are good lecturers, and if our decisions

are of no intrinsic value (we don't pretend they are particularly), the increase in knowledge and interest is very considerable; and there is the great thing of meeting live contemporaries. The latter holds particular attraction for me, I'm lonely here.

Thursday 11th

A day of cynical memories for many; merely memories of pre-war hypocrisy for me. The poppies for the school, stupidly ordered from Holt, did not arrive.

... prep fairly quiet, no punishments—and some perhaps deserved. It remains to be seen if the principle of no use for punishment is practical, or if people are going to take advantage of it.

Kiev bulge swelling rapidly. Churchill talks tactlessly of 1944 [for a second front], *while Stalin has just spoken of 1943, and while Italy creeps funereally ...*

Monday 15th

... Explosives blitz [a search] *through school; in (early) extra PSN showed some of the results, including sawn open rounds to remove cordite—some bloody fools in the world ...*

Am reading Strachey's 'What are we to do', which is helping considerably to resolve my conflict (Wed. Oct. 20th '43—see earlier).

Tuesday 16th

After a lovely vivid sunrise, a wet day. Read Strachey most of spare time. Indoor miscellaneous signals.

Good biology extra both biologically and sociologically—discussing drinking, masturbation and hence segregation.

Wednesday 17th

A photograph in the paper of Yugoslav men, women and a child or two come to Italy—they were wearing uniforms, and on their hats were five pointed stars. I begin to feel comradely pleasure at such sights.

The dominant role of the communists in the Yugoslav partisans was now being acknowledged.

I finished Strachey's book, which has left me considerably wiser and more decided …

Letter from Daddy saying he's prouder of my 1st XV colours than me—perhaps it is really an inverted form of snobbery …

Excellent Soc. Soc.—American on American education. Salient points: high school universal; … religion confined to 10+ verses of bible and the Lord's prayer without comment; … private schools worse than others, no economic privilege. He did not mention, however, negroes—but a very decent fellow.

Tuesday 23rd

Took two books from the library—Marx's 'Capital' [but I do not think I ever read it!] *and 'Moscow rehearsals'—Soviet drama. Strachey's book has clarified my mind considerably—my conflict was in effect Fabian vs. Marxian socialism, and the fact that capitalism is a disruptive, decaying force in its old age leaves the Marxist method the only possible …*

Another punishment set in prep [by me] *on T, for Habershon imitation which distracted others—600 words on the imitative faculties of the Apes as manifested in infantile humans! Not v. funny, but necessary. Make punishment fit crime …*

Wednesday 24th

Off to Truro by the 12.10 to play a very very muddy game which we lost. … Read 'They died with their boots clean' [a book about the Coldstream Guards by Gerald Kersh, 1941] *on the journey—a good book but I do NOT want to join the Guards.*

OG [old Greshamian] *G (I gave him a black eye in '41 train fight) is down,* [now in the] *Irish Guards—same as book.*

I heard later that he lost a leg in North Africa.

Friday 26th

… We had a prefects' meeting in the evening—Max suggested (fairly violently) that we were not here "to try out our own educational ideas", i.e. we are but yes-men to enforce already established school rules. I shall

never make a good prefect if that is what he wants; I will never bring myself to punish for what I do not regard as unreasonable—rules or not.

In fact, Max and I are not going to get on very well. It is inconceivable that I should merely be a Max idea machine—I intend to use my own discretion freely—I will either cease being a prefect, or become what is my conception of a reasonable and just one.

Tuesday 30th

A long very wise letter from Daddy on the question of the correct attitude to my prefectorial powers, which has balanced my attitude—how nice to have such parents whose wisdom is on tap, and such kindly wisdom …

December

Wednesday 1st

The Russian Kiev drive seems to have overstretched itself a bit, and Korestan has been abandoned. We're advancing in Italy …

Soc. Soc. was Dr. Mace on Psychology—chiefly on learning—very interesting indeed on psychological experiments, fatigue curves etc. Back with latter pretty low, and then some potatoes to be peeled until near midnight.

Friday 3rd

… I borrowed yesterday's papers on the debate on Mosley [in the House of Commons; he had been released from internment on the grounds of ill health]—*this is what was said* [in support of his release]*:*

(1) thrombosis (2) principles of civil liberty (3) still power over him. While against: (1) thrombosis does not require 7 mile walks, most char[ladie]*s and MPs have it anyway; (2) we're fighting Fascism, this man is the British symbol of Fascism; popular disgust at release. Morrison winding up made a lot of very dirty lying cracks about the CP; the motion deploring his release was beaten very easily, which only shows how out of touch is Parliament from the people.*

Monday 6th

… bad back—kidney I think, not lumbago. Saw Miss Milner re: games. She rubbed in embrocation and told me to drink lots of water. Blast it. La

Uncle Bill got tonsillitis—off school for the first time since 1923!

Tuesday 7th

A signallers' classification exam in the afternoon, which proved to be a complete farce—no officer could come, and all they tested us on was receiving buzzer at six and lamp and flex. Futile.

After tea I mooned around until the concert, then up to Pentire. All went well, but for Miss E. on the 'cello coming in a bar early at the beginning of the movement. Complete catastrophe was avoided, however. After the first exposed flute passage my heart was going at a fearful rate, thumping away—it calmed off eventually, and I perpetrated (?) no sins of commission, but of necessity some of omission. Anyhow it was a grand experience for which I am very glad.

Back 9 o'clock, to rehearse.

Wednesday 8th

… After tea we rehearsed, and Lawrence Taylor came round in 3rd prep and we did Acts 2-3, which went very well. Taylor then played some of his swing compositions—quite amusing and, as that sort of thing goes, good.

I see opposite a rough draft of the article which may now be, or will soon be, in 'Phoenix'. Reading through, after five weeks of prefectship, I find no reason to alter my attitude.

Have just read Gollancz's 'Shall our children live or die', which struck me as very wise and sound [this argued against post-war revenge on the German people].

Rough draft in summer holiday, '43—printed in Xmas '43.

Training for democracy?

This is a criticism of the internal organisation of schools, and a broad indication of the changes I believe to be necessary to ensure a greater development of the democratic spirit and way of thought …

My chief contention is that education for life in a democratic state must entail to some extent the practice of democracy, while the existing forms of school government are essentially authoritarian. Nobody will deny that discipline is essential for the proper running of any community, but I contend that the essence of democracy is that this discipline should be, to the greatest possible extent, self-imposed.

How far this principle of self-imposed discipline can be applied to schools can only be shown by experiment; a democracy is always limited by the maturity of its members. As things are, orders from above with no discernible basis of reason, and rules with no apparent basis of necessity, have disastrous effects; besides being unnecessarily cramping to the individual, they cause all rules, whether reasonable or not, to be regarded with contempt, and popular approval is even accorded to the law breaker who is not found out …

So far I have spoken of the school system from the point of view of one who is yet to attain the dizzy heights of prefectship, and my remarks cannot be applied altogether to these exalted beings … [but] *I have only too frequently suffered, and been angered by, the gropings of prefects after a proper attitude to their power, and I have observed with interest the development, through stages of officiousness or of negligence, of the ability to lead, or shall I say to order without rousing resentment?*

No doubt this process has been very valuable to them, especially as preparation for service as officers in the armed forces, but I am dubious if it has been the best means of inculcating, in them or in us, a proper sense of citizenship …

I can well believe that during the latter period of colonial expansion, when our school system was established, leadership—especially military—was in great demand, and I can well imagine that any kind of conscience would have been a restricting burden. However, it is to be hoped that we are at the dawn of a more enlightened era and so, I submit, we require a more enlightened form of school discipline ...

Friday 10th
A letter for Anthony Ryall today asking me to be chairman of one of the commissions at the conference—having been unanimously chosen by the ISC as one worthy of the office, which is gratifying, and which I speedily proceeded to accept ...

Another inter-schools conference was to be held in London in January.

Tuesday 14th
News—German Kiev counter-attack pass over to the defensive. USSR send military mission to Tito's forces in YugoSlavia, good. King Peter [of Yugoslavia] *(in Cairo) is anti—so unity is lacking—but I'm very glad they've done it.*

During the day I slept whenever possible, which was not often [tired from performance the evening before, and late night]. *PSN read from 'An Unknown Disciple'* [a novel about Christ] *in Divinity, which struck me as very good ...*

Thursday 16th
[End of term] ... *A reply from David Gellman (ISC) thanking me for accepting chairmanship, and a copy of Phoenix including (quite a good—I think) article called 'Training for Democracy' by Anthony Ryle. The paper makes me feel happy—a breath of the conference spirit of hope and energy towards a purpose.*

There was a letter from Margaret saying—she's got in touch with a friend in the Pressed Steel factory at Oxford who might be able to introduce some young enthusiastic working class comrades. Margaret says, and I know the feeling exactly, "I have contacted a group of people—and you have a nice warm sort of feeling, that you belong, they accept you, knowing that you're working in the same direction".

Perhaps when I next read this I shall be in Oxford, instead of warming my legs by a blue electric fire here …

to Oxford

Friday 17th
… I carried two v. heavy packages (suitcase and box of books) home to Kybald St.; Mommy and Daddy both in, Daddy engaged with a Mad Irish doctor with coloured geometrical interpretations of life. Mommy with flu. Home.

Saturday 18th
Went with Mommy in the new car—a 1937 Morris 8, taking Daddy to the Dept, and we arrived back to find Martin and two fellow boffins, who had called in to thaw on the way to Farnborough. Martin fairly cheery. Wood [who lived near Oxford] *arrived at 11.15 (per arrangement), and we went and—after searching—found a Mr. Williams at the dept of Pathology who is to take us for two hourly periods weekly on Chemistry (for 12/6 a time!) …*

Sunday 19th
… I spent the whole day very lazily, largely reading Eve Curie's 'Journey among warriors', which I think is very good [a journalist's report from the main war fronts in late 1941 and early 1942] …

Monday 20th
Wood round for lunch … our Chemistry extra was very efficient and worthwhile ...

An Air Transport command MO—old Guy's man—came round to supper, a German Jew, rather nice I thought …

Friday 24th
Can't remember a bloody thing of the early part of the day. In the evening we (Daddy, Margaret and I) went to a party given by the Univ. firewatchers—about 40 there, quite fun—silly games, and unfortunately dancing. Then carols. Daddy left early. Margaret and I to our surprise

enjoyed it quite a lot. We got back to find Martin just arrived, having worked all day.

Saturday 25th
Christmas day—a day of much eating after much preparation by Mother. Very nice food. Lots of presents. … Thoroughly extravagant, thoroughly lovely. We walked before lunch, and slept after, also 'New World' [symphony]. *Mickey* [Margaret's friend] *came to lunch and tea …*

After a late supper we went again to firewatchers' party—rather similar, quite amusing, not quite so good as before. Several very decorative girls—Martin quite enjoyed it, talking to one observer corps girl a lot of the time.

Martin is cheerfuller than before, but John is beastly with him—John I think despises him for lack of Toughness—which shows lack of sensitivity on his part. Anyhow we kept fairly happy all day.

Tuesday 28th
Felt Pretty bloody. Wood to lunch, I managed to stomach only cornflakes. A useful chemi. lesson, followed by an interesting discussion on penicillin and etc.—he showed us where he is growing some new stuff—a yield of 2 grams in six months, this is all he's got—he's trying to find the formula C32. A bit of a job. I came back, and retired to bed and sleep. John left in the evening. I had diarrhoea and felt sick.

Wednesday 29th
In bed, not feeling too good. Good news—the 'Scharnhorst' sunk off N. Cape—no losses.

The Scharnhorst had been damaged in previous engagements. She constituted a threat to the convoys taking supplies to Russia from Britain and to the Atlantic convoys. She was sunk by the convoy's escorts. Despite the German air and sea forces in northern Norway, convoys to Russia were maintained to 1945, under 10% of the merchant ships being lost.

Thursday 30th
… 3 destroyers and a blockade runner sunk in the bay of Biscay. Enormous Russian breakthrough. I was moved to the drawing room after tea; a Pressed Steel arc welder CP friend of Margaret's came to supper—is going to put me in touch with some contemporaries in Oxford. … He was extraordinarily nice and interesting.

Friday 31st
Up at 11, to spend a very lazy day happily browsing through books, to bed just before next year. Mother went to a Univ. New Year party for which she had made some jellies—she did not stay very long. Funny Louis MacNeice wireless play—wise in parts.

Diary for 1944

January

Saturday 1st
… there was a Mommy-Margaret scene because Margaret turned on the kettle without any water—fortunately I discovered that it was not burnt out, but automatically switched off. Then we went to see Oxford rep. at the 'Playhouse' perform 'Charlie's Aunt'—which I did enjoy—Margaret a bit stern, as she is unfortunately apt to be on frivolous occasions …

The following day I went to London for the next inter-schools conference (at Central Hall, Westminster), staying with friends of my parents.

Monday 3rd
I am writing this after tea today, having a lot of time before me and no company or other engagements to distract me, and therefore I feel it a good time for stock-taking of myself—a diary being an introspective instrument to avoid the embarrassment from intimacy.

First, however, I must record today's happenings, which were enjoyable. … I walked down Whitehall to the abbey. Crowds of youth, preponderantly feminine. After a while I went up to the Hall and sat down—up came EZ to say hullo—she brought along some fellow Paulines, and unfortunately I could not keep a seat later. I will leave her now as she will fit into the general review.

The introductory speeches were not very inspiring ... Noel Baker giving a fairly good general talk. The Racial Problems talk was adequate apart from a complete silence on economic factors—rather a serious omission!

Then a long break for lunch, followed by commission meetings. We started off tepid, and throughout our adult leader—a pleasant Pole—led rather too much; we got warmed up, but were definitely too woolly. We concentrated on anti-semitism—with a personal account from an extraordinarily beautiful Jewish girl and a German refugee. Informal chat—discussion after, then back by bus, having arranged to meet Elizabeth tomorrow before the lecture.

Elizabeth is not pretty, but attractive, vivacious, and charming and sensible (ISC) [i.e. a member of the inter-schools committee]. *I feel I'll like her, a lot; she impressed me greatly at the last conference and last term, in sexless, lonely, school, I used to weave fantasies around her memory. I have been deplorably reticent in my diary writing—very regrettably so; for who else is going to read these pages anyway? I think I will be capable of living a very full sexual life in its widest meaning, and I do feel very strongly the absence of feminine intimacy—I hope that my hopes towards such intimacy are not too rosy-tinted; Mother and Father's lives comfort any doubts I may have in that direction. I feel that Elizabeth may to some extent fill that gap. Perhaps I shall find out. The dreams of youth are pleasant dreams ---*

That briefly is a large part of the emotional resumé of the past few months; during that time I wrote [to a] *certain extent; some poetry—some I see as hopeless in a few days, some in a few weeks, others still seem poetry, and those I keep.*

Politically I have advanced, but I do feel often how little I have done of real thinking on the subject; I often suddenly see where a failure to be objective has produced an idea which I have accepted for a long time and then suddenly realised its falsity. Such realisations lead me to question my present beliefs, which is right and proper, I only hope I do it enough …

Tuesday 4th

… The morning lectures were, first, international co-operation, which was only fairly able—the barriers put up by capitalism are I think a very important subject, which the speaker ignored—an uneducated but highly relevant socialist-to-be (hark at the mature old man!) asked a question on this, but was largely evaded.

… the secretary of the National Union of Students gave an extraordinarily good talk—briefly on what we (Youth) have got to do. Then Tom Elkins of Willesden gave a good sort-of-an appeal for a fund in schools for rebuilding schools in Europe—a good idea and a good morning.

The papers have fully covered this [conference]*, and we're to be featured in Picture Post; the News Chronicle reported our commission—when I'd asked for a vote on the banning of anti-semitic propaganda (unanimous against) and then on the desirability of government sponsored anti-anti-semitic propaganda (wrongly reported unanimous for, actually only about 60%). The 'Sketch' had awful blurb on 'these young Atlases bearing with a worried frown all the troubles of the world', and regretted that we preferred this to pantomimes. oof.*

Our commission was lead by an army lieutenant (at 10 mins. notice)—again rather woolly, the group is too big and people are continually irrelevant, but eventually we reached one or two conclusions—a good discussion, if unorganised.

I then took Elizabeth out to tea … I learnt this much about her today: (1) name is Zaiman, came from Russia two generations ago, Irish mother; (2) Medical student [prospective]*, exactly my contemporary ? Oxford; (3) Father has gastric ulcer, doesn't like her going to theatre or being out late; she is a complete balletomane; (4) she remembers more about me at* [the] *Queenswood* [conference] *than vice-versa; (5) as much as I know her, I like her a lot.*

Wednesday 5th

… We first had a talk on the CEWC, ISC etc. by assorted people, which was good, and after it I conferred with [3 others] *on the necessity for agitation at school. Then Bill Beveridge himself, in a long and very good speech, followed by good questions. I bear him a grudge, however, for Elizabeth went and spent the lunch 1½ hours having lunch with him; I spent it walking to Westminster bridge—looking up the Thames there was big Ben and hazy buildings … and lovely orange sun on the water.*

Then I went back and prepared a short talk on comprehensive National medical service. The chairman got people to prepare short pro and con talks, and the discussion was energetic, to the point, very enjoyable, and very successful. We unanimously (almost) decided on [a] *state national service.*

… the Social was too much dancing and very hot, I quite enjoyed it and wish I could dance. At 6.30 I left and went to Leicester Sq. [with Elizabeth] *and there parted, Elizabeth going on the Northern and I on the ~~Piccadilly~~ Bakerloo via ~~Charing Cross~~ Piccadilly Circus, I forget which and it does not matter. I think if I were to be perfectly frank with myself (as I should be but find difficult in carrying out) I would confess that I was just a little in love—there I've done it! Back by tube to St. Johns Wood, pensive.*

Thursday 6th

This is being written at some unearthly hour in the morning, it having happened thuswise: about two hours ago I woke up, and commenced thinking about emotional experiences of the last few days; that is to say about Elizabeth. I began also thinking that today is to be the last day I shall see her … and having heard that there are no possible-for-me (or probably her) conferences next Easter … thought whimsically how nice if she could stay at Glatting … but I couldn't very well ask her all alone, it would be too embarrassing—then there dawned the IDEA, which is this: why ask her alone? Why not have a party of 8 or 10 nice conference people down to Glatting, then Glatting would be filled as Glatting should. … The idea was so persistent I have had to write this down to calm myself …

After a slightly hurried breakfast, I said a grateful goodbye [to my hosts], *… and off to Central Hall. Elisabeth (note s not z) there, we spent most of the day together …*

John Marrach on 'World plans for Food and Agriculture', which was good … MoI film 'World of Plenty', which is extraordinarily good. Then I took Elisabeth to lunch at a Lyons cafeteria—eating little myself. … She likes Browning, and acting, but not Barry.

Back for the reports of the commissions (after meeting regional leaders)—they were of necessity inconclusive; on the whole, however, fairly satisfactory. Then Priestley on the 'New Citizen'—despite unprepossessing appearance and a bad beginning, it was very good. Although the BBC was broadcasting it, he was very definitely political-socialist, good …

Elisabeth says she is a very bad correspondent; I hope not too bad. … I caught a 5.12 train, changing at Didcot and arriving at Oxford at 9.30, going straight home. All well and as before, happy. … having Elizabeth to write to will be lovely. And mother suggested impromptu that I should ask some people down to Glatting, so that is a very definite possibility—we will see …

at Oxford

Friday 7th
… At 6.15 we went to 'The Merry Widow'—Mother, Melody [very pregnant] *and I—Daddy was up in London at a committee. It was colourful and gay, … while not deeply satisfying …*

What I most remembered is that the company were shortly going to the Middle East and all had plasters on their arms where they had been vaccinated.

Saturday 8th
…Reflecting on EZ, what I have previously written has been sincere entirely—I say this as it does contrast with my tendency to reticence even in my diary. She is the first girl I know who is wholly intelligent and charming; she is sensitive, appreciating art, and the same forms of it

as I do; she is intelligent, holding generally the same views as I do. … Really I cannot discuss her, because my feelings towards her just are …

Previous diary entries concerning my feeling lonely and longing for a like-minded (girl)friend make it clear that there was, in my mind, a relationship waiting to happen. Little came of this one.

Sunday 9th
… I went and dug in the garden … a satisfactory occupation, for it gives one pleasant exercise, and leaves ones mind free to think and dream … I also finished off a Biology science prelim essay.

Stefan [Gawel] *came to tea—not too happy about the terms announced by the USSR today. These say the Curzon line is approximately the new* [Polish] *boundary—not Atlantic Charter principles, but then she was never asked. There may be better reasons than revenge for 1920 and traditional rivalry—and perhaps those Poles are now pro-Soviet—but it will cause bitterness, and will not help towards understanding of the Soviet Union.*

Monday 10th
… We decided to go to a flick, except Daddy; we … walked back through a moonlight Oxford. Evidence of American profligacy and juvenile delinquency was only too widespread, but Oxford spires by moonlight are very lovely.

Tuesday 11th
As I lay in bed wondering if today would bring a letter, Daddy did, so I was very pleased. It was a long nice letter … I replied in the morning having thought of so much to say—it's nice to have tangible evidence in the shape of a letter, as before all I had was her address, and memories of all the things I should have said but did not …

I spent the morning after writing the letter doing a chemistry essay (compare and contrast the properties of aldehydes and hetones—oof). … Melody still quite fit—baby is at action stations so it can't be long now.

Father was up in London today doing a recording for the BBC social medicine talk. … A letter from Margaret's CP friend Gwyn Davies in the evening inviting me to a CP meeting tomorrow and supper the next night—good.

Wednesday 12th

The conference was not in this week's issue of Picture Post, but at 11 o'clock there was a schools broadcast … not awfully thrilling but good for the uninitiated …

After an early supper I went to the Union Debating Hall … to the CP meeting. Interesting types—mostly youngish factory workers, a few old men and middle-aged women, a few students. Only about 80 there.

Ted Bramley, London CP district secretary, … explained how Mosely was a symbol of the capitalist reaction which even now is banning TU activity etc.—one of the hardest jobs the CP is facing is stopping strikes. Their programme seems to me eminently sensible: (i) win the war (ii) strong united Labour movement for social reform, starting with the nationalisation of the basic industries, followed by whole scale socialisation. He was good on pointing out how then everyone would be able to enjoy the culture at present restricted to the 15% capitalist class. His medical programme was excellent.

After him spoke a factory girl, saying why we should join and why she had … followed by two recent converts—I could not help being reminded of Salvation Army prayer meetings, but it was all free from emotion and ritual and thus alright.

There are several reasons why I won't join the CP, yet at least. (1) Not being permanently resident anywhere I could never get down to useful work; (2) I am not entirely convinced on the rightness of their methods, but actually I think there is probably no alternative. I do not like the stupid manifestations of class war which sneers at 'toffs'—it is from these people that most culture comes—by virtue of their good fortune, but it is childish to dislike them from envy.

… Gwyn Davies … introduced me to a young medical student (who remembered Margaret), whom I invited to tea tomorrow to discuss. Then he took me and Comrade Mariel (that is to say bourgeois but safe Mrs. Gillet jr.) to a snack bar, where we talked.

… Family reaction fairly OK, but I think parents would rather I did not get too involved—fearing perhaps Margaret's grimness—? I don't know, I don't think they'll object to me going my own way if I think first. Anyway an exhilarating evening.

Thursday 13th

… Mother went 'Soldiers, Sailors and Airforce Families Association' visiting—she has some very interesting cases, as well as stopping unnecessary demands for the return of husbands from the Forces …

The [CP] *medical student whom I'd invited … was very interesting and pleasant—a French (and Greek) who escaped after Dunkirk. … Final advice was study the CP hard before joining, to get your shocks over. I certainly will …*

He later left the CP, and gave me a group photograph of the Central Committee of the Soviet Communist Party with those already killed indicated.

At 8.20 I made my way to the Taj Mahal to meet Gwyn Davies—we talked about politics, and his various experiences etc.—he is an extraordinarily wise, widely experienced and—despite leaving school at the age of 13½—cultured man. His jobs include dirt-track rider, butcher, coffee stall keeper, arc welder, government inspector --- and he has always kept a diary which is a jolly good effort.

He says that the ordinary working man has neither the time and energy nor the training to think, which is a very terrible truth to a large extent. I tackled him on class hatred towards individuals, and he agreed but thought it inevitable, and thought it was up to converted bourgeoisie to convert their fellows …

Friday 14th

… I walked round Christ Church meadows—the Cher was lovely with streaky reflections of overhanging trees and bright yellow and red shoots, with lovely blue through the trees—like nice Chinese painting, but lovelier colours even than that. I saw a kingfisher, and dabchicks

fishing—one with a wriggling silver fish in its mouth. Two stately swans were standing on the bank, with lovely reflections.

... I wound [crank-started] *the car for Mother to go visiting, and returned to clear the gravel path of weeds and earth. ... Good Russian news, big American day raids as ever.*

Saturday 15th

... Melo went off to the Radcliffe to be jipped up with castor oil. ... Mother went to the Radcliffe after supper (also at 3) to see Melo—slight pains every five minutes—started. What a business.

Big raid on Brunswick, Poles want discussions ...

Sunday 16th

A hectic day. First of all Daddy had a bilious attack and was intermittently sick all night; thus neither he nor Mommy slept. Then in the morning Melo's pains had stopped.

Daddy had a committee all day, here ... All went away for lunch—Daddy off to sleep, we had lunch, and I packed Mother off to bed for a short rest. Back at three to talk, with a break for tea, until 6 o'clock ...

Patric Gardner and a woman doctor friend came in, and we chatted cheerfully about infantile diarrhoea, sex education, Basques etc.—she's very startling and refreshing. ... Now Mother's in the bath—I'll go and prepare for mine.

to Newquay

Tuesday 18th

... [on the train] *to Bristol, talked to quite a nice American whom I tackled on the colour question—he was ignorantly prejudiced in a conventional way. Also a silly parson and wife.*

... missing one connection ... [Martin Wood and I] *explored part of dirty Bristol. ... Then we shared* [a compartment] *... with two Negresses, two charming little 3ish-year old piccaninnies and a little 5-month old one—awfully jolly—very sleepy.*

School-filled train to Newquay, bus, supper—and, oh joy of joys, a long letter from Elisabeth which was very, very cheering. Bless her …

Wednesday 19th

… After [breakfast] *I unpacked violently, and got it over … up to the Pentire to discuss with fellow conference-goers* [some others had attended the last one] *the formation of our discussion group. I was quite cheered by their determination …*

PSN and Hales had both heard of my Phoenix article, Kitson had read and approved, Max borrowed it and (of course) said "Jolly good"!—I'm almost famous from it. I saw Picture Post's conference pictures—awful photo of crowd. … Quite a respectful write-up, though. There have been cracks about the conference as connected with the fair sex ---.

Thursday 20th

Off with a bang. Treble ARSS [Mr. Stony-Smith] *Physics, followed by new* [teacher] *Mr. Spencer, English—he told us what we're going to do, and then set an essay on what we thought we ought to do.*

1st game hockey, not bad for a first game, I'm pretty paralytic though after 4 weeks sedentary …

Friday 21st

… I realised I've more to do than there's time for, but can't do anything about it so don't think about it. … Double Physics study—my mind is too inclined to wander when I'm bored with my work, which is usually.

Letter from Mommy; I'm the uncle of a fine girl, whom Melody produced with ease on Wednesday night—apart from the blue clothes I hope she's satisfied …

Weighing and measuring in the evening—11.3 and 6′ 1 ½″. Russians take Novgorod …

Sunday 23rd

… off up Penpoll Creek. Very little wild life. On the way back I got caught in a thunderstorm (in January!)—rain, then hard hail. The wind

was roaring up the Gannel, and crossing the slippery footbridge was quite an effort …

Daddy's 'Social Medicine' broadcast at 1 o'clock—Max told everyone when I'd asked if I might listen, so as it was in prep, many came. The voice was unrecognisable—I think a good talk.

… up to the Pentire for Debating Society committee meeting. … We decided for the first debate 'This house would support socialism (or back Bolshevism)'—which I'll enjoy enormously.

Monday 24th

Short letter from Daddy, pleased with an 8 lb pink grand daughter ...

I've started Anna Karenina, which is naughty—it's far too good to stop though—easier to get into than War and Peace, just as hard to get out …

Tuesday 25th

More filthy weather. A letter from Elisabeth—good—she's started school; included dissertation on politics—I'm glad we can discuss such things too …

Wednesday 26th

… A nasty accident in Chemi. Wood was melting down some lead for a weight, and it suddenly exploded (delayed boiling ?)—L and G were right over it—the latter had specs, but I turned to see L writhing on the floor.

I rushed off and fetched a matron, arriving back to find L—doubtless suffering from considerable shock and with both eyes unable to see—surrounded by half the form scraping lead off his face with a scalpel, cutting off his eyelashes, and cooling him with slooshes of water—my God. Later he had one eye operated on—a nasty business.

Saturday 29th

… first meeting of the Literary Society—we read 'Journey's End' (cut)—quite fun—I read Stanhope …

Sunday 30th

... WAS [World Affairs Society] *inaugural meeting—despite time, 2.15, and weather, first fine* [day] *this week—was attended by 15—good!! I'm librarian.*

... back via sunny Splash point, to finish Anna Karenina—a grand book combining tragic 'eternal triangles' with heroine's philosophical development—I've enjoyed it immensely.

Short chapel, snoozed in sermon. Read to Juniors ...

Monday 31st

... There was an awfully nice letter from Tom Elkins—he's our district representative on the ISC, a communist with a London accent who speaks well—first to say that there ain't another group in Cornwall; and then re: my Phoenix article, of which he seemed to approve.

Finally he said this: 'Although I hardly met you at the conference, ever since then I have been hearing from Barbara P. or Elisabeth Zaiman ... "Oh, Anthony Ryle says this, or thinks that", so I really know more about you than you might imagine'. Well !!? I wrote a letter back ...

February

Tuesday 1st

... Indoor JTC RT [radio transmission] *procedure (lecture on same by L./Cpl. A. Ryle—who knew no more than the people he was addressing—who knew all). Futile Physics, followed by rage on same ...*

News lately largely of enormous night and day [air] *raids* [on Germany].

Wednesday 2nd

... Orchestra practice was much more of a success than last week—lots of my bits were OK, and I enjoyed it a lot.

Soc. Soc. was Prof. Fletcher (Education, Bristol) on the new education bill—very able and interesting, I hope we'll be able to tap him tomorrow to argue in first period (PSN's plan).

Thursday 3rd
… We had Fletcher 1st period—re: religious education, he wants Christian teaching universal, and apparently refuses to recognise the possibility of fundamental differences of opinion …

In the evening the [unofficial] *night op.; signalling had a special scheme of their own—I and Wood with an 18* [radio]*—all went well, nice moon; chatted with a niceish American soldier, sentry behind the Fistral …*

Friday 4th
Filthy icy gale. I had shivers, goose skin and a headache all day, in the evening a spot on my head, so I'm wondering … if I've chicken pox …

Saturday 5th
I had indeed—woke up with a spotty chest. Fortunately last night my premonition made me prepare the books I'll need—if I can get 'em past the fumigation barrier. The latter also vetoes letters—but Max typed a note out to home, and I'll have to try and disinfect and smuggle out one to Elisabeth—or if necessary get Max to type a short note.

Max brought me up to the San. … Dozed in the afternoon; the original culprit H [first chicken pox victim] *brought me up an orange—he's been here three weeks—if I'm that long I'll scream! WAS tonight too, socialism debate on Saturday, work pressing … and no letters out officially. Hell.*

Bored evening dipping into books and dozing—food good. Life by year [ear] *and through a window gives a sense of detachment—I could see my bedclothes airing from my window, and the bus seems to pass very frequently.*

Tuesday 8th
With the aid of dope I had a lovely night, and slept on after breakfast to about 12 o'clock, when Max arrived with two letters—Elisabeth and Tom Elkins. Former a lovely long one—on ballet, explanation thereof, and woffle on people [to invite] *re: Glatting. … Letter improved morale a lot.*

Tom Elkins wrote … saying Glatting was a marvellous, if rather brave, idea. He described the 'awful band of would-be politicians in the ISC', even the ones I knew; confessed a weakness for EZ …

I spent a lazyish afternoon. … Quite content. Danger of becoming lazy?

Wednesday 9th

… In future years, when I'm the Pope, I may be interested in my present philosophy of life, which is this. There is no ultimate meaning to life; what meaning there is in one's life depends on what meaning one gives it. It is obvious to a rational, imaginative being that happiness is only possible if everyone, particularly (due to Mutual Aid Instinct) oneself, … is what is commonly called 'good'. Being 'good' must therefore be the philosophy of life one forms for oneself, if one is rational.

It's silly to argue (as Prof. Fletcher did) that without ultimate eternal truths one would revert to force—but that would <u>not</u> lead to happiness. This needs an educated people, and does away with the need for eternal truths, future lives and the clergy—all small losses. I think it's quite a satisfying philosophy. I haven't explained beauty, but explain it by God and you have to explain God—probably there is, or will be, a biological or psychological explanation.

Thursday 10th

Letter from Mommy … John very happy, and paternally successful at calming his daughter.

I got up, read and worked and ate; and wrote and wrecked 3 letters with Dettol, re-wrote two, won't use Dettol—I'm sure I'm safe enough anyway …

Friday 11th

Worked quite a lot. Crantock beach walk afternoon, posting letters home, to EZ and Tom. Comforting letter EZ, nice one from Roger—a very good friend. … I'm fairly content—face covered in long lank hairs and a few spots, head bumpy—ugly, but not itchy. Roger may not be able to manage Glatting …

Saturday 12th

... went for a walk up the Gannel—a grey César-Franck symphony day—all the houses ugly, and the people meaningless, and the gulls sad. There was a conceited little redshank bowing at his reflection. I got back and read straight through, with a break for tea (now downstairs), Charles Morgan's 'Portrait in a Mirror'—I think a very beautiful love-story—it moved and impressed me a lot ...

Sunday 13th

... up Penpol—lots of bird song, mostly robins. Saw Wallop and chatted while he removed (with permission) an accumulator from the old [abandoned] *van up by Penpol. I helped carry it back, keeping a good distance apart.*

Little school news, socialism defeated [in school debate] *27–25, all speakers pro, Kennedy spoke badly. Back, tea, I read 'The Circle of Life' by Kenneth Walker—many striking similarities to Daddy's 'Fears may be Liars', but he came to a conclusion which I don't quite understand. Sometimes, perhaps not often enough, I realise just how little I do understand.*

News: Big Russian victories with many cut off [German] *divisions in the past week—S. front. Italy bridgehead* [Anzio] *has been a little precarious. Churchill wrote another letter for Conservative bye-election candidate—Party truce = vote Right. Some hereditary Duke or something, who got leave for the nomination by ? means, but you can't blame the young fellow, he knows nothing of politics—as Maxton (?)* [a veteran left-wing MP] *said. Bevan made a fuss re-corruption in the house—exaggerated, but started useful discussion I think.*

* * *

A further volume of the diary was lost. The last entries show that I was becoming less isolated from my contemporaries, and was approaching my 17th birthday with 'that precarious gait some call experience' (Emily Dickinson). The end of the war was still eighteen ferocious months away, and the last entries record continuing military uncertainties. But in both individual and worldwide spheres there was a sense of a new phase beginning.

Woodlands House ca. 1942. The author is in the fourth row, second from right.

Chapter 6: Retrospect

I was surprised, when reading through this text, to find that some passages produced a felt re-experience of the people, linked in some cases with an eerie foreknowledge of their later fates. The group photograph of 'Woodlands' from '42 or '43 contains most of the individuals named in the diary, and I am surprised to be able to name well over half the boys. I have no idea of what happened to most of them, but know that there is one future President of the Royal Academy and one internationally famous theatrical director, and within a few years, there was one who died on his first RAF operation, one who died of poliomyelitis, one who died in a road accident, and two who became schizophrenic.

I was also struck by the limits of my self-scrutiny, despite expressed good intentions; was disappointed that my extensive reading yielded judgments but few critical insights; and amused to see that the recorded responses to girls, when I finally encountered them, were based on evaluations of their political development.

In this postscript I reflect on what became of some of the characteristics and beliefs of my seventeen-year-old self through the sixty-seven years since the last diary entry—in particular in respect of the influence of my parents, my political beliefs, and my hatred of war.

I was struck by how fond of (or perhaps unduly attached to) my parents I was. This dependency was transformed into a caretaking role by my father's successive heart attacks and my mother's associated anxiety and depression, and later by her being widowed. Although I was the youngest, the dispersion of the family during and after the war meant that I became the main emotional support.

I had qualified as a doctor seven weeks before my father died. He had another coronary thrombosis soon after I started as house physician to Max Rosenheim at University College Hospital, who very kindly drove 60 miles to visit my father (whose doctor was incompetent), and gave me leave so that I could be with him through his last few days. My father was glad to meet my much respected chief, and to know that I was launched on a career in medicine. My choice of medicine had obviously been influenced by the family tradition and I have never regretted it, and am pleased that one son and one granddaughter have followed the same course.

I was lucky in my parents, but their need of me blunted any normal adolescent challenge, notably in respect of their puritanical views on sex. It was also difficult to separate my admiration of my father from my mother's idealisation of him. My formation as a caretaker was not always a good influence on my personal relationships, but it eventually found a useful expression in my becoming a psychotherapist.

The political atmosphere of the home in the pre-war years, which I described in the first chapter, had not freed me from the residual class attitudes evident in the 1940–1942 diaries. But influenced by the atmosphere of wartime Britain, and by my involvement in socialist and communist activity and reading, I became firmly egalitarian. My disillusion with the Soviet Union did not alter my valuing the Marxist analysis of class society.

Re-reading the diaries I found something enviable—but dangerously naive—in my optimism about the future. My life went on through the terrible war years, and it has gone on through the terrible 65 years since that war ended, during which wars have continued. There has been no nuclear holocaust, but the mass bombing of civilians, which I had come to question by 1944, has become normal practice. It was employed without shame by Britain and the USA in Korea and Iraq, and by the USA in Vietnam. Worldwide arms sales by the developed nations have made a major contribution to other, smaller wars, including those in Africa, the Balkans and Afghanistan.

My hopes for a fairer society were to some extent realised by the development in Britain of the Welfare State, but as I write it is being dismantled by a government of millionaire old Etonians, whose rhetoric about withholding help because of the need for people to be responsible for their lives could be taken verbatim from the statements of the government which closed the soup kitchens at the height of the Irish potato famine.

While the technological advances and economic developments of the past half century have made life easier for many in the developed countries, they have done nothing to reduce the gross inequalities within and between nations, and have been accompanied by an unsustainable plundering and poisoning of the natural world. We should, but do not, include in the cosmic casualty lists the thousands who die from poverty-related causes every day.

In re-reading my diaries, I realised that—in relation to the continuing violence, deprivations and dangers in the world—I have been as much on the edge as I was in my witnessing of the war. What I see now indicates a clearer, and ultimately irresolvable, personal moral dimension. I have continued to embrace life, while far away it is being extinguished; and to enjoy eating, in the knowledge of world hunger. I have continued to occupy a privileged position in the privileged society of Britain. My children and grandchildren have never known hunger or fear, and have received education and health care as beneficiaries of the post-war reforms which mitigated the injustices of the pre-war years. As a doctor I had been able to play a part in delivering these reforms, and I comforted myself—I now think excessively—that putting my energies into my professional work made up for my political disillusion and impotence.

I remain a socialist critic of capitalism, but a general weakening of socialist thinking has resulted from the revelations of the full horrors of the 'actually existing socialism' of Stalinism, the weakening of the Trade Unions as a result of our shrinking industrial base, consumerism, the direct assaults of Thatcher, the betrayals of Blair, and the bias of the media. Wartime adversity, and the memory of recent poverty, made rationing acceptable in Britain; and a shared sense of community supported the reforms of the immediate post-war years. But this has largely faded away.

Most ordinary citizens do still seek to live ordinary lives which include concern for each other and for the future but, all too easily, they are rendered passive or complacent by the systematic omissions and distortions of the media, and the distractions of the electronic equivalents of Rome's bread and circuses. Market forces promote greed, while failing to meet many basic human needs, and in the developed world obesity has replaced malnutrition as a major health concern.

When the global casino of international finance capitalism lurches into one of its recurrent economic crises, which it is doing conspicuously as I write, explanations are offered as if these were natural phenomena like tsunamis, rather than the results of human action. Governments are not free to follow policies which conflict with the interests of international capital. In response to the crisis, social care is whittled away, but the banks are protected. Actually existing capitalism has much to answer for.

It is hard not to feel sadness and anger and fear for the future. What is to be done? The dangerously unstable and destructive system of post-industrial finance capitalism controls the world, even though it cannot control itself. Effective political opposition needs to recover its voice, and sustain a sense of what human society and human individuals might become; recognizing and challenging how human consciousness is shaped by the system, resisting each erosion of human values, and freeing ourselves from what Blake described as 'mind forg'd manacles'.